Henry Miller on Writing

To Henry Miller, who brought me to life.
—Thomas H. Moore

also by Henry Miller

Henry Miller

on Writing

Selected by Thomas H. Moore

from the Published and Unpublished Works

of Henry Miller

A New Directions Paperbook

The author, editor and publishers are grateful to the following for permission to reprint selections from works by Henry Miller, first published or copyrighted by others, as indicated:

Carrefour, Edition du Laurier, and Daphne Fraenkel, for the selection from *Hamlet*, Third Printing 1962, London.

Editions du Chêne, Paris, for selections from *Nexus* (Copyright © 1959 by Henry Miller): *Black Spring*, first published by Obelisk Press, Paris, 1936. Copyright © 1958 by Editions du Chêne; and *Nexus* © 1960 by Editions du Chêne.

Grove Press, Inc. and Barney Rosset, New York, for the selections from *Black Spring*. (Copyright © 1963 by Grove Press, Inc.); *Tropic of Cancer* (Copyright © 1961 by Grove Press, Inc.); *Tropic of Capricorn* (Copyright © 1961 by Grove Press, Inc.); and a selection from *Nexus*, which appeared in *The Evergreen Review*, Vol. III, No. 10 (Copyright © 1959 by Grove Press, Inc.).

Olympia Press and Maurice Girodias, Paris, for selections from *Plexus* (Copyright 1953. All Rights Reserved.)

Putnam & Company, Ltd., London, and McClelland & Stewart Ltd., Toronto, for selections from *Art and Outrage* (Copyright © 1959 by Putnam & Company, Ltd.)

Bern Porter for "Work Schedule" from *Henry Miller Miscellanea*, edited and published by Bern Porter 1945, reprinted by special arrangement with Bern Porter.

Henry Miller Literary Society, 3748 Park Ave., So., 7, Minneapolis, Minnesota, and Edward P. Schwartz for the "First Letter to Trygve Hirsch" which was first issued and circulated in mimeographed form by them in 1957. It was first published in *Henry Miller—Between Heaven and Hell*, © 1961 by Emile White.

The previously unpublished manuscript notes, reproduced here in facsimile, are the property of Robert Fink, who kindly made the originals available.

Published simultaneously in Canada by McClelland & Stewart, Ltd.

Manufactured in the United States of America
New Directions Books are published by James Laughlin at Norfolk, Connecticut. New York Office: 333 Sixth Avenue (14).

978

Contents

Part III   The Author at Work   159

Part IV   Writing and Obscenity   173

Preface

It was several years ago that I first began making notes of certain passages in the works of Henry Miller on the subject of writing. Since then I have received letters remarking on the stimulating effect of some of these selections. This encouraged me in my then vague idea of collecting them into a volume. I finally decided to go ahead with the book after reading the passage from *Art and Outrage* reprinted here as an epigraph.

In the first section, "The 'Literary' Writer," are to be found the selections dealing with Henry Miller's struggles to perfect his style by imitating various writers he admired. The section covers the period from about 1917 to 1927.

The second section, "Finding His Own Voice," is a record of his successful search within himself for his own way of writing. It begins about 1930 and continues into the present time.

The third section, "The Author at Work," attempts to show, in a small way, the methods Henry Miller used in preparing his books.

The fourth section, "Writing and Obscenity," contains the most important writings by Henry Miller on obscenity and its relation to his own idea of the artist as writer. I think it is very important for an understanding of Henry Miller's works.

I was fortunate in being able to obtain the help of Henry Miller in the final selection of the passages.

To conclude, I feel that, first of all, the selections will be found enjoyable reading. I also know that they will be an inspiration and a stimulus to those who are, or ever hope to be, writers.

THOMAS H. MOORE

... I proved to my satisfaction that, like any other mortal, I too could write. But since I wasn't really meant to be a writer, all that was permitted me to give expression to was this business of writing and being a writer; in short, my own private struggle with this problem. My grief, in other words. Out of the lack I made my song. Very much as if a warrior, challenged to mortal combat and having no weapons, must first forge them himself. And in the process, one that takes all his life, the purpose of his labors gets forgotten or sidetracked.

—*Art and Outrage*

I The "Literary" Writer

My Anchorage
—Tropic of Capricorn

During this period when I was drifting from door to door, job to job, friend to friend, meal to meal, I did try nevertheless to rope off a little space for myself which might be an anchorage; it was more like a life-buoy in the midst of a swift channel. To get within a mile of me was to hear a huge dolorous bell tolling. Nobody could see the anchorage—it was buried deep in the bottom of the channel. One saw me bobbing up and down on the surface, rocking gently sometimes or else swinging backwards and forwards agitatedly. What held me down safely was the big pigeon-holed desk which I put in the parlor. This was the desk which had been in the old man's tailoring establishment for the last fifty years, which had given birth to many bills and many groans, which had housed strange souvenirs in its compartments, and which finally I had filched from him when he was ill and away from the establishment, and now it stood in the middle of the floor in our lugubrious parlor on the third floor of a respectable brown-stone house in the dead center of the most respectable neighborhood in Brooklyn. I had to fight a tough battle to install it there, but I insisted that it be there in the midmost midst of the shebang. It was like putting a mastodon in the center of a dentist's office. But since the wife had no friends to visit her and since my friends didn't give a fuck if it were suspended from the chandelier, I kept it in the parlor and I put all the extra chairs we had around it in a big circle and then I sat down comfortably and I put my feet up on the desk and dreamed of what I would write if I could write. I had a spittoon alongside of the desk, a big brass one from the same establishment, and I would spit in it now and then to remind myself that it was there. All the pigeon-holes were empty and all the drawers were empty; there wasn't a thing on the desk or in it except a sheet of white paper on which I found it impossible to put so much as a pot-hook.

When I think of the titanic efforts I made to canalize the hot lava which was bubbling inside me, the efforts I repeated thousands of times to bring the funnel into place and capture *a* word, *a* phrase, I think inevitably of the men of the old stone age. A hundred thousand, two hundred thousand years, three hundred thousand years to arrive at the idea of the paleolith. A phantom struggle, because they weren't dreaming of such a thing as the paleolith. It came without effort, born of a second, a miracle you might say, except that everything which happens is miraculous. Things happen or they don't happen, that's all. Nothing is accomplished by sweat and struggle. Nearly everything which we call life is just insomnia, an agony because we've lost the habit of falling asleep. We don't know how to let go. We're like a Jack-in-the-box perched on top of a spring and the more we struggle the harder it is to get back in the box.

I think if I had been crazy I couldn't have hit upon a better scheme to consolidate my anchorage than to install this Neanderthal object in the middle of the parlor. With my feet on the desk, picking up the current, and my spinal column snugly socketed in a thick leather cushion, I was in an ideal relation to the flotsam and jetsam which was whirling about me, and which, because they were crazy and part of the flux, my friends were trying to convince me was life. I remember vividly the first contact with reality that I got through my feet, so to speak. The million words or so which I had written previously, which were intelligible words, mind you, well ordered, well connected, were as nothing to me—crude ciphers from the old stone age—because the contact was through the head and the head is a useless appendage unless you're anchored in mid-channel deep in the mud. Everything I had written before was museum stuff, and most writing is still museum stuff and that's why it doesn't catch fire, doesn't inflame the world. I was only a mouth-piece for the ancestral race which was talking through me; even my dreams were not authentic, not bona fide Henry Miller dreams. To sit still and think one thought which would come up out of me, out of the life-buoy, was a Herculean task. I didn't lack thoughts nor words nor the power of expression—I lacked something much more important: the lever which would shut off the juice. The bloody machine wouldn't stop, that was the difficulty. I was not only in the middle of the current but the current was running through me and I had no control over it whatever.

I remember the day I brought the machine to a dead stop and how the other mechanism, the one that was signed with my own initials and which I had made with my own hands and my own blood slowly began to function. I had gone to the theatre nearby to see a vaudeville show; it was the matinee and I had a ticket for the balcony. Standing on line in the lobby, I already experienced a strange feeling of consistency. It was as though I were coagulating, becoming a recognizable consistent mass of jelly. It was like the ultimate stage in the healing of a wound. I was at the height of normality, which is a very abnormal condition. Cholera might come and blow its foul breath in my mouth—it wouldn't matter. I might bend over and kiss the ulcers of a leprous hand, and no harm could possibly come to me. There was not just a balance in this constant warfare between health and disease, which is all that most of us may hope for, but there was a plus integer in the blood which meant that, for a few moments at least, disease was completely routed. If one had the wisdom to take root in such a moment, one would never again be ill or unhappy or even die. But to leap to this conclusion is to make a jump which would take one back farther than the old stone age. At that moment I wasn't even dreaming of taking root; I was experiencing for the first time in my life the meaning of the miraculous. I was so amazed when I heard my own cogs meshing that I was willing to die then and there for the privilege of the experience.

What happened was this. . . . As I passed the doorman, holding the torn stub in my hand, the lights were dimmed and the curtain went up. I stood a moment slightly dazed by the sudden darkness. As the curtain slowly rose I had the feeling that throughout the ages man had always been mysteriously stilled by this brief moment which preludes the spectacle. I could feel the curtain rising *in man*. And immediately I also realized that this was a symbol which was being presented to him endlessly in his sleep and that if he had been awake the players would never have taken the stage but he, Man, would have mounted the boards. I didn't think this thought—it was a realization, as I say, and so simple and overwhelmingly clear was it that the machine stopped dead instantly and I was standing in my own presence bathed in a luminous reality. I turned my eyes away from the stage and beheld the marble staircase which I should take to go to my seat in the balcony. I saw a man slowly mounting the steps, his hand laid across the balustrade. The man could have been myself, the old self which had been sleep-walking ever since I was born. My eye didn't take in the entire staircase just the few steps which the man had climbed or was climbing in the moment that I took it all in. The man never reached the top of the stairs and his hand was never removed from the marble balustrade. I felt the curtain descend, and for another few moments I was behind the scenes moving amidst the sets like the property man suddenly roused from his sleep and not sure whether he is still dreaming or looking at a dream which is being enacted on the stage. It was as fresh and green, as strangely new as the bread and cheese lands which the Biddenden maidens saw every day of their long life joined at the hips. I saw only that which was alive; the rest faded out in a penumbra. And it was in order to keep the world alive that I rushed home without waiting to see the performance and sat down to describe the little patch of staircase which is imperishable.

It was just about this time that the Dadaists were in full swing to be followed shortly by the Surrealists. I never heard of either group until some ten years later; I never read a French book and I never had a French idea. I was perhaps the unique Dadaist in America, and I didn't know it. I might just as well have been living in the jungles of the Amazon for all the contact I had with the outside world. Nobody understood what I was writing about or why I wrote that way. I was so lucid that they said I was daffy. I was describing the New World—unfortunately a little too soon because it had not yet been discovered and nobody could be persuaded that it existed. It was an ovarian world, still hidden away in the Fallopian tubes. Naturally nothing was clearly formulated: there was only the faint suggestion of a backbone visible, and certainly no arms or legs, no hair, no nails, no teeth. Sex was the last thing to be dreamed of; it was the world of Chronos and his ovicular progeny. It was the world of the iota, each iota being indispensable, frighteningly logical, and absolutely unpredictable. There was no such thing as a *thing*, because the concept "thing" was missing.

I say it was a New World I was describing, but like the New World which Columbus discovered it turned out to be a far older world than any we have known. I saw beneath the superficial physiognomy of skin and bone the indestructible world which man has always carried within him; it was neither old nor new, really, but the eternally true world which changes from moment to moment. Everything I looked at was palimpsest and there was no layer of writing too strange for me to decipher. When my companions left me of an evening I would often sit down and write to my friends the Australian Bushmen or to the Mound Builders of the Mississippi Valley or to the Igorotes in the Philippines. I had to write English, naturally, because it was the only language I spoke, but between my language and the telegraphic code employed by my bosom friends there was a world of difference. Any primitive man would have understood me, any man of archaic epochs would have understood me: only those about me, that is to say, a continent of a hundred million people, failed to understand my language. To write intelligibly for them I would have been obliged first of all to kill something, secondly, to arrest time. I had just made the realization that life is indestructible and that there is no such thing as time, only the present. Did they expect me to deny a truth which it had taken me all my life to catch a glimpse of? They most certainly did. The one thing they did not want to hear about was that life is indestructible. Was not their precious new world reared on the destruction of the innocent, on rape and plunder and torture and devastation? Both continents had been violated; both continents had been stripped and plundered of all that was precious—*in things*. No greater humiliation, it seems to me, was meted out to any man than to Montezuma; no race was ever more ruthlessly wiped out than the American Indian; no land was ever raped in the foul and bloody way that California was raped by the gold-diggers. I blush to think of our origins—our hands are steeped in blood and crime. And there is no let-up to the slaughter and the pillage, as I discovered at first hand traveling throughout the length and breadth of the land. Down to the closest friend every man is a potential murderer. Often it wasn't necessary to bring out the gun or the lasso or the branding iron—they had found subtler and more devilish ways of torturing and killing their own. For me the most excruciating agony was to have the world annihilated before it had even left my mouth. I learned, by bitter experience, to hold my tongue; I learned to sit in silence, and even smile, when actually I was foaming at the mouth. I learned to shake hands and say how do you do to all these innocent-looking fiends who were only waiting for me to sit down in order to suck my blood.

How was it possible, when I sat down in the parlor at my prehistoric desk, to use this code language of rape and murder? I was alone in this great hemisphere of violence, but I was not alone as far as the human race was concerned. I was lonely amidst a world of *things* lit up by phosphorescent flashes of cruelty. I was delirious with an energy which could not be unleashed except in the service of death and futility. I could not begin with a full statement—it would have meant the strait-jacket or the electric chair. I was like a man who had been too long incarcerated in a dungeon—I had to feel my way slowly, falteringly, lest I stumble and be run over. I had to accustom myself gradually to the penalties which freedom involves. I had to grow a new epidermis which would protect me from this burning light in the sky.

The ovarian world is the product of a life rhythm. The moment a child is born it becomes part of a world in which there is not only the life rhythm but the death rhythm. The frantic desire to live, to live at any cost, is not a result of the life rhythm in us, but of the death rhythm. There is not only no need to keep alive at any price, but, if life is undesirable, it is absolutely wrong. This keeping oneself alive, out of a blind urge to defeat death, is in itself a means of sowing death. Everyone who has not fully accepted life, who is not incrementing life, is helping to fill the world with death. To make the simplest gesture with the hand can convey the utmost sense of life; a word spoken with the whole being can give life. Activity in itself means nothing: it is often a sign of death. By simple external pressure, by force of surroundings and example, by the very climate which activity engenders, one can become part of a monstrous death machine, such as America, for example. What does a dynamo know of life, of peace, of reality? What does any individual American dynamo know of the wisdom and energy, of the life abundant and eternal possessed by a ragged beggar sitting under a tree in the act of meditation? What is *energy*? What is *life*? One has only to read the stupid twaddle of the scientific and philosophic text-books to realize how less than nothing is the wisdom of these energetic Americans. Listen, they had me on the run, these crazy horse-power fiends; in order to break their insane rhythm, their death rhythm, I had to resort to a wave-length which, until I found the proper sustenance in my own bowels, would at least nullify the rhythm they had set up. Certainly I did not need this grotesque, cumbersome, antediluvian desk which I had installed in the parlor; certainly I didn't need twelve empty chairs placed around it in a semi-circle; I needed only elbow room in which to write and a thirteenth chair which would take me out of the zodiac they were using and put me in a heaven beyond heaven. But when

you drive a man almost crazy and when, to his own surprise
perhaps, he finds that he still has some resistance, some powers
of his own, then you are apt to find such a man acting very
much like a primitive being. Such a man is apt not only to become stubborn and dogged, but superstitious, a believer in magic
and a practicer of magic. Such a man is beyond religion—it is his
religiousness he is suffering from. Such a man becomes a mono-
maniac, bent on doing one thing only and that is to break the
evil spell which has been put upon him. Such a man is beyond
throwing bombs, beyond revolt; he wants to stop reacting,
whether inertly or ferociously. This man, of all men on earth,
wants the act to be a manifestation of life. If, in the realization
of his terrible need, he begins to act regressively, to become unsocial, to stammer and stutter, to prove so utterly unadapted as
to be incapable of earning a living, know that this man has found
his way back to the womb and source of life and that tomorrow,
instead of the contemptible object of ridicule which you have
made of him, he will stand forth as a *man* in his own right and
all the powers of the world will be of no avail against him.

Out of the crude cipher with which he communicates from
his prehistoric desk with the archaic men of the world a new
language builds up which cuts through the death language of
the day like wireless through a storm. There is no magic in this
wave-length, any more than there is magic in the womb. Men are
lonely and out of communication with one another because
all their inventions speak only of death. Death is the automaton
which rules the world of activity. Death is silent, because it has
no mouth. Death has never *expressed* anything.

Death is wonderful too—*after life*. Only one like myself who
has opened his mouth and spoken, only one who has said Yes,
Yes, Yes, and again Yes! can open wide his arms to death and
know no fear. Death as a reward, yes! Death as a result of fulfillment, yes! Death as a crown and shield, yes! But not death from
the roots, isolating men, making them bitter and fearful and
lonely, giving them fruitless energy, filling them with a will
which can only say No! The first word any man writes when
he has found himself, his own rhythm, which is the life rhythm.

is Yes! Everything he writes thereafter is Yes, Yes, Yes,—Yes in a
thousand million ways. No dynamo, no matter how huge—not
even a dynamo of a hundred million dead souls—can combat one
man saying Yes!

The war was on and men were being slaughtered, one million,
two million, five million, ten million, twenty million, finally a
hundred million, then a billion, everybody, man, woman and
child, down to the last one. "*No!*" they were shouting, "*No!
they shall not pass!*" And yet everybody passed; everybody got
a free pass, whether he shouted Yes or No. In the midst of this
triumphant demonstration of spiritually destructive osmosis I sat
with my feet planted on the big desk trying to communicate with
Zeus the Father of Atlantis and with his lost progeny, ignorant
of the fact that Apollinaire was to die the day before the Armistice in a military hospital, ignorant of the fact that in his "new
writings" he had penned these indelible lines:

> Be forbearing when you compare us
> With those who were the perfection of order.
> We who everywhere seek adventure,
> We are not your enemies.
> We would give you vast and strange domains
> Where flowering mystery waits for him would pluck it.

Ignorant that in this same poem he had also written:

> Have compassion on us who are always fighting on
>   the frontiers
> Of the boundless future,

Compassion for our errors, compassion for our sins. I was ignorant of the fact that there were men then living who went by the
outlandish names of Blaise Cendrars, Jacques Vaché, Louis
Aragon, Tristan Tzara, René Crevel, Henri de Montherlant,
André Breton, Max Ernst, George Grosz; ignorant of the fact
that on July, 14, 1916, at the Saal Waag, in Zurich, the first Dada
Manifesto had been proclaimed—"manifesto by monsieur antipyrine"—that in this strange document it was stated: "Dada is
life without slippers or parallel. . . severe necessity without disci-

pline or morality and we spit on humanity." Ignorant of the fact
that the Dada Manifesto of 1918 contained these lines: "I am writing a manifesto and I want nothing, yet I say certain things, and I
am against manifestoes as a matter of principle, as I am also
against principles. . . . I write this manifesto to show that one
may perform opposed actions together, in a single fresh respira-
tion; I am against action; for continual contradiction, for affirma-
tion also, I am neither for nor against and I do not explain for I
hate good sense. . . . There is a literature which does not reach
the voracious mass. The work of creators, sprung from a real
necessity on the part of the author, and for himself. Consciousness of a supreme egotism where the stars waste away. . . . Each
page must explode, either with the profoundly serious and heavy,
the whirlwind, dizziness, the new, the eternal, with the overwhelming hoax, with an enthusiasm for principles or with the
mode of typography. On the one hand a staggering fleeing
world, affianced to the jinglebells of the infernal gamut, on the
other hand: *new beings.* . . ."

Thirty-two years later and I am still saying Yes! Yes, Monsieur Antipyrine! Yes, Monsieur Tristan Bustanoby Tzara! Yes,
Monsieur Max Ernst Geburt! Yes! Monsieur René Crevel, now
that you are dead by suicide, yes, the world is crazy, you were
right. Yes, Monsieur Blaise Cendrars, you were right to kill.
Was it the day of the Armistice that you brought out your little
book—*J'ai tué?* Yes, "keep on my lads, humanity. . . ." Yes,
Jacques Vaché, quite right—"Art ought to be something funny
and a trifle boring." Yes, my dear dead Vaché, how right you
were and how funny and how boring and touching and tender
and true: "It is of the essence of symbols to be symbolic." Say
it again, from the other world! Have you a megaphone up there?
Have you found all the arms and legs that were blown off during
the melee? Can you put them together again? Do you remember
the meeting at Nantes in 1916 with André Breton? Did you
celebrate the birth of hysteria together? Had he told you, Breton,
that there was only the marvelous and nothing but the marvelous
and that the marvelous is always marvelous—and isn't it marvelous to hear it again, even though your ears are stopped? I

want to include here, before passing on, a little portrait of you by Emile Bouvier for the benefit of my Brooklyn friends who may not have recognized me then but who will now, I am sure. . . .

". . . he was not at all crazy, and could explain his conduct when occasion required. His actions, none the less, were as disconcerting as Jarry's worst eccentricities. For example, he was barely out of hospital when he hired himself out as a stevedore, and he thereafter passed his afternoons in unloading coal on the quays along the Loire. In the evening, on the other hand, he would make the rounds of the cafés and cinemas, dressed in the height of fashion and with many variations of costume. What was more, in time of war, he would strut forth sometimes in the uniform of a lieutenant of Hussars, sometimes in that of an English officer, of an aviator or of a surgeon. In civil life, he was quite as free and easy, thinking nothing of introducing Breton under the name of André Salmon, while he took unto himself, but quite without vanity, the most wonderful titles and adventures. He never said good morning nor good evening nor good-bye, and never took any notice of letters, except those from his mother, when he had to ask for money. He did not recognize his best friends from one day to another. . . ."

Do you recognize me, lads? Just a Brooklyn boy communicating with the red-haired albinos of the Zuni region. Making ready, with feet on the desk, to write "strong works, works forever incomprehensible," as my dead comrades were promising. These "strong works"—would you recognize them if you saw them? Do you know that of the millions who were killed not one death was necessary to produce "the strong work"? *New beings*, yes! We have need of new beings still. We can do without the telephone, without the automobile, without the high-class bombers—but we can't do without new beings. If Atlantis was submerged beneath the sea, if the Sphinx and the Pyramids remain an eternal riddle, it is because there were no more new beings being born. Stop the machine a moment! Flash back! Flash back to 1914, to the Kaiser sitting on his horse. Keep him sitting there a moment with his withered arm clutching the

bridle rein. Look at his moustache! Look at his haughty air of
pride and arrogance! Look at his cannon-fodder lined up in
strictest discipline, all ready to obey the word, to get shot, to get
disemboweled, to be burned in quick-lime. Hold it a moment,
now, and look at the other side: the defenders of our great and
glorious civilization, the men who will war to end war. Change
their clothes, change uniforms, change horses, change flags,
change terrain. My, is that the Kaiser I see on a white horse?
Are those the terrible Huns? And where is Big Bertha? Oh, I
see—I thought it was pointing towards Notre Dame? Humanity,
me lads, humanity always marching in the van . . . And the
strong works we were speaking of? Where are the strong works?
Call up the Western Union and dispatch a messenger fleet of
foot—not a cripple or an octogenarian, but a young one! Ask
him to find the great work and bring it back. We need it. We
have a brand new museum ready waiting to house it—and cello-
phane and the Dewey Decimal system to file it. All we need is
the name of the author. Even if he has no name, even if it is
an anonymous work, we won't kick. Even if it has a little mustard
gas in it we won't mind. Bring it back dead or alive—there's a
$25,000 reward for the man who fetches it.

And if they tell you that these things had to be, that things
could not have happened otherwise, that France did her best and
Germany her best and that little Liberia and little Ecuador and
all the other allies also did their best, and that since the war
everybody has been doing his best to patch things up or to forget, tell them that their best is not good enough, that we don't
want to hear any more this logic of "doing the best one can,"
tell them we don't want the best of a bad bargain, we don't believe in bargains good or bad, nor in war memorials. We don't
want to hear about the logic of events—or any kind of logic.
"*Je ne parle pas logique,*" said Montherlant, "*je parle générosité.*"
I don't think you heard it very well, since it was in French. I'll
repeat it for you, in the Queen's own language: "I'm not talking
logic, I'm talking generosity." That's bad English, as the Queen
herself might speak it, but it's clear. *Generosity*—do you hear?
You never practice it, any of you, either in peace or in war. You

don't know the meaning of the word. You think to supply guns and ammunition to the winning side is generosity; you think sending Red Cross nurses to the front, or the Salvation Army, is generosity. You think a bonus twenty years too late is generosity; you think a little pension and a wheel-chair is generosity; you think if you give a man his old job back it's generosity. You don't know what the fucking word means, you bastards! To be generous is to say Yes before the man even opens his mouth. To say Yes you have to first be a Surrealist or a Dadaist, because you have understood what it means to say No. You can even say Yes and No at the same time, provided you do more than is expected of you. Be a stevedore in the day time and a Beau Brummell in the night time. Wear any uniform so long as it's not yours. When you write your mother ask her to cough up a little dough so that you may have a clean rag to wipe your ass with. Don't be disturbed if you see your neighbor going after his wife with a knife: he probably has good reason to go after her, and if he kills her you may be sure he has the satisfaction of knowing *why* he did it. If you're trying to improve your mind, stop it! There's no improving the mind. Look to your heart and gizzard—the brain is in the heart.

Ah yes, if I had known then that these birds existed—Cendrars, Vaché, Grosz, Ernst, Apollinaire—if I had known that then, if I had known that in their own way they were thinking exactly the same things as I was, I think I'd have blown up. Yes, I think I'd have gone off like a bomb. But I was ignorant. Ignorant of the fact that almost fifty years previously a crazy Jew in South America had given birth to such startlingly marvelous phrases as "doubt's duck with the vermouth lips" or "I have seen a fig eat an onager"—that about the same time a Frenchman, who was only a boy, was saying: "Find flowers that are chairs" . . . "my hunger is the black air's bits" . . . "his heart, amber and spunsk." Maybe at the same time, or thereabouts, while Jarry was saying "in eating the sound of moths," and Apollinaire repeating after him "near a gentleman swallowing himself," and Breton murmuring softly "night's pedals move uninterruptedly," perhaps "in the air beautiful and black" which the lone Jew had found

under the Southern Cross another man, also lonely and exiled
and of Spanish origin, was preparing to put down on paper these
memorable words: "I seek, all in all, to console myself for my
exile, for my exile from eternity, for that un-earthing *(destierro)*
which I am fond of referring to as my unheavening ... At present, I think that the best way of writing this novel is to tell how
it should be written. It is the novel of the novel, the creation of
creation. Or God of God, *Deus de Deo*." Had I known he was going to add this, this which follows, I would surely have gone off
like a bomb. ... "By being crazy is understood losing one's reason. Reason, but not the truth, for there are madmen who speak
truths while others keep silent. . . ." Speaking of these things,
speaking of the war and the war dead, I cannot refrain from
mentioning that some twenty years later I ran across this in
French by a Frenchman, O miracle of miracles! *"Il faut le dire,
il y a des cadavres que je ne respecte qu'à moitié."* Yes, yes, and
again yes! O, let us do some rash thing—for the sheer pleasure of
it! Let us do something live and magnificent, even if destructive!
Said the mad cobbler: "All things are generated out of the
grand mystery, and proceed out of one degree into another.
Whatever goes forward in its degree, the same receives no
abominate."

Everywhere in all times the same ovarian world announcing
itself. Yet also, parallel with these announcements, these proph-
ecies, these gynecological manifestoes, parallel and contempo-
raneous with them new totem poles, new taboos, new war dances.
While into the air so black and beautiful the brothers of man,
the poets, the diggers of the future, were spitting their magic
lines, in this same time, O profound and perplexing riddle, other
men were saying: "Won't you please come and take a job in
our ammunition factory. We promise you the highest wages,
the most sanitary and hygienic conditions. The work is so easy
that even a child could do it." And if you had a sister, a wife, a
mother, an aunt, as long as she could manipulate her hands, as
long as she could prove that she had no bad habits, you were
invited to bring her or them along to the ammunition works. If
you were shy of soiling your hands they would explain to you

very gently and intelligently just how these delicate mechanisms
operated, what they did when they exploded, and why you
must not waste even your garbage because . . . et ipso facto e
pluribus unum. The thing that impressed me, going the rounds
in search of work, was not so much that they made me vomit
every day (assuming I had been lucky enough to put something
into my gut), but that they always demanded to know if you
were of good habits, if you were steady, if you were sober, if
you were industrious, if you had ever worked before and if not
why not. Even the garbage, which I had gotten the job of collecting for the municipality, was precious to them, the killers.
Standing knee-deep in the muck, the lowest of the low, a coolie,
an outcast, still I was part of the death racket. I tried reading the
Inferno at night, but it was in English and English is no language
for a catholic work. "Whatever enters in itself into its self-hood,
viz., into its own lubet . . ." *Lubet!* If I had had a word like that
to conjure with then, how peacefully I might have gone about
my garbage collecting! How sweet, in the night when Dante is
out of reach and the hands smell of muck and slime, to take unto
oneself this word which in the Dutch means "lust" and in Latin
"lubitum" or the divine, *beneplacitum.* Standing knee-deep in
the garbage I said one day what Meister Eckhart is reported to
have said long ago: "I truly have need of God, but God has
need of me too." There was a job waiting for me in the slaughter-
house, a nice little job of sorting entrails, but I couldn't raise the
fare to get to Chicago. I remained in Brooklyn, in my own palace
of entrails, and turned round and round on the plinth of the
labyrinth. I remained at home seeking the "germinal vesicle,"
"the dragon castle on the floor of the sea," "the Heavenly Heart,"
"the field of the square inch," "the house of the square foot," "the
dark pass," "the space of former Heaven." I remained locked in,
a prisoner of Forculus, god of the door, of Cardea, god of the
hinge, and of Limentius, god of the threshold. I spoke only with
their sisters, the three goddesses called Fear, Pallor and Fever. I
saw no "Asian luxury," as had St. Augustine, or as he imagined
he had. Nor did I see "the two twins born, so near together, that
the second held the first by the heel." But I saw a street called

Myrtle Avenue, which runs from Borough Hall to Fresh Pond Road, and down this street no saint ever walked (else it would have crumbled), down this street no miracle ever passed, nor any poet, nor any species of human genus, nor did any flower ever grow there, nor did the sun strike it squarely, nor did the rain ever wash it. For the genuine Inferno which I had to postpone for twenty years I give you Myrtle Avenue, one of the innumerable bridle-paths ridden by iron monsters which lead to the heart of America's emptiness. If you have only seen Essen or Manchester or Chicago or Levallois-Perret or Glasgow or Hoboken or Canarsie or Bayonne, you have seen nothing of the magnificent emptiness of progress and enlightenment. Dear reader, you must see Myrtle Avenue before you die, if only to realize how far into the future Dante saw. You must believe me that on this street, neither in the houses which line it nor the cobble-stones which pave it, nor the elevated structure which cuts it atwain, neither in any creature that bears a name and lives thereon, neither in any animal, bird or insect passing through it to slaughter or already slaughtered, is there hope of "lubet," "sublimate" or "abominate." It is a street not of sorrow, for sorrow would be human and recognizable, but of sheer emptiness: it is emptier than the most extinct volcano, emptier than a vacuum, emptier than the word God in the mouth of an unbeliever.

My First Book
—*Tropic of Capricorn*

When it came time for my vacation—I hadn't taken one for three years, I was so eager to make the company* a success!—I took three weeks instead of two and I wrote the book about the twelve little men. I wrote it straight off, five, seven, sometimes

---

* "I entered the Western Union as personnel manager in 1920 and left towards the end of 1924. About 1922, I think it was, I wrote my first book, while on a three week vacation. I forget the title but it was about twelve messengers I had studied."—Unpublished letter to Huntington Cairns, 1939.

eight thousand words a day. I thought that a man, to be a writer, must do at least five thousand words a day. I thought he must say everything all at once—in one book—and collapse afterwards. I didn't know a thing about writing. I was scared shitless. But I was determined to wipe Horatio Alger out of the North American consciousness. I suppose it was the worst book any man has ever written. It was a colossal tome and faulty from start to finish. But it was my first book and I was in love with it. If I had had the money, as Gide had, I would have published it at my own expense. If I had had the courage that Whitman had, I would have peddled it from door to door. Everybody I showed it to said it was terrible. I was urged to give up the idea of writing. I had to learn, as Balzac did, that one must write volumes before signing one's own name. I had to learn, as I soon did, that one must give up everything and not do anything else but write, that one must write and write and write, even if everybody in the world advises you against it, even if nobody believes in you. Perhaps one does it just because nobody believes; perhaps the real secret lies in making people believe. That the book was inadequate, faulty, bad, *terrible*, as they said, was only natural. I was attempting at the start what a man of genius would have undertaken only at the end. I wanted to say the last word at the beginning. It was absurd and pathetic. It was a crushing defeat, but it put iron in my backbone and sulphur in my blood. I knew at least what it was to fail. I knew what it was to attempt something big. Today, when I think of the circumstances under which I wrote that book, when I think of the overwhelming material which I tried to put into form, when I think of what I hoped to encompass, I pat myself on the back, I give myself a double A. I am proud of the fact that I made such a miserable failure of it; had I succeeded I would have been a monster. Sometimes, when I look over my notebooks, when I look at the names alone of those whom I thought to write about, I am seized with vertigo. Each man came to me with a world of his own; he came to me and unloaded it on my desk; he expected me to pick it up and put it on my shoulders. I had no time to make a world of my own: I had to stay fixed like Atlas, my feet on the elephant's back and the elephant on the tortoise's back. To inquire on what the tortoise stood would be to go mad.

I didn't dare to think of anything then except the "facts." To get beneath the facts I would have had to be an artist, and one doesn't become an artist overnight. First you have to be crushed, to have your conflicting points of view annihilated. You have to be wiped out as a human being in order to be born again an individual. You have to be carbonized and mineralized in order to work upwards from the last common denominator of the self. You have to get beyond pity in order to feel from the very roots of your being. One can't make a new heaven and earth with "facts." There are no "facts"—there is only *the fact* that man, every man everywhere in the world, is on his way to ordination. Some men take the long route and some take the short route. Every man is working out his destiny in his own way and nobody can be of help except by being kind, generous and patient.

Why Don't You Try to Write?
—Sexus

. . . Instead of rushing out of the house immediately after dinner that evening, as I usually did, I lay on the couch in the dark and fell into a deep reverie. "*Why don't you try to write?*" That was the phrase which had stuck in my crop all day, which repeated itself insistently, even as I was saying thank you to my friend MacGregor for the ten-spot which I had wrung from him after the most humiliating wheedling and cajoling.

In the darkness I began to work my way back to the hub. I began to think of those most happy days of childhood, the long summer days when my mother took me by the hand, led me over the fields to see my little friends, Joey and Tony. As a child it was impossible to penetrate the secret of that joy which comes from a sense of superiority. That extra sense, which enables one to participate and at the same time to observe one's participation, appeared to me to be the normal endowment of every one. That I enjoyed everything more than other boys my age I was unaware of. The discrepancy between myself and others only dawned on me as I grew older.

To write, I meditated, must be an act devoid of will. The word, like the deep ocean current, has to float to the surface of its own impulse. A child has no need to write, he is innocent. A man writes to throw off the poison which he has accumulated because of his false way of life. He is trying to recapture his innocence, yet all he succeeds in doing (by writing) is to inoculate the world with the virus of his disillusionment. No man would set a word down on paper if he had the courage to live out what he believed in. His inspiration is deflected at the source. If it is a world of truth, beauty and magic that he desires to create, why does he put millions of words between himself and the reality of that world? Why does he defer action—unless it be that, like other men, what he really desires is power, fame, success. "Books are human actions in death," said Balzac. Yet, having perceived the truth, he deliberately surrendered the angel to the demon which possessed him.

A writer woos his public just as ignominiously as a politician or any other mountebank; he loves to finger the great pulse, to prescribe like a physician, to win a place for himself, to be recognized as a force, to receive the full cup of adulation, even if it be deferred a thousand years. He doesn't want a new world which might be established immediately, because he knows it would never suit him. He wants an impossible world in which he is the uncrowned puppet ruler dominated by forces utterly beyond his control. He is content to rule insidiously—in the fictive world of symbols—because the very thought of contact with rude and brutal realities frightens him. True, he has a greater grasp of reality than other men, but he makes no effort to impose that higher reality on the world by force of example. He is satisfied just to preach, to drag along in the wake of disasters and catastrophes, a death-croaking prophet always without honor, always stoned, always shunned by those who, however unsuited for their tasks, are ready and willing to assume respon-

sibility for the affairs of the world. The truly great writer does
not want to write: he wants the world to be a place in which he
can live the life of the imagination. The first quivering word he
puts to paper is the word of the wounded angel: pain. The process of putting down words is equivalent to giving oneself a nar-
cotic. Observing the growth of a book under his hands, the
author swells with delusions of grandeur. "I too am a conqueror
—perhaps the greatest conqueror of all! My day is coming. I will
enslave the world—by the magic of words. . . ." Et cetera ad
nauseam.

The little phrase—*Why don't you try to write?*—involved me,
as it had from the very beginning, in a hopeless bog of confusion.
I wanted to enchant but not to enslave; I wanted a greater, richer
life, but not at the expense of others; I wanted to free the imagination of all men at once because without the support of the
whole world, without a world imaginatively unified, the freedom
of the imagination becomes a vice. I had no respect for writing
per se any more than I had for God *per se*. Nobody, no principle,
no idea has validity in itself. What is valid is only that much—of
anything, God included—which is realized by all men in common. People are always worried about the fate of the genius. I
never worried about the genius: genius takes care of the genius
in a man. My concern was always for the nobody, the man who
is lost in the shuffle, the man who is so common, so ordinary, that
his presence is not even noticed. One genius does not inspire another. All geniuses are leeches, so to speak. They feed from the
same source—the blood of life. The most important thing for the
genius is to make himself useless, to be absorbed in the common
stream, to become a fish again and not a freak of nature. The
only benefit, I reflected, which the act of writing could offer me
was to remove the differences which separated me from my
fellow-man. I definitely did not want to become the artist, in the
sense of becoming something strange, something apart and out
of the current of life.

The best thing about writing is not the actual labor of putting
word against word, brick upon brick, but the preliminaries, the
spade work, which is done in silence, under any circumstances,

in dream as well as in the waking state. In short, the period of gestation. No man ever puts down what he intended to say: the original creation, which is taking place all the time, whether one writes or doesn't write, belongs to the primal flux: it has no dimensions, no form, no time element. In this preliminary state, which is creation and not birth, what disappears suffers no destruction; something which was already there, something imperishable, like memory, or matter, or God, is summoned and in it one flings himself like a twig into a torrent. Words, sentences, ideas, no matter how subtle or ingenious, the maddest flights of poetry, the most profound dreams, the most hallucinating visions, are but crude hieroglyphs chiseled in pain and sorrow to commemorate an event which is untransmissible. In an intelligently ordered world there would be no need to make the unreasonable attempt of putting such miraculous happenings down. Indeed, it would make no sense, for if men only stopped to realize it, who would be content with the counterfeit when the real is at everyone's beck and call? Who would want to switch in and listen to Beethoven, for example, when he might himself experience the ecstatic harmonies which Beethoven so desperately strove to register? A great work of art, if it accomplishes anything, serves to remind us, or let us say to set us dreaming, of all that is fluid and intangible. Which is to say, *the universe*. It cannot be understood; it can only be accepted or rejected. If accepted we are revitalized; if rejected we are diminished. Whatever it purports to be it is not: it is always something more for which the last word will never be said. It is all that we put into it out of hunger for that which we deny every day of our lives. If we accepted *ourselves* as completely, the work of art, in fact *the whole world of art*, would die of malnutrition. Every man Jack of us moves without feet at least a few hours a day, when his eyes are closed and his body prone. The art of dreaming when wide awake will be in the power of every man one day. Long before that books will cease to exist, for when men are wide awake *and* dreaming their powers of communication (with one another and with the spirit that moves all men) will be so enhanced as to make writing seem like the harsh and raucous squawks of an idiot.

I think and know all this, lying in the dark memory of a summer's day, without having mastered, or even half-heartedly attempted to master, the art of the crude hieroglyph. Before ever I begin I am disgusted with the efforts of the acknowledged masters. Without the ability or the knowledge to make so much as a portal in the façade of the grand edifice, I criticize and lament the architecture itself. If I were only a tiny brick in the vast cathedral of this antiquated façade I would be infinitely happier; I would have life, the life of the whole structure, even as an infinitesimal part of it. But I am outside, a barbarian who cannot make even a crude sketch, let alone a plan, of the edifice he dreams of inhabiting. I dream a new blazingly magnificent world which collapses as soon as the light is turned on. A world that vanishes but does not die, for I have only to become still again and stare wide-eyed into the darkness and it reappears. . . . There is then a world in me which is utterly unlike any world I know of. I do not think it is my exclusive property—it is only the angle of my vision which is exclusive in that it is unique. If I talk the language of my unique vision nobody understands; the most colossal edifice may be reared and yet remain invisible. The thought of that haunts me. What good will it do to make an invisible temple?

*   *   *

It was in Ulric's studio not so many months ago that I had finished my first book—the book about the twelve messengers. I used to work in his brother's room where some short time previously a magazine editor, after reading a few pages of an unfinished story, informed me cold-bloodedly that I hadn't an ounce of talent, that I didn't know the first thing about writing —in short that I was a complete flop and the best thing to do, my lad, is to forget it, try to make an honest living. Another nincompoop who had written a highly successful book about Jesus-the-carpenter had told me the same thing. And if rejection slips mean anything there was simple corroboration to support the criticism of these discerning minds. "Who *are* these shits?" I used to say to

Ulric. "Where do they get off to tell me these things? What have they done, except to prove that they know how to make money?"

Well, I was talking about Joey and Tony, my little friends. I was lying in the dark, a little twig floating in the Japanese current. I was getting back to simple abracadabra, the straw that makes bricks, the crude sketch, the temple which must take on flesh and blood and make itself manifest to all the world. I got up and put on a soft light. I felt calm and lucid, like a lotus opening up. No violent pacing back and forth, no tearing the hair out by the roots. I sank slowly into a chair by the table and with a pencil I began to write. I described in simple words how it felt to take my mother's hand and walk across the sun-lit fields, how it felt to see Joey and Tony rushing towards me with arms open, their faces beaming with joy. I put one brick upon another like an honest brick-layer. Something of a vertical nature was happening—not blades of grass shooting up but something structural, something planned. I didn't strain myself to finish it; I stopped when I had said all I could. I read it over quietly, what I had written. I was so moved that the tears came to my eyes. It wasn't something to show an editor: it was something to put away in a drawer, to keep as a reminder of natural processes, as a promise of fulfillment.

Every day we slaughter our finest impulses. That is why we get a heart-ache when we read those lines written by the hand of a master and recognize them as our own, as the tender shoots which we stifled because we lacked the faith to believe in our own powers, our own criterion of truth and beauty. Every man, when he gets quiet, when he becomes desperately honest with himself, is capable of uttering profound truths. We all derive from the same source. There is no mystery about the origin of things. We are all part of creation, all kings, all poets, all musicians; we have only to open up, only to discover what is already there.

What happened to me in writing about Joey and Tony was tantamount to revelation. It was revealed to me that I could say what I wanted to say—if I thought of nothing else, if I concentrated upon that exclusively —*and* if I were willing to bear the consequences which a pure act always involves.

Creation
—*Sexus*

The world would only begin to get something of value from me the moment I stopped being a serious member of society and became—*myself*. The State, the nation, the united nations of the world, were nothing but one great aggregation of individuals who repeated the mistakes of their forefathers. They were caught in the wheel from birth and they kept at it till death— and this treadmill they tried to dignify by calling it "life." If you asked anyone to explain or define life, what was the be-all and the end-all, you got a blank look for answer. Life was something which philosophers dealt with in books that no one read. Those in the thick of life, "the plugs in harness," had no time for such idle questions. "*You've got to eat, haven't you?*" This query, which was supposed to be a stop-gap, and which had already been answered, if not in the absolute negative at least in a disturbingly relative negative by those who knew, was a clue to all the other questions which followed in a veritable Euclidian suite. From the little reading I had done I had observed that the men who were most *in* life, who were molding life, who were life itself, ate little, slept little, owned little or nothing. They had no illusions about duty, or the perpetuation of their kith and kin, or the preservation of the State. They were interested in truth and in truth alone. They recognized only one kind of activity— *creation*. Nobody could command their services because they had of their own pledged themselves to give all. They gave gratuitously, because that is the only way to give. This was the way of life which appealed to me: it made sound sense. It *was* life—not the simulacrum which those about me worshipped.

I had understood all this—with my mind at the very brink of

manhood. But there was a great comedy of life to be gone through before this vision of reality could become the motivating force. The tremendous hunger for life which others sensed in me acted like a magnet; it attracted those who needed my particular kind of hunger. The hunger was magnified a thousand times. It was as if those who clung to me (like iron filings) became sensitized and attracted others in turn. Sensation ripens into experience and experience engenders experience.

What I secretly longed for was to disentangle myself of all those lives which had woven themselves into the pattern of my own life and were making my destiny a part of theirs. To shake myself free of these accumulating experiences which were mine only by force of inertia required a violent effort. Now and then I lunged and tore at the net, but only to become more enmeshed. My liberation seemed to involve pain and suffering to those near and dear to me. Every move I made for my own private good brought about reproach and condemnation. I was a traitor a thousand times over. I had lost even the right to become ill—because "they" needed me. I wasn't *allowed* to remain inactive. Had I died I think they would have galvanized my corpse into a semblance of life.

"I stood before a mirror and said fearfully: 'I want to see how I look in the mirror with my eyes closed.' "

These words of Richter's, when I first came upon them, made an indescribable commotion in me. As did the following, which seems almost like a corollary of the above—from Novalis:

"The seat of the soul is where inner world and outer world touch each other. For nobody knows himself, if he is only himself and not also another one at the same time."

"To take possession of one's transcendental I, to be the I of one's I, at the same time," as Novalis expressed it again.

There is a time when ideas tyrannize over one, when one is just a hapless victim of another's thoughts. This "possession" by another seems to occur in periods of depersonalization, when the warring selves come unglued, as it were. Normally one is impervious to ideas; they come and go, are accepted or rejected,

put on like shirts, taken off like dirty socks. But in those periods
which we call crises, when the mind sunders and splinters like
a diamond under the blows of a sledge-hammer, these innocent
ideas of a dreamer take hold, lodge in the crevices of the brain,
and by some subtle process of infiltration bring about a definite,
irrevocable alteration of the personality. Outwardly no great
change takes place; the individual affected does not suddenly behave differently; on the contrary, he may behave in more "normal" fashion than before. This seeming normality assumes more
and more the quality of a protective device. From surface deception he passes to inner deception. With each new crisis, however, he becomes more strongly aware of a change which is no
change, but rather an intensification of something hidden deep
within. Now when he closes his eyes he can really look at himself. He no longer sees a mask. He sees without seeing, to be
exact. Vision without sight, a fluid grasp of intangibles: the merg-
ing of sight and sound: the heart of the web. Here stream the
distant personalities which evade the crude contact of the senses;
here the overtones of recognition discreetly lap against one another in bright, vibrant harmonies. There is no language employed, no outlines delineated.

When a ship founders it settles slowly; the spars, the masts,
the rigging float away. On the ocean floor of death the bleeding
hull bedecks itself with jewels; remorselessly the anatomic life
begins. What was ship becomes the nameless indestructible.

Like ships, men founder time and again. Only memory saves
them from complete dispersion. Poets drop their stitches in the
loom, straws for drowning men to grasp as they sink into extinction. Ghosts climb back on watery stairs, make imaginary
ascents, vertiginous drops, memorize numbers, dates, events, in
passing from gas to liquid and back again. There is no brain
capable of registering the changing changes. Nothing happens
in the brain, except the gradual rust and detrition of the cells.
But in the mind, worlds unclassified, undenominated, unassimi-
lated, form, break, unite, dissolve and harmonize ceaselessly. In
the mind-world ideas are the indestructible elements which form
the jeweled constellations of the interior life. We move within

their orbits, freely if we follow their intricate patterns, enslaved or possessed if we try to subjugate them. Everything external is but a reflection projected by the mind machine.

Creation is the eternal play which takes place at the borderline; it is spontaneous and compulsive, obedient to law. One removes from the mirror and the curtain rises. *Séance permanente.* Only madmen are excluded. Only those who "have lost their mind," as we say. For these never cease to dream that they are dreaming. They stood before the mirror with eyes open and fell sound asleep; they sealed their shadow in the tomb of memory. In them the stars collapse to form what Hugo called "a blinding menagerie of suns which, through love, make themselves the poodles and the Newfoundlands of immensity."

The creative life! Ascension. Passing beyond oneself. Rocketing out into the blue, grasping at flying ladders, mounting, soaring, lifting the world up by the scalp, rousing the angels from their ethereal lairs, drowning in stellar depths, clinging to the tails of comets. Nietzsche had written of it ecstatically—and then swooned forward into the mirror to die in root and flower. "Stairs and contradictory stairs," he wrote, and then suddenly there was no longer any bottom; the mind, like a splintered diamond, was pulverized by the hammer-blows of truth.

There was a time when I acted as my father's keeper. I was left alone for long hours, cooped up in the little booth which we used as an office. While he was drinking with his cronies I was feeding from the bottle of creative life. My companions were the free spirits, the overlords of the soul. The young man sitting there in the mingy yellow light became completely unhinged; he lived in the crevices of great thoughts, crouched like a hermit in the barren folds of a lofty mountain range. From truth he passed to imagination and from imagination to invention. At this last portal, through which there is no return, fear beset him. To venture farther was to wander alone, to rely wholly upon oneself.

The purpose of discipline is to promote freedom. But freedom leads to infinity and infinity is terrifying. Then arose the comforting thought of stopping at the brink, of setting down in words

the mysteries of impulsion, compulsion, propulsion, of bathing
the senses in human odors. To become utterly human, the com-
passionate fiend incarnate, the locksmith of the great door leading beyond and away and forever isolate. . . .

Men founder like ships. Children also. There are children who
settle to the bottom at the age of nine, carrying with them the
secret of their betrayal. There are perfidious monsters who look
at you with the bland, innocent eyes of youth; their crimes are
unregistered, because we have no names for them.

Why do lovely faces haunt us so? Do extraordinary flowers
have evil roots?

Studying her morsel by morsel, feet, hands, hair, lips, ears,
breasts, traveling from navel to mouth and from mouth to eyes,
the woman I fell upon, clawed, bit, suffocated with kisses, the
woman who had been Mara and was now Mona, who had been
and would be other names, other persons, other assemblages of
appendages, was no more accessible, penetrable, than a cool statue
in a forgotten garden of a lost continent. At nine or earlier, with
a revolver that was never intended to go off, she might have
pressed a swooning trigger and fallen like a dead swan from the
heights of her dream. It might well have been that way, for in
the flesh she was dispersed, in the mind she was as dust blown
hither and thither. In her heart a bell tolled, but what it signified
no one knew. Her image corresponded to nothing that I had
formed in my heart. She had intruded it, slipped it like thinnest
gauze between the crevices of the brain in a moment of lesion.
And when the wound closed the imprint had remained, like a
frail leaf traced upon a stone.

Haunting nights when, filled with creation, I saw nothing but
her eyes and in those eyes, rising like bubbling pools of lava,
phantoms came to the surface, faded, vanished, reappeared,
bringing dread, apprehension, fear, mystery. A being constantly
pursued, a hidden flower whose scent the blood-hounds never
picked up. Behind the phantoms, peering through the jungle
brush, stood a shrinking child who seemed to offer herself las-
civiously. Then the swan dive, slow, as in motion pictures, and
snow-flakes falling with the falling body, and then phantoms and

more phantoms, the eyes becoming eyes again, burning like lignite, then glowing like embers, then soft like flowers; then nose, mouth, cheeks, ears looming out of chaos, heavy as the moon, a mask unrolling, flesh taking form, face, feature.

Night after night, from words to dreams, to flesh, to phantoms. Possession and depossession. The flowers of the moon, the broad-backed palms of jungle growth, the baying of blood-hounds, the frail white body of a child, the lava bubbles, the rallentando of the snow-flakes, the floorless bottom where smoke blooms into flesh. And what is flesh but moon? and what is moon but night? Night is longing, longing, longing, beyond all endurance.

"Think of *us!*" she said that night when she turned and flew up the steps rapidly. And it was as if I could think of nothing else. We two and the stairs ascending infinitely. Then "contradictory stairs": the stairs in my father's office, the stairs leading to crime, to madness, to the portals of invention. How *could* I think of anything else?

Creation. To create the legend in which I could fit the key which would open her soul.

A woman trying to deliver her secret. A desperate woman, seeking through love to unite herself with herself. Before the immensity of mystery one stands like a centipede that feels the ground slipping beneath its feet. Every door that opens leads to a greater void. One must swim like a star in the trackless ocean of time. One must have the patience of radium buried beneath a Himalayan peak.

It is about twenty years now since I began the study of the photogenic soul; in that time I have conducted hundreds of experiments. The result is that I know a little more—about myself. I think it must be very much the same with the political leader or the military genius. One discovers nothing about the secrets of the universe; at the best one learns something about the nature of destiny.

In the beginning one wants to approach every problem directly. The more direct and insistent the approach, the more quickly and surely one succeeds in getting caught in the web. No one is more helpless than the heroic individual. And no one can produce more tragedy and confusion than such a type. Flashing his sword above the Gordian knot, he promises speedy deliverance. A delusion which ends in an ocean of blood.

The creative artist has something in common with the hero. Though functioning on another plane, he too believes that he has solutions to offer. He gives his life to accomplish imaginary triumphs. At the conclusion of every grand experiment, whether by statesman, warrior, poet or philosopher, the problems of life present the same enigmatic complexion. The happiest peoples, it is said, are those which have no history. Those which have a history, those which have made history, seem only to have emphasized through their accomplishments the eternality of struggle. These disappear too, eventually, just as those who made no effort, who were content merely to live and to enjoy.

The creative individual (in wrestling with his medium) is supposed to experience a joy which balances, if it does not outweigh, the pain and anguish which accompany the struggle to express himself. He lives in his work, we say. But this unique kind of life varies extremely with the individual. It is only in the measure that he is aware of more life, the life abundant, that he may be said to live in his work. If there is no realization, there is no purpose or advantage in substituting the imaginative life for the purely adventurous one of reality. Everyone who lifts himself above the activities of the daily round does so not only in the hope of enlarging his field of experience, or even of enriching it, but of quickening it. Only in this sense does struggle have any meaning. Accept this view, and the distinction between failure and success is nil. And this is what every great artist comes to learn en route—that the process in which he is involved has to do with another dimension of life, that by identifying himself with this process he *augments* life. In this view of things he is permanently removed—and protected—from that insidious death which seems to triumph all about him. He divines that the great secret will never be apprehended but incorporated in his very substance. He has to make himself a part of the mystery, live *in* it as well as with it. Acceptance is the solution: it is an art, not an egotistical performance on the part of the intellect. Through art then, one finally establishes contact with reality: that is the great discovery. Here all is play and invention; there is no solid foothold from which to launch the projectiles which will pierce the miasma of folly, ignorance and greed. The world has *not* to be put in order: the world *is* order incarnate. It is for us to put ourselves in unison with this order, to know what is the world order in contradistinction to the wishful-thinking orders which we seek to impose on one another. The power which we long to possess, in order to establish the good, the true and the beautiful, would prove to be, if we could have it, but the means of destroying one another. It is fortunate that we are powerless. We have first to acquire vision, then discipline and forbearance. Until we have the humility to acknowledge the existence of a vision beyond our own, until we have faith and trust in superior powers, the blind must lead the blind. The men who believe that work and brains will accomplish everything must ever be deceived by the quixotic and unforeseen turn of events. They are the ones who are perpetually disappointed; no longer able to blame the gods, or God, they turn on their fellow-men and vent their impotent rage by crying "Treason! Stupidity!" and other hollow terms.

The great joy of the artist is to become aware of a higher order of things, to recognize by the compulsive and spontaneous manipulation of his own impulses the resemblance between human creation and what is called "divine" creation. In works of fantasy the existence of law manifesting itself through order is even more apparent than in other works of art. Nothing is less mad, less chaotic, than a work of fantasy. Such a creation, which is nothing less than pure invention, pervades all levels, creating, like water, its own level. The endless interpretations which are offered up contribute nothing, except to heighten the significance of what is seemingly unintelligible. This unintelligibility somehow makes profound sense. Everyone is affected, including those who pretend not to be affected. Something is present, in works of fantasy, which can only be likened to an elixir. This mysterious element, often referred to as "pure nonsense," brings with it the flavor and the aroma of that larger and utterly impenetrable

world in which we and all the heavenly bodies have their being.
The term nonsense is one of the most baffling words in our vocabulary. It has a negative quality only, like death. Nobody can
explain nonsense: it can only be demonstrated. To add, moreover, that sense and nonsense are interchangeable is only to labor
the point. Nonsense belongs to other worlds, other dimensions, and the gesture with which we put it from us at times, the
finality with which we dismiss it, testifies to its disturbing nature
Whatever we cannot include within our narrow framework of
comprehension we reject. Thus profundity and nonsense may
be seen to have certain unsuspected affinities.

Why did I not launch into sheer nonsense immediately? Because, like others, I was afraid of it. And deeper than that was
the fact that, far from situating myself in a beyond, I was caught
in the very heart of the web. I had survived my own destructive
school of Dadaism: I had progressed, if that is the word, from
scholar to critic to pole-axer. My literary experiments lay in
ruins, like the cities of old which were sacked by the vandals. I
wanted to build, but the materials were unreliable and the plan
had not even become blueprints. If the substance of art is the
human soul, then I must confess that with dead souls I could
visualize nothing germinating under my hand.

To be caught in a glut of dramatic episodes, to be ceaselessly
participating, means among other things that one is unaware of
the outlines of that bigger drama of which human activity is but
a small part. The act of writing puts a stop to one kind of activity
in order to release another. When a monk, prayerfully meditating, walks slowly and silently down the hall of a temple, and
thus walking sets in motion one prayerwheel after another, he
gives a living illustration of the act of sitting down to write. The
mind of the writer, no longer preoccupied with observing and
knowing, wanders meditatively amidst a world of forms which
are set spinning by a mere brush of his wings. No tyrant, this
wreaking his will upon the subjugated minions of his ill-gotten
kingdom. An explorer, rather, calling to life the slumbering enti-
ties of his dream. The act of dreaming, like a draught of fresh
air in an abandoned house, situates the furniture of the mind in

a new ambiance. The chairs and tables collaborate; an effluvia is given off, a game is begun.

To ask the purpose of this game, how it is related to life, is idle. As well ask the Creator why volcanos? why hurricanes? since obviously they contribute nothing but disaster. But, since disasters are disastrous only for those who are engulfed in them, whereas they can be illuminating for those who survive and study them, so it is in the creative world. The dreamer who returns from his voyage, if he is not shipwrecked en route, may and usually does convert the collapse of his tenuous fabric into other stuff. For a child the pricking of a bubble may offer nothing but astonishment and delight. The student of illusions and mirages may react differently. A scientist may bring to a bubble the emotional wealth of a world of thought. The same phenomenon which causes the child to scream with delight may give birth, in the mind of an earnest experimenter, to a dazzling vision of truth. In the artist these contrasting reactions seem to combine or merge, producing that ultimate one, the great catalyzer called *realization*. Seeing, knowing, discovering, enjoying—these faculties or powers are pale and lifeless without realization. The artist's game is to move over into reality. It is to see beyond the mere "disaster" which the picture of a lost battlefield renders to the naked eye. For, since the beginning of time the picture which the world has presented to the naked human eye can hardly seem anything but a hideous battle ground of lost causes. It has been so and will be so until man ceases to regard himself as the mere seat of conflict. Until he takes up the task of becoming the "I of his I."

Reading the Face of the World
—Plexus

There exists a curious book by an American anarchist, Benjamin R. Tucker, entitled INSTEAD OF A BOOK BY A MAN TOO BUSY TO WRITE ONE. The title describes my new-found situation to a T. My creative energy suddenly released, I spilled over in all directions at once. Instead of a book, the first thing I sat down to write was a prose poem about Brooklyn's backyard. I was so in love with the idea of being a writer that I could scarcely write. The amount of physical energy I possessed was unbelievable. I wore myself out in preparation. It was impossible for me to sit down quietly and just turn on the flow; I was dancing inside. I wanted to describe the world I knew and be in it at the same time. It never occurred to me that with just two or three hours of steady work a day I could write the thickest book imaginable. It was my belief then that if a man sat down to write he should remain glued to his seat for eight or ten hours at a stretch. One ought to write and write until he dropped from exhaustion. That was how I imagined writers went about their task. If only I had known then the program which Cendrars describes in one of his books! Two hours a day, before dawn, and the rest of the day to oneself. What a wealth of books he has given the world, Cendrars! All *en marge*. Employing a similar procedure—two or three hours a day regularly every day of one's life—Rémy de Gourmont had demonstrated, as Cendrars points out, that it is possible for a man to read virtually everything of value which has ever been written.

But I had no order, no discipline, no set goal. I was completely at the mercy of my impulses, my whims, my desires. My frenzy to live the life of the writer was so great that I overlooked the vast reservoir of material which had accumulated during the years leading up to this moment. I felt impelled to write about the immediate, about what was happening outside my very door. *Something fresh*, that's what I was after. To do this was compulsive because, whether I was aware of it or not, the material which I had stored up had been chewed to a frazzle during the years of frustration, doubt and despair when everything I had to say was written out in my head. Add to this that I felt like a boxer or wrestler getting ready for the big event. I needed a work-out. These first efforts then, these fantasies and fantasias, these prose poems and rambling divagations of all sorts, were like a grand tuning up of the instrument. It satisfied my vanity (which was enormous) to set off Roman candles, pin-wheels, sputtering firecrackers. The big cannon crackers I was reserving for the night of the Fourth of July. It was morning now, a long, lazy morning of a holiday that was to last forever. I had elected to occupy a choice seat in Paradise. It was definite and certain. I could therefore afford to take my time, could afford to dawdle away the glorious hours ahead of me during which I would still be part of the world and its senseless routine. Once I ascended to the heavenly seat I would join the chorus of angels, the seraphic choir which never ceases to give forth hymns of joy.

If I had long been reading the face of the world with the eyes of a writer, I now read it anew with even greater intensity. Nothing was too petty to escape my attention. If I went for a walk—and I was constantly seeking excuses to take a walk, "to explore," as I put it—it was for the deliberate purpose of transforming myself into an enormous eye. Seeing the common, everyday things in this new light I was often transfixed. The moment one gives close attention to anything, even a blade of grass, it becomes a mysterious, awesome, indescribably magnified world in itself. Almost an "unrecognizable" world. The writer waits in ambush for these unique moments. He pounces on his little grain of nothingness like a beast of prey. It is the moment of full awakening, of union and absorption, and it can never be forced. Sometimes one makes the mistake or commits the sin, shall I say, of trying to fix the moment, trying to pin it down in words. It took me ages to understand why, after having made exhaustive efforts to induce these moments of exaltation and release, I should be so incapable of recording them. I never dreamed that it was an end in itself, that to experience a moment of pure bliss, of pure awareness, was the end-all and be-all.

Many is the mirage I chased. Always I was overreaching myself. The oftener I touched reality, the harder I bounced back to the world of illusion, which is the name for everyday life. "Experience! More experience!" I clamored. In a frantic effort to arrive at some kind of order, some tentative working program, I would sit down quietly now and then and spend long, long hours mapping out a plan of procedure. Plans, such as architects and engineers sweat over, were never my forte. But I could always visualize my dreams in a cosmogonic pattern. Though I could never formulate a plot I could balance and weigh opposing forces, characters, situations, events, distribute them in a sort of heavenly lay-out, always with plenty of space between, always with the certitude that there is no end, only worlds within worlds *ad infinitum*, and that wherever one left off one had created *a* world, a world finite, total, complete.

Like a finely trained athlete, I was easy and uneasy at the same time. Sure of the final outcome, but nervous, restless, impatient, fretful. And so, after I had set off a few fireworks, I began to think in terms of light artillery. I began to align my pieces, so to speak. First of all, I reasoned, to have any effect my voice must be heard. I would have to find some outlet for my work—in newspapers, magazines, almanacs or house organs. Somewhere, somehow. What was my range, what my firing power? Though I wasn't one to bore my friends with private readings, now and then in moments of unbridled enthusiasm I was guilty of such misconduct. Rare as they were, these lapses, they had a tonic effect upon me. It was seldom, I noticed, that any of my friends grew intoxicated over my efforts. This silent criticism which friends often give is, I believe, worth infinitely more than the belabored, hostile shafts of the paid critic. The fact that my friends failed to laugh uproariously at the right moment, the fact that they did not applaud vociferously when I terminated my readings, conveyed more than a torrent of words. Sometimes, to be sure, I salved my pride by thinking of them as obtuse or too reserved. Not often, however. To Ulric's appraisals I was particularly sensitive. It was foolish of me, perhaps, to give such keen attention to his comments, since our tastes (in literature) were widely different, but he was so very, very close to me, the one friend I had whom it was imperative to convince of my ability. He was not easy to please either, my Ulric. What he enjoyed most was the fireworks, that is to say, the unusual words, the striking references, the fine brocades, the senseless jeremiads. Often he would thank me, in parting, for the string of new words I had added to his vocabulary. Sometimes we would spend another evening, an entire evening, looking up these bizarre words in the dictionary. Some we never found—because I had made them up.

But to get back to the grand plan. . . . Since I was convinced that I could write about anything under the sun, and excitingly, it seemed the most natural thing in the world to make up a list of themes which I thought of interest and submit them to editors of magazines in order that they might select what appealed to them. This entailed writing dozens and dozens of letters. Long, fatuous letters they were, too. It also meant keeping files, as well as observing the idiotic rules and regulations of a hundred and one editorial bodies. It involved altercations and disputes, fruitless errands to editorial offices, vexation, disgruntlement, rage, despair, ennui. *And postage stamps!* After weeks of turmoil and effervescence there might appear one day a letter from an editor saying that he would condescend to read my article if and if and if and but. Never daunted by the ifs and buts, I would regard such a letter as a bona fide pledge, a commission. Good! So I was at liberty, let us say, to write something about Coney Island in winter. If they liked it it would appear in print, my name would be signed to it, and I could show it to my friends, carry it about with me, put it under my pillow at night, read it surreptitiously, over and over, because the first time you see yourself in print you're beside yourself, you've at last proved to the world that you really are a writer, and you *must* prove it to the world, at least once in your life, or you will go mad from believing it all by yourself.

And so to Coney Island on a wintry day. Alone, of course. It wouldn't do to have one's reflections and observations diverted by a trivial-minded friend. A new pad in my pocket and a sharp pencil.

It's a long, dreary ride to Coney Island in midwinter. Only convalescents and invalids, or demented ones, seem to be trekking there. I feel as though I were slightly mad myself. Who wants to hear about a Coney Island which is all boarded up? I

must have put this theme down in a moment of exaltation, believing that nothing could be more inspiring than a picture of
desolation.

Desolate is hardly the word for it. As I walk along the boardwalk, the icy wind whistling through my breeches, everything
closed tight, it dawns on me that I couldn't possibly have chosen
a more difficult subject to write about. There is absolutely nothing to take note of, unless it be the silence. I see it better through
Ulrich's eyes than my own. An illustrator might have a good
time of it here, what with the bleak, crazy, tumbling edifices,
the snarling piles and planks, the still, empty Ferris wheel,
the noiseless roller coasters, rusting under a feeble sun. Just
to assure myself that I am on the job, I make a few notes
about the crazy look of the razzle-dazzle, the yawning mouth
of George C. Tilyou, and so forth. . . . A hot frankfurter
and a cup of steaming hot coffee would do me good, I think.
I find a little booth open on a side street off the boardwalk. There
is a shooting gallery open a few doors away. Not a customer in
sight: the owner is shooting at the clay pigeons himself, for practice, no doubt. A drunken sailor comes lurching along; a few
feet away from me he doubles up and lets go. (No need to take
note of this.) I go down to the beach and watch the sea gulls.
I'm looking at the sea gulls and thinking about Russia. A picture
of Tolstoy seated at a bench mending shoes obsesses me. What
was the name of his abode again? Yasna Polyana? No, Yasnaya
Polyana. Well, anyway, what the hell am I speculating on this
for? Wake up! I shake myself and push forward into the icy
gale. Driftwood lying all about. Fantastic forms. (So many
stories about bottles with messages inside them.) I wish now I
had thought to ask MacGregor to come along. That idiotic,
pseudo-serious line of his sometimes stimulated me in a perverse
way. How he would laugh to see me pacing the beach in search
of material! "Well, you're working anyhow," I can hear him
chirping. "That's something. But why in hell did you have to
pick this for a subject? You know damned well nobody will be
interested in it. You probably just wanted a little outing. Now

you've got a good excuse, haven't you? Jesus, Henry, you're just the same as ever—*nuts*, completely nuts."

As I board the train to go home I realize that I have made just three lines of notes. I haven't the slightest idea what I shall say when I sit down to the machine. My mind is a blank. A frozen blank. I sit staring out the window and not even the tremor of a thought assails me. The landscape itself is a frozen blank. The whole world is locked in snow and ice, mute, helpless. I've never known such a bleak, dismal, gruesome, lack-lustre day.

That night I went to bed rather chastened and humbled. Doubly so, because before retiring I had picked up a volume of Thomas Mann (in which there was the Tonio Kröger story) and had been overwhelmed by the flawless quality of the narrative. To my astonishment, however, I awoke the next day full of piss and vinegar. Instead of going for my usual morning stroll—"to get my blood up"—I sat down at the machine immediately after breakfast. By noon I had finished my article on Coney Island. It had come without effort. Why? Because instead of forcing it out I had gone to sleep—after due surrender of the ego, *certes*. It was a lesson in the futility of struggle. Do your utmost and let Providence do the rest! A petty victory, perhaps, but most illuminating.

The article, of course, was never accepted. (Nothing was ever accepted.) It went the rounds from one editor to another. Nor did it make the rounds alone. Week after week I was turning them out, sending them forth like carrier pigeons, and week after week they came back, always with the stereotyped rejection slip. Nevertheless, nothing daunted, as they say, "always merry and bright," I adhered rigidly to my program. There it was, the program, on a huge sheet of wrapping paper, tacked up on the wall. Beside it was another big sheet of paper on which were listed the exotic words I was endeavoring to annex to my vocabulary. The problem was how to hitch these words to my texts without having them stick out like sore thumbs. Often I tried them out beforehand, in letters to my friends, in letters to "all and sundry." The letter writing was for me what shadow boxing is to a pugilist. But imagine a pugilist spending so much time fighting his shadow that when he hooks up with a sparring partner he has no fight left! I could spend two or three hours writing a story, or article, and another six or seven explaining them to my friends by letter. The real effort was going into the letter writing, and perhaps it was best so, now that I look back on it, because it preserved the speed and naturalness of my true voice. I was far too self-conscious, in the early days, to use my own voice. I was the literary man through and through. I made use of every device I discovered, employed every register, assumed a thousand different stances, always confusing the mastery of technique with creation. Experience and technique, those were the two goads that drove me on. To triumph in the world of experience, as I formulated it, I would have to live at least a hundred lives. To acquire the right, or shall I say the complete, technique, I would have to live to be a hundred, not a day less.

My Two Lives
—Plexus

"I feel in myself a life so luminous," says Louis Lambert, "that I might enlighten a world, and yet I am shut up in a sort of mineral." This statement, which Balzac voices through his double, expresses perfectly the secret anguish of which I was then a victim. At one and the same time I was leading two thoroughly divergent lives. One could be described as "the merry whirl," the other as the contemplative life. In the role of active being everybody took me for what I was, or what I appeared to be; in the other role no one recognized me, least of all myself. No matter with what celerity and confusion events succeeded one another, there were always intervals, self-created, in which through contemplation I lost myself. It needed only a few moments, seemingly, of shutting out the world for me to be restored. But it required much longer stretches—of being alone with myself—to write. As I have frequently pointed out, the business of writing never ceased. But from this interior process to the process of translation is always, and was then very definitely, a big step. Today it is often hard for me to remember when or where I made this or that utterance, to remember whether I actually said it somewhere or whether I intended to say it sometime or other. There is an ordinary kind of forgetting and a special kind; the latter is due, more than likely, to the vice of living in two worlds at once. One of the consequences of this tendency is that you live everything out innumerable times. Worse, whatever you succeed in transmitting to paper seems but an infinitesimal fraction of what you've already written in your head. That delicious experience with which everyone is familiar, and which occurs with haunting impressiveness in dreams—I mean of falling into a familiar groove: meeting the same person over and over, going down the same street, confronting the identically same situation—this experience often happens to me in waking moments. How often I rack my brains to think where it was I made use of a certain thought, a certain situation, a certain character! Frantically I wonder if "it" occurred in some manuscript thoughtlessly destroyed. And then, when I've forgotten all about it, suddenly it dawns on me that "it" is one of the perpetual themes which I carry about inside me, which I am writing in the air, which I have written hundreds of times already, but never set down on paper. I make a note to write it out at the first opportunity, so as to be done with it, so as to bury it once and for all. I make the note—and I forget it with alacrity. . . . It's as though there were two melodies going on simultaneously: one for private exploitation and the other for the public ear. The whole struggle is to squeeze into that public record some tiny essence of the perpetual inner melody.

It was this inner turmoil which my friends detected in my comportment. And it was the lack of it, in my writings, which they deplored. I almost felt sorry for them. But there was a streak in me, a perverse one, which prevented me from giving the essential self. This "perversity" always voiced itself thus: "Reveal your true self and they will mutilate you." "They" meant not my friends alone but the world.

Once in a great while I came across a being whom I felt I could give myself to completely. Alas, these beings existed only in books. They were worse than dead to me—they had never existed except in imagination. Ah, what dialogues I conducted with kindred, ghostly spirits! Soul-searching colloquies, of which not a line has ever been recorded. Indeed, these "excriminations," as I chose to style them, defied recording. They were carried on in a language that does not exist, a language so simple, so direct, so transparent, that words were useless. It was not a silent language either, as is often used in communication with "higher beings." It was a language of clamor and tumult—the heart's clamor, the heart's tumult. But noiseless. If it were Dostoievski whom I summoned, it was "the complete Dostoievski," that is to say, the man who wrote the novels, diaries and letters we know, *plus* the man we also know by what he left unsaid, unwritten. It was type and archetype speaking, so to say. Always full, resonant, veridic; always the unimpeachable sort of music which one credits him with, whether audible or inaudible, whether recorded or unrecorded. A language which could emanate *only* from Dostoievski.

After such indescribably tumultuous communions I often sat down to the machine thinking that the moment had at last arrived. "Now I can say it!" I would tell myself. And I would sit there, mute, motionless, drifting with the stellar flux. I might sit that way for hours, completely rapt, completely oblivious to everything about me. And then, startled out of the trance by some unexpected sound or intrusion, I would wake with a start, look at the blank paper, and slowly, painfully tap out a sentence or perhaps only a phrase. Whereupon I would sit and stare at these words as if they had been written by some unknown hand. Usually somebody arrived to break the spell. If it were Mona she would of course burst in enthusiastically (seeing me sitting there at the machine) and beg me to let her glance at what I had written. Sometimes, still half-drugged, I would sit there like an automaton while she stared at the sentence, or the little phrase. To her bewildered queries I would answer in a hollow, empty voice, as if I were far away, speaking through a microphone.

Other times I would spring out of it like a Jack-in-the-box, hand
her a whopping lie (that I had concealed "the other pages," for
instance), and begin raving like a lunatic. Then I could really
talk a blue streak! It was as if I were reading from a book. All to
convince her—and even more myself!—that I had been deep in
work, deep in thought, deep in creation. Dismayed, she would
apologize profusely for having interrupted me at the wrong
moment. And I would accept her apology lightly, airily, as
though to say—"What matter? There's more where that came
from. . . . I have only to turn it on or off. . . . I'm a prestidigitator,
I am." And from the lie I would make truth. I'd spool it off (my
unfinished opus) like a man possessed—themes, sub-themes,
variations, detours, parentheses—as if the only thing I thought
about the live-long day was creation. With this of course went
considerable clowning. I not only invented the characters and
events, I acted them out. And poor Mona exclaiming: "Are you
really putting all that into the story? or the book?" (Neither
of us, in such moments, ever specified *what* book.) When the
word book sprang up it was always assumed that it was *the* book,
that is to say, the one I would soon get started on—or else it was
the one I was writing secretly, which I would show her only
when finished. (She always acted as if she were certain this
secret travail was going on. She even pretended that she had
searched everywhere for the script during my periods of absence.) In this sort of atmosphere it was not at all unusual, therefore, that reference be made occasionally to certain chapters, or
certain passages, chapters and passages which never existed, to be
sure, but which were "taken for granted" and which, no doubt,
had a greater reality (for us) than if they were in black and
white. Mona would sometimes indulge in this kind of talk in the
presence of a third person, which led, of course, to fantastic and
often most embarrassing situations. If it were Ulric who happened to be listening in, there was nothing to worry about. He
had a way of entering into the game which was not only gallant
but stimulating. He knew how to rectify a bad slip in a humorous
and fortifying way. For example, he might have forgotten for a
moment that we were employing the present tense and begun

using the future tense. ("I know you *will* write a book like that someday!") A moment later, realizing his error he would add: "I didn't mean *will* write—I meant the book you *are* writing— and very obviously writing, too, because nobody on God's earth could talk the way you do about something in which he wasn't deeply engrossed. Perhaps I'm being *too* explicit—forgive me, won't you?" At such junctures we all enjoyed the relief of letting go. We would indeed laugh uproariously. Ulric's laughter was always the heartiest—and the dirtiest, if I may put it that way. "Ho! Ho!" he seemed to laugh, "but aren't we all wonder- ful liars! I'm not doing so bad myself, by golly. If I stay with you people long enough I won't even know I'm lying any more. Ho Ho Ho! Haw Haw! Ha Ha! Hee Hee!" And he would slap his thighs and roll his eyes like a darkie, ending with a smacking of the lips and a mute request for a wee bit of schnapps. . . . With other friends it didn't go so well. They were too inclined to ask "impertinent" questions, as Mona put it. Or else they grew fidgety and uncomfortable, made frantic efforts to get back to terra firma. Kronski, like Ulric, was one who knew how to play the game. He did it somewhat differently from Ulric, but it seemed to satisfy Mona. *She could trust him.* That's how she put it to herself, I felt. The trouble with Kronski was that he played the game too well. He was not content to be a mere accomplice, he wanted to improvise as well. This zeal of his, which was not altogether diabolical, led to some weird discussions—discussions about the progress of the mythical book, to be sure. The critical moment always announced itself by a salvo of hysterical laughter —from Mona. It meant that she didn't know where she was any more. As for myself, I made little or no effort to keep up with the others, it being no concern of mine what went on in this realm of make believe. All I felt called upon to do was to keep a straight face and pretend that everything was kosher. I would laugh when I felt like it, or make criticism and correction, but under no circumstances, neither by word, gesture or implication did I let on that it was just a game. . . .

My Doomsday Book
—*Nexus*

. . . About five that afternoon, in a mood of utter despair, I sat down at the typewriter to outline the book I told myself I must write one day. My Domesday Book. It was like writing my own epitaph.

I wrote rapidly, in telegraphic style, commencing with the evening I first met her. For some inexplicable reason I found myself recording chronologically, *and without effort*, the long chain of events which filled the interval between that fateful evening and the present. Page after page I turned out, and always there was more to put down.

Hungry, I knocked off to walk to the village and get a bite to eat. When I returned to the office I again sat down to the machine. As I wrote I laughed and wept. Though I was only making notes it seemed as if I were actually writing the book there and then; I relived the whole tragedy over again step by step, day by day.

It was long after midnight when I finished. Thoroughly exhausted, I lay down on the floor and went to sleep. I awoke early, walked to the village again for a little nourishment, then strolled leisurely back to resume work for the day.

Later that day I read what I had written during the night. There were only a few insertions to be made. How did I ever remember so accurately the thousand and one details I had recorded? And, if these telegraphic notes were to be expanded into a book, would it not require several volumes to do justice to the subject? The very thought of the immensity of this task staggered me. When would I ever have the courage to tackle a work of such dimensions?

Musing thus, an appalling thought suddenly struck me. It was this—our love is ended. That could be the only meaning for planning such a work. I refused, however, to accept this con-

clusion. I told myself that my true purpose was merely to relate—"merely"!—the story of my misfortunes. But is it possible
to write of one's sufferings while one is still suffering? Abélard
had done it, to be sure. A sentimental thought now intruded. I
would write the book for her—to her—and in reading it she
would understand, her eyes would be opened, she would help
me bury the past, we would begin a new life, a life together . . .
true togetherness.

How naive! As if a woman's heart, once closed, can ever be
opened again!

I squelched these inner voices, these inner promptings which
only the Devil could inspire. I was more hungry than ever for
her love, more desperate far than ever I had been. There came
then the remembrance of a night years before when seated at the
kitchen table (my wife upstairs in bed), I had poured my heart
out to her in a desperate, suicidal appeal. And the letter had had
its effect. I *had* reached her. Why then would a book not have
an even greater effect? Especially a book in which the heart was
laid bare? I thought of that letter which one of Hamsun's characters had written to his Victoria, the one he penned with "God
looking over his shoulder." I thought of the letters which had
passed between Abélard and Héloïse and how time could never
dim them. Oh, the power of the written word!

That evening, while the folks sat reading the papers, I wrote
her a letter such as would have moved the heart of a vulture.
(I wrote it at that little desk which had been given me as a
boy.) I told her the plan of the book and how I had outlined it
all in one uninterrupted session. I told her that the book was for
her, that it *was* her. I told her that I would wait for her if it
took a thousand years.

It was a colossal letter, and when I had finished I realized that
I could not dispatch it—because she had forgotten to give me her
address. A fury seized me. It was as if she had cut out my tongue.
How could she have played such a scurvy trick on me? Where-
ever she was, in whomever's arms, couldn't she sense that I was
struggling to reach her? In spite of the maledictions I heaped

upon her my heart was saying "I love you, I love you, I love
you. . . ."

And as I crept into bed, repeating this idiotic phrase, I groaned.
I groaned like a wounded grenadier.

To Write as One Talks
—Nexus

. . . After we had had a good snack—*pâté de foie gras*, cold turkey,
cole slaw, washed down with a delicious Moselle—I felt as if I
could go to the machine and really write. Perhaps it was the talk,
the mention of travel, of strange cities . . . of a new life. Or that
I had successfully prevented our talk from degenerating into a
quarrel. (It was such a delicate subject, Stasia.) Or perhaps it
was the Jew, Sid Essen, and the stir of racial memories. Or perhaps nothing more than the rightness of our quarters, the feeling
of snugness, cosiness, at-homeness.

Anyway, as she was clearing the table, I said: "If only one
could write as one talks . . . write like Gorky, Gogol or Knut
Hamsun!"

She gave me a look such as a mother sometimes directs at the
child she is holding in her arms.

"Why write like them?" she said. "Write like you are, that's
so much better."

"I wish I thought so. Christ! Do you know what's the matter
with me? I'm a chameleon. Every author I fall in love with I
want to imitate. If only I could imitate myself!"

"When are you going to show me some pages?" she said. "I'm
dying to see what you've done so far."

"Soon," I said.

"Is it about us?"

"I suppose so. What else could I write about?"

"You could write about anything, Val."

"That's what *you* think. You never seem to realize my limitations. You don't know what a struggle I go through. Sometimes I feel thoroughly licked. Sometimes I wonder what ever gave me the notion that I could write. A few minutes ago, though, I was writing like a madman. In my head, again. But the moment I sit down to the machine I become a clod. It gets me. It gets me down."

"Did you know," I said, "that toward the end of his life Gogol went to Palestine? A strange fellow, Gogol. Imagine a crazy Russian like that dying in Rome! I wonder where I'll die."

"What's the matter with you, Val? What are you talking about? You've got eighty more years to live. *Write!* Don't talk about dying."

I felt I owed it to her to tell her a little about the novel. "Guess what I call myself in the book!" I said. She couldn't. "I took your uncle's name, the one who lives in Vienna. You told me he was in the Hussars, I think. Somehow I can't picture him as the colonel of a death's head regiment. And a Jew. But I like him. . . . I like everything you told me about him. That's why I took his name. . . ."

Pause.

"What I'd like to do with this bloody novel—only Pop might not feel the same way—is to charge through it like a drunken Cossack. *Russia, Russia, where are you heading? On, on, like the whirlwind!* The only way I can be myself is to smash things. I'll never write a book to suit the publishers. I've written too many books. Sleep-walking books. You know what I mean. Millions and millions of words—all in the head. They're banging around up there, like gold pieces. I'm tired of making gold pieces. I'm sick of these cavalry charges . . . in the dark. Every word I put down now must be an arrow that goes straight to the mark. A poisoned arrow. I want to kill off books, writers, publishers, readers. To write for the public doesn't mean a thing to me. What I'd like is to write for madmen—or for the angels."

I paused and a curious smile came over my face at the thought which had entered my head.

"That landlady of ours, I wonder what she'd think if she heard me talking this way? She's too good to us, don't you think? She doesn't *know* us. She'd never believe what a walking pogrom I am. Nor has she any idea why I'm so crazy about Sirota and that bloody synagogue music." I pulled up short. "What the hell has Sirota got to do with it anyway?"

"Yes, Val, you're excited. Put it in the book. Don't waste yourself in talk!"

Such Exquisite Torture
—Nexus

Sometimes I would sit at the machine for hours without writing a line. Fired by an idea, often an irrelevant one, my thoughts would come too fast to be transcribed. I would be dragged along at a gallop, like a stricken warrior tied to his chariot.

On the wall at my right there were all sorts of memoranda tacked up: a long list of words, words that bewitched me and which I intended to drag in by the scalp if necessary; reproductions of paintings, by Uccello, della Francesca, Breughel, Giotto, Memling; titles of books from which I meant to deftly lift passages; phrases filched from my favorite authors, not to quote but to remind me how to twist things occasionally; for example: "The worm that would gnaw her bladder" or "the pulp which had deglutinized behind his forehead." In the Bible were slips of paper to indicate where gems were to be found. The Bible was a veritable diamond mine. Every time I looked up a passage I became intoxicated. In the dictionary were place marks for lists of one kind or another: flowers, birds, trees, reptiles, gems, poisons, and so on. In short, I had fortified myself with a complete arsenal.

But what was the result? Pondering over a word like praxis, for example, or pleroma, my mind would wander like a drunken wasp. I might end up in a desperate struggle to recall the name of that Russian composer, the mystic, or Theosophist, who had left unfinished his greatest work. The one of whom someone had written—"He, the messiah in his own imagination, who had dreamed of leading mankind toward 'the last festival,' who had imagined

himself God, and everything, including himself, his own creation, who had dreamed by the force of his tones to over-
throw the universe, died of a pimple." *Scriabin*, that's who it was.
Yes, Scriabin could derail me for days. Every time his name
popped into my head I was back on Second Avenue, in the rear
of some café, surrounded by Russians (white ones usually) and
Russian Jews, listening to some unknown genius reel off the
sonatas, preludes and études of the divine Scriabin. From Scriabin
to Prokofiev, to the night I first heard him, Carnegie Hall probably, high up in the gallery, and so excited that when I stood up
to applaud or to yell—we all yelled like madmen in those days—
I nearly tumbled out of the gallery. A tall, gaunt figure he was,
in a frock coat, like something out of the *Dreigroschenoper*,
like Monsieur les Pompes Funèbres. From Prokofiev to Luke
Ralston, now departed, an ascetic also, with a face like the death
mask of Monsieur Arouet. A good friend, Luke Ralston, who
after visiting the merchant tailors up and down Fifth Avenue
with his samples of imported woolens, would go home and practice German lieder while his dear old mother, who had ruined
him with her love, would make him pigs' knuckles and sauerkraut
and tell him for the ten thousandth time what a dear, good son
he was. His thin, cultivated voice too weak, unfortunately, to
cope with the freight-laden melodies of his beloved Hugo Wolf
with which he always larded his programs. At thirty-three he
dies—of pneumonia, they said, but it was probably a broken
heart. . . . And in between come memories of other forgotten
figures—minnesinger, flutists, 'cellists, pianists in skirts, like the
homely one who always included Schubert's *Carnaval* on her program. (Reminded me so much of Maude: the nun become vir-
tuoso.) There were others too, short-haired and long-haired, all
perfectos, like Havana cigars. Some, with chests like bulls, could
shatter the chandeliers with their Wagnerian shrieks. Some were
like lovely Jessicas, their hair parted in the middle and pasted
down: benign madonnas (Jewish mostly) who had not yet taken
to rifling the ice-box at all hours of the night. And then the
fiddlers, in skirts, left-handed sometimes, often with red hair or
dirty orange, and bosoms which got in the way of the bow. . . .

Just looking at a word, as I say. Or a painting, or a book. The title alone, sometimes. Like *Heart of Darkness* or *Under the Autumn Star*. How did it begin again, that wonderful tale? Have a look-see. Read a few pages, then throw the book down. Inimitable. And how had I begun? I read it over once again, my imaginary Paul Morphy opening. Weak, wretchedly weak. Something falls off the table. I get down to search for it. There, on hands and knees, a crack in the floor intrigues me. It reminds me of something. *What?* I stay like that, as if waiting to be "served," like a ewe. Thoughts whirl through my bean and out through the vent at the top of my skull. I reach for a pad and jot down a few words. More thoughts, plaguey thoughts. (What dropped from the table was a match-box.) How to fit these thoughts into the novel. Always the same dilemma. And then I think of *Twelve Men.* If only somewhere I could do one little section which would have the warmth, the tenderness, the pathos of that chapter on Paul Dressler. But I'm not a Dreiser. And I have no brother Paul. It's far away, the banks of the Wabash. Farther, much farther, than Moscow or Kronstadt, or the warm, utterly romantic Crimea. *Why?*

Russia, where are you leading us? Forward! Ech konee, konee!

I think of Gorky, the baker's helper, his face white with flour, and the big fat peasant (in his nightshirt) rolling in the mud with his beloved sows. *The University of Life.* Gorky: mother, father, comrade. Gorky, the beloved vagabond, who whether tramping, weeping, pissing, praying or cursing, writes. Gorky: who wrote in blood. A writer true as the sun dial. . . .

Just looking at a title, as I say.

Thus, like a piano concerto for the left hand, the day would slip by. Lucky if there were a page or two to show for all the torture and the inspiration. Writing! It was like pulling up poison oak by the roots. Or searching for mangolds.

When now and then she asked: "How is it coming, dear Val?" I wanted to bury my head in my hands and sob.

"Don't push yourself, Val!"

But I have pushed. I've pushed and pushed till there's not a drop of caca in me. Often it's just when she says, "Dinner's

ready!" that the flow begins. What the hell! Maybe after dinner.
Maybe after she's gone to sleep. *Mañana*.

At table I talk about the work as if I were another Alexandre
Dumas or a Balzac. Always what I intend to do, never what I
have done. I have a genius for the impalpable, for the inchoate,
for the not yet born.

"And *your* day?" I'll say sometimes. "What was *your* day
like?" (More to get relief from the devils who plagued me than
to hear the trivia which I already knew by heart.)

Listening with one ear I could see Pop waiting like a faithful
hound for the bone he was to receive. Would there be enough
fat on it? Would it splinter in his mouth? And I would remind
myself that it wasn't really the book pages he was waiting for
but a more juicy morsel—*her*. He would be patient, he would
be content—for a while at least—with literary discussions. As
long as she kept herself looking lovely, as long as she continued
to wear the delightful gowns which he urged her to select for
herself, as long as she accepted with good grace all the little
favors he heaped upon her. As long, in other words, as she
treated him like a human being. As long as she wasn't ashamed
to be seen with him. (Did he really think, as she averred, that
he looked like a toad?) With eyes half-closed I could see him
waiting, waiting on a street corner, or in the lobby of a semi-
fashionable hotel, or in some outlandish café (in another incarnation), a café such as "Zum Hiddigeigei." I always saw
him dressed like a gentleman, with or without spats and cane.
A sort of inconspicuous millionaire, fur trader or stockbroker,
not the predatory type but, as the paunch indicated, the kind
who prefers the good things of life to the almighty dollar. A
man who once played the violin. A man of taste, indisputably.
In brief, no dummox. Average perhaps, but not ordinary. Conspicuous by his inconspicuousness. Probably full of watermelon
seeds and other pips. And saddled with an invalid wife, one he
wouldn't dream of hurting. ("Look, darling, see what I've
brought you! Some Maatjes herring, some lachs, and a jar of
pickled antlers from the reindeer land.")

And when he reads the opening pages, this pipsqueaking millionaire, will he exclaim: "Aha! I smell a rat!" Or, putting his wiry brains to sleep, will he simply murmur to himself: "A lovely piece of tripe, a romance out of the Dark Ages."

And our landlady, the good Mrs. Skolsky, what would *she* think if she had a squint at these pages? Would she wet her panties with excitement? Or would she hear music where there were only seismographic disturbances? (I could see her running to the synagogue looking for rams' horns.) One day she and I have got to have it out, about the writing business. Either more strudels, more Sirota, or—the *garrotte*. If only I knew a little Yiddish!

"Call me Reb!" Those were Sid Essen's parting words.

Such exquisite torture, this writing humbuggery! Bughouse reveries mixed with choking fits and what the Swedes call *mardrömmen*. Squat images roped with diamond tiaras. Baroque architecture. Cabalistic logarithms. Mezuzahs and prayer-wheels. Portentous phrases. ("Let no one," said the auk, "look upon this man with favor!") Skies of blue-green copper, filigreed with lacy striata; umbrella ribs, obscene graffiti. Balaam the ass licking his hind parts. Weasels spouting nonsense. A sow menstruating. . . .

All because, as she once put it, I had "the chance of a lifetime."

Sometimes I sailed into it with huge black wings. Then everything came out pell-mell and arsey-versy. Pages and pages. Reams of it. None of it belonged in the novel. Nor even in *The Book of Perennial Gloom*. Reading them over I had the impression of examining an old print: a room in a medieval dwelling, the old woman sitting on the pot, the doctor standing by with red-hot tongs, a mouse creeping towards a piece of cheese in the corner near the crucifix. A ground-floor view, so to speak. A chapter from the history of everlasting misery. Depravity, insomnia, gluttony posing as the three graces. All described in quicksilver, benzine and potassium permanganate.

Another day my hands might wander over the keys with the felicity of a Borgia's murderous paw. Choosing the staccato tech-

nique, I would ape the quibblers and quipsters of the Ghibellines.
Or put it on, like a *saltimbanque* performing for a feeble-minded
monarch.

The next day a quadruped: everything in hoof beats, clots of
phlegm, snorts and farts. A stallion *(ech!)* racing over a frozen
lake with torpedoes in his bowels. All bravura, so to say.

And then, as when the hurricane abates, it would flow like a
song—quietly, evenly, with the steady lustre of magnesium. As
if hymning the Bhagavad Gita. A monk in a saffron robe ex-
tolling the work of the Omniscient One. No longer a writer. A
saint. A saint from the Sanhedrin sent. God bless the author!
(Have we a David here?)

What a joy it was to write like an organ in the middle of a
lake!

Bite me, you bed lice! Bite while I have the strength!

The Book of Life
—Nexus

"Val, you're a dreamer."

"Sure I am. But I'm an active dreamer. There's a difference."

Then I added: "We're all dreamers, only some of us wake up
in time to put down a few words. Certainly I want to write. But
I don't think it's the end-all and be-all. How shall I put it? Writing is like the caca that you make in your sleep. Delicious caca,
to be sure, but first comes life, then the caca. Life is change,
movement, quest . . . a going forward to meet the unknown, the
unexpected. Only a very few men can say of themselves, 'I have
lived!' That's why we have books—so that men may live vicariously. But when the author also lives vicariously——!"

She broke in. "When I listen to you sometimes, Val, I feel
that you want to live a thousand lives in one. You're eternally
dissatisfied—with life as it is, with yourself, with just about
everything. You're a Mongol. You belong on the steppes of Cen-
tral Asia."

"You know," I said, getting worked up now, "one of the reasons why I feel so disjointed is that there's a little of everything in me. I can put myself in any period and feel at home in it. When I read about the Renaissance I feel like a man of the Renaissance; when I read about one of the Chinese dynasties I feel exactly like a Chinese of that epoch. Whatever the race, the period, the people, Egyptian, Aztec, Hindu or Chaldean, I'm thoroughly in it, and it's always a rich, tapestried world whose wonders are inexhaustible. That's what I crave—a humanly created world, a world responsive to man's thoughts, man's dream's, man's desires. What gets me about *this* life of ours, this American life, is that we kill everything we touch. Talk of the Mongols and the Huns—they were cavaliers compared to us. This is a hideous, empty, desolate land. I see my compatriots through the eyes of my ancestors. I see clean through them—and they're hollow, worm-eaten. . . ."

I took the bottle of Gevrey-Chambertin and refilled the glasses. There was enough for one good swallow.

"To Napoleon!" I said. "A man who lived life to the fullest."

"Val, you frighten me sometimes, the way you speak about America. Do you really hate it that much?"

"Maybe it's love," I said. "Inverted love. I don't know."

"I hope you're not going to work any of that off in the novel."

"Don't worry. The novel will be about as unreal as the land it comes from. I won't have to say, 'All the characters in this book are fictitious' or whatever it is they put in the front of books. Nobody will recognize anybody, the author least of all. A good thing it will be in your name. What a joke if it turned out to be a best seller! If reporters came knocking at the door to interview *you!*"

The thought of this terrified her. She didn't think it funny at all.

"Oh," I said, "you called me a dreamer a moment ago. Let me read you a passage—it's short—from *The Hill of Dreams.* You should read the book sometime; it's a dream of a book."

I went to the bookshelf and opened to the passage I had in mind.

"He's just been telling about Milton's *Lycidas,* why it was probably the most perfect piece of pure literature in existence. Then says Machen: 'Literature is the sensuous art of causing exquisite impressions by means of words.' But here's the passage . . . it follows right after that: 'And yet there was something more; besides the logical thought, which was often a hindrance, a troublesome though inseparable accident, besides the sensation, always a pleasure and a delight, besides these there were the indefinable, inexpressible images which all fine literature summons to the mind. As the chemist in his experiments is sometimes astonished to find unknown, unexpected elements in the crucible or the receiver, as the world of material things is considered by some a thin veil of the immaterial universe, so he who reads wonderful prose or verse is conscious of suggestions that cannot be put into words, which do not rise from the logical sense, which are rather parallel to than connected with the sensuous delight. The world so disclosed is rather the world of dreams, rather the world in which children sometimes live, instantly appearing, and instantly vanishing away, a world beyond all expression or analysis, neither of the intellect nor of the senses. . . .'"

"It *is* beautiful," she said, as I put the book down. "But don't *you* try to write like that. Let Arthur Machen write that way, if he wishes. You write your own way."

I sat down at the table again. A bottle of Chartreuse was standing beside my coffee. As I poured a thimbleful of the fiery green liqueur into my glass, I said: "There's only one thing missing now: *a harem.*"

"Pop supplied the Chartreuse," she said. "He was so delighted with those pages."

"Let's hope he'll like the next fifty pages as much."

"You're not writing the book for him, Val. You're writing it for *us.*"

"That's true," I said. "I forget that sometimes."

It occurred to me then that I hadn't told her anything yet about the outline of the real book. "There's something I have to tell you," I began. "Or should I? Maybe I ought to keep it to myself a while longer."

She begged me not to tease.

"All right, I'll tell you. It's about the book I intend to write one day. I've got the notes for it all written out. I wrote you a long letter about it, when you were in Vienna or God knows where. I couldn't send the letter because you gave me no address. Yes, this will really be a book . . . a huge one. About you and me."

"Didn't you keep the letter?"

"No. I tore it up. Your fault! But I've got the notes. Only I won't show them to you yet."

"Why?"

"Because I don't want any comments. Besides, if we talk about it I may never write the book. Also, there are some things I wouldn't want you to know about until I had written them out."

"You can trust me," she said. She began to plead with me.

"No use," I said, "you'll have to wait."

"But supposing the notes got lost?"

"I could write them all over again. That doesn't worry me in the least."

She was getting miffed now. After all, if the book was about her as well as myself . . . And so on. But I remained adamant.

Knowing very well that she would turn the place upside down in order to lay hands on the notes, I gave her to understand that I had left them at my parents' home. "I put them where they'll never find them," I said. I could tell from the look she gave me that she wasn't taken in by this. Whatever her move was, she pretended to be resigned, to think no more of it.

To sweeten the atmosphere I told her that if the book ever got written, if it ever saw the light of day, she would find herself immortalized. And since that sounded a bit grandiloquent I added, "You may not always recognize yourself but I promise you this, when I get through with your portrait you'll never be forgotten."

She seemed moved by this. "You sound awfully sure of yourself," she said.

"I have reason to. This book I've *lived*. I can begin anywhere and find my way around. It's like a lawn with a thousand sprinklers: all I need do is turn on the faucet." I tapped my head. "It's all there, in invisible . . . I mean indelible . . . ink."

"Are you going to tell the truth—*about us?*"

"I certainly am. About everyone, not just us."

"And you think there'll be a publisher for such a book?"

"I haven't thought about that," I replied. "First I've got to write it."

"You'll finish the novel first, I hope?"

"Absolutely. Maybe the play too."

"The play? Oh Val, that would be wonderful."

That ended the conversation.

Once again the disturbing thought arose: how long will this peace and quiet last? It was almost too good, the way things were going. I thought of Hokusai, his ups and downs, his 947 changes of address, his perseverance, his incredible production. What a life! And I, I was only on the threshold. Only if I lived to be ninety or a hundred would I have something to show for my labors.

Another almost equally disturbing thought entered my head. *Would I ever write anything acceptable?*

The answer which came at once to my lips was: "*Fuck a duck!*"

Still another thought now came to mind. *Why was I so obsessed about truth?*

And the answer to that also came clear and clean. *Because there is only the truth and nothing but the truth.*

But a wee small voice objected, saying: "*Literature is something else again.*"

Then to hell with literature! *The book of life*, that's what I would write.

And whose name will you sign to it?

The Creator's.

That seemed to settle the matter.

The thought of one day tackling such a book—*the book of life*

–kept me tossing all night. It was there before my closed eyes, like the *Fata Morgana* of legend. Now that I had vowed to make it a reality, it loomed far bigger, far more difficult of accomplishment than when I had spoken about it. It seemed overwhelming, indeed. Nevertheless, I was certain of one thing—it would flow once I began it. It wouldn't be a matter of squeezing out drops and trickles. I thought of that first book I had written, about the twelve messengers. What a miscarriage! I *had* made a little progress since then, even if no one but myself knew it. But what a waste of material that was! My theme should have been the whole eighty or a hundred thousand whom I had hired and fired during those sizzling cosmococcic years. No wonder I was constantly losing my voice. Merely to talk to that many people was a feat. But it wasn't the talk alone, it was their faces, the expressions they wore—grief, anger, deceit, cunning, malice, treachery, gratitude, envy, and so on—as if, instead of human beings, I were dealing with totemistic creatures: the fox, the lynx, the jackal, the crow, the lemming, the magpie, the dove, the musk-ox, the snake, the crocodile, the hyena, the mongoose, the owl. . . Their images were still fresh in my memory, the good and the bad, the crooks and the liars, the cripples, the maniacs, the tramps, the gamblers, the leeches, the perverts, the saints, the martyrs, all of them, the ordinary ones and the extraordinary ones. Even down to a certain lieutenant of the Horse Guard whose face had been so mutilated—by the Reds or the Blacks—that when he laughed he wept and when he wept he jubilated. Whenever he addressed me—usually to make a complaint—he stood at attention, as if he were the horse not the guard. And the Greek with the long equine face, a scholar unquestionably, who wanted to read from *Prometheus Bound*—or was it *Unbound?* Why was it, much as I liked him, that he always roused my scorn and ridicule? How much more interesting and more lovable was that wall-eyed Egyptian with sex on the brain! Always in hot water, especially if he failed to jerk off once or twice a day. And that Lesbian, *Iliad*, she called herself—why Iliad?—so lovely, so demure, so coy . . . an excellent musician too. I know because she brought her fiddle to the office one evening and played for me. And after

she had rendered her Bach, her Mozart, her Paganini repertoire
she has the gall to inform me that she's tired of being a Lesbian
wants to be a whore, and wouldn't I please find her a better
office building to work in, one where she could drum up a little
business.

They were all there parading before me as of yore—with their
tics, their grimaces, their supplications, their sly little tricks
Every day they were dumped on my desk out of a huge flou
sack, it seemed—they, their troubles, their problems, their ache
and pains. Maybe when I was selected for this odious job someone
had tipped off the big Scrabblebuster and said: "Keep this mar
good and busy! Put his feet in the mud of reality, make his hai
stand on end, feed him bird lime, destroy his every last illusion!"
And whether he had been tipped off or not, that old Scrabble
buster had done just that. That and a little more. He made me
acquainted with grief and sorrow.

However . . . among the thousands who came and went, who
begged, whistled and wept before me naked, bereft, making
their last call, as it were, before turning themselves in at the
slaughter-house, there appeared now and then a jewel of a guy
usually from some far-off place, a Turk perhaps or a Persian
And like that, there happened along one day this Ali something
or other, a Mohammedan, who had acquired a divine calligraphy
somewhere in the desert, and after he gets to know me, know
that I am a man with big ears, he writes me a letter, a letter
thirty-two pages long, with never a mistake, never a comma or
semicolon missing, and in it he explains (as if it were important
for me to know) that the miracles of Christ—he went into them
one by one—were not miracles at all, that they had all been per
formed before, even the Resurrection, by unknown men, men
who understood the laws of nature, laws which, he insisted, ou
scientists know nothing about, but which were eternal laws and
could be demonstrated to produce so-called miracles wheneve
the right man came along . . . and he, Ali, was in possession of th
secret, but I was not to make it known because he, Ali, had
chosen to be a messenger and "wear the badge of servitude" fo
a reason known only to him and to Allah, bless his name, but

when the time came I had only to say the word and so forth and so on. . . .

How had I managed to leave out all these divine behemoths and the ruckus they were constantly creating, me up on the carpet every few days to explain this and explain that, as if I had instigated their peculiar, inexplicably screwy behavior. Yeah, what a job trying to convince the big shot (with the brain of a midget) that the flower of America was seeded from the loins of these crack-pots, these monsters, these harebrained idiots who, whatever the mischief, were possessed of strange talents such as the ability to read the Cabala backwards, multiply ten columns of figures at a time or sit on a cake of ice and manifest signs of fever. None of these explanations, of course, could alleviate the horrendous fact that an elderly woman had been raped the night before by a swarthy devil delivering a death message.

It was tough. I never could make things clear to him. Any more than I could present the case for Tobachnikov, the Talmudic student, who was the nearest replica of the living Christ that ever walked the streets of New York with Happy Easter messages in his hand. How could I say to him, this owl of a boss: "This devil needs help. His mother is dying of cancer, his father peddles shoelaces all day, the pigeons are crippled. (The ones that used to make the synagogue their home.) He needs a raise. He needs food in his belly."

To astonish him or intrigue him, I would sometimes relate little anecdotes about my messengers, always using the past tense as if about someone who had once been in the service (though he was there all the time, right up my sleeve, securely hidden away in Px or FU office.) Yes, I'd say, he was the accompanist of Johanna Gadski, when they were on tour in the Black Forest. Yes (about another), he once worked with Pasteur at the famous Institute in Paris. Yes (still another), he went back to India to finish his *History of the World* in four languages. Yes (a parting shot), he was one of the greatest jockeys that ever lived; made a fortune after he left us, then fell down an elevator shaft and smashed his skull.

And what was the invariable response? "Very interesting, in-

deed. Keep up the good work. Remember, hire nothing but
nice clean boys from good families. No Jews, no cripples, no ex-
convicts. We want to be proud of our messenger force."

"Yes, *sir*!"

"And by the way, see that you clean out all these niggers
you've got on the force. We don't want our clients to be scared
out of their wits."

"Yes, *sir*!"

And I would go back to my perch, do a little shuffling,
scramble them up a bit, but never fire a soul, not even if he were
as black as the ace of spades.

How did I ever manage to leave them out of the messenger
book, all these lovely dementia praecox cases, these star rovers,
these diamond-backed logicians, these battle-scarred epileptics,
thieves, pimps, whores, defrocked priests and students of the
Talmud, the Cabala and the Sacred Books of the East? *Novels!*
As if one could write about such matters, such specimens, in a
novel. Where, in such a work, would one place the heart, the
liver, the optic nerve, the pancreas or the gall bladder? They
were not fictitious, they were alive, every one of them and, besides being riddled with disease, they ate and drank every day,
they made water, they defecated, fornicated, robbed, murdered,
gave false testimony, betrayed their fellow-men, put their children out to work, their sisters to whoring, their mothers to begging, their fathers to peddling shoelaces or collar buttons and to
bringing home cigarette butts, old newspapers and a few coppers
from the blind man's tin cup. What place is there in a novel for
such goings-on?

Yes, it was beautiful coming away from Town Hall of a
snowy night, after hearing the Little Symphony perform. So
civilized in there, such discreet applause, such knowing comments. And now the light touch of snow, cabs pulling up and
darting away, the lights sparkling, splintering like icicles, and
Monsieur Barrère and his little group sneaking out the back entrance to give a private recital at the home of some wealthy
denizen of Park Avenue. A thousand paths leading away from
the concert hall and in each one a tragic figure silently pursues

is destiny. Paths criss-crossing everywhere: the low and the mighty, the meek and the tyrannical, the haves and the have nots.

Yes, many's the night I attended a recital in one of these hallowed musical morgues and each time I walked out I thought not of the music I had heard but of one of my foundlings, one of the bleeding cosmococcic crew I had hired or fired that day and the memory of whom neither Haydn, Bach, Scarlatti, Beethoven, Beelzebub, Schubert, Paganini or any of the wind, string, horn or cymbal clan of musikers could dispel. I could see him, poor devil, leaving the office with his messenger suit wrapped in a brown parcel, heading for the elevated line at the Brooklyn Bridge, where he would board a train for Fresh Pond Road or Pitkin Avenue, or maybe Kosciusko Street, there to descend into the warm, grab a sour pickle, dodge a kick in the ass, peel the potatoes, clean the lice out of the bedding and say a prayer for his great grandfather who had died at the hand of a drunken Pole because the sight of a beard floating in the wind was anathema to him. I could also see myself walking along Pitkin Avenue, or Kosciusko Street, searching for a certain hovel, or was it a kennel, and thinking to myself how lucky to be born a Gentile and speak English so well. (Is this still Brooklyn? Where am I?) Sometimes I could smell the clams in the bay, or perhaps it was the sewer water. And wherever I went, searching for the lost and the damned, there were always fire escapes loaded with bedding, and from the bedding there fell like wounded cherubim an assortment of lice, bedbugs, brown beetles, cockroaches and the scaly rinds of yesterday's salami. Now and then I would treat myself to a succulent sour pickle or a smoked herring wrapped in newspaper. Those big fat pretzels, how good they were! The women all had red hands and blue fingers—from the cold, from scrubbing and washing and rinsing. (But the son, a genius already, would have long, tapering fingers with calloused tips. Soon he would be playing in Carnegie Hall.) Nowhere in the upholstered Gentile world I hailed from had I ever run into a genius, or even a near genius. Even a book shop was hard to find. Calendars, yes, oodles of them, supplied by the butcher or grocer. Never a Hol-

bein, a Carpaccio, a Hiroshige, a Giotto, nor even a Rembrandt.
Whistler possibly, but only his mother, that placid-looking creature all in black with hands folded in her lap, so resigned, so
eminently respectable. No, never anything among us dreary
Christians that smelled of art. But luscious pork stores with tripe
and gizzards of every variety. And of course linoleums, brooms,
flower pots. Everything from the animal and vegetable kingdom,
plus hardware, German cheese cake, knackwurst and sauerkraut.
A church on every block, a sad-looking affair, such as only Lu-
therans and Presbyterians can bring forth from the depths of
their sterilized faith. And Christ was a carpenter! He had built
a church, but not of sticks and stones.

Not I, But the Father within Me
—*Nexus*

"Why should we always go out of our way to describe the
wretchedness and the imperfections of our life, and to unearth
characters from wild and remote corners of our country?"

Thus Gogol begins Part II of his unfinished novel.

I was now well into the novel—my own—but still I had no clear
idea where it was leading me, nor did it matter, since Pop was
pleased with all that had been shown him thus far, the money
was always forthcoming, we ate and drank well, the birds were
scarcer now but still they sang, Thanksgiving had come and
gone, and my chess game had improved somewhat. Moreover, no
one had discovered our whereabouts, none of our pestilential
cronies, I mean. Thus I was able to explore the streets at will,
which I did with a vengeance because the air was sharp and
biting, the wind whistled, and my brain ever in a whirl drove
me on face forward, forced me to ferret out streets, memories,
buildings, odors (of rotting vegetables), abandoned ferry slips,
storekeepers long dead, saloons converted into dime stores, ceme-
teries still redolent with the punk of mourners.

The wild and remote corners of the earth were all about me,

only a stone's throw from the boundary which marked off our aristocratic precinct. I had only to cross the line, the *Grenze*, and I was in the familiar world of childhood, the land of the poor and happily demented, the junk yard where all that was dilapidated, useless and germ-ridden was salvaged by the rats who refused to desert the ship.

As I roamed about gazing into shop windows, peering into alleyways, and never anything but drear desolation, I thought of the Negroes whom we visited regularly and of how uncontaminated they appeared to be. The sickness of the Gentiles had not destroyed their laughter, their gift of speech, their easy-going ways. They had all our diseases to combat and our prejudices as well, yet they remained impervious.

The one who owned the collection of erotica had grown very fond of me; I had to be on guard lest he drive me into a corner and pinch my ass. Never did I dream that one day he would be seizing my books too and adding them to his astounding collection. He was a wonderful pianist, I should add. He had that dry pedal technique I relished so much in Count Basie and Fats Waller. They could all play some instrument, these lovable souls. And if there were no instrument they made music with fingers and palms—on table tops, barrels or anything to hand.

I had introduced no "unearthed characters" as yet in the novel. I was still timid. More in love with words than with psychopathic "devaginations." I could spend hours at a stretch with Walter Pater, or even Henry James, in the hope of lifting a beautifully turned phrase. Or I might sit and gaze at a Japanese print, say "The Fickle Type" of Utamaro, in the effort to force a bridge between a vague, dreamy fugue of an image and a living colored wood-block. I was ever frantically climbing ladders to pluck a ripe fig from some exotic overhanging garden of the past. The illustrated pages of a magazine like the *Geographic* could hold me spellbound for hours. How work in a cryptic reference to some remote region of Asia Minor, some little known site, for example, where a Hittite monster of a monarch had left colossal statues to commemorate his flea-blown ego? Or I might dig up an old history book—one of Mommsen's, let us say—in order to

fetch up with a brilliant analogy between the skyscrapered can-
yons of Wall Street and the congested districts of Rome under
the Emperors. Or I might become interested in sewers, the great
sewers of Paris, or some other metropolis, whereupon it would
occur to me that Hugo or some other French writer had made
use of such a theme, and I would take up the life of this novelist
merely to find out what had impelled him to take such an interest
in sewers.

Meanwhile, as I say, "the wild and remote corners of our
country" were right to hand. I had only to stop and buy a bunch
of radishes to unearth a weird character. Did an Italian funeral
parlor look intriguing I would step inside and inquire the price of
a coffin. Everything that was beyond the *Grenze* excited me.
Some of my most cherished cosmococcic miscreants, I discovered,
inhabited this land of desolation. Patrick Garstin, the Egyp-
tologist, was one. (He had come to look more like a gold-digger
than an archaeologist.) Donato lived here too. Donato, the Sicilian
lad, who in taking an axe to his old man had luckily chopped off
only one arm. What aspirations he had, this budding parricide!
At seventeen he was dreaming of getting a job in the Vatican. In
order, he said, to become better acquainted with St. Francis!

Making the rounds from one alkali bed to another, I brought
my geography, ethnology, folk lore and gunnery up to date. The
architecture teemed with atavistic anomalies. There were dwell-
ings seemingly transplanted from the shores of the Caspian, huts
out of Andersen's fairy tales, shops from the cool labyrinths of
Fez, spare cart wheels and sulkies without shafts, bird cages
galore and always empty, chamber pots, often of majolica and
decorated with pansies or sun flowers, corsets, crutches and the
handles and ribs of umbrellas . . . an endless array of bric-a-brac
all marked "manufactured in Hagia Triada." And what midgets!
One, who pretended to speak only Bulgarian—he was really a
Moldavian—lived in a dog kennel in the rear of his shack. He ate
with the dog—out of the same tin plate. When he smiled he
showed only two teeth, huge ones, like a canine's. He could bark
too, or sniff and growl like a cur.

None of this did I dare to put into the novel. No, the novel I kept like a boudoir. No *Dreck*. Not that all the characters were respectable or impeccable. Ah no! Some whom I had dragged in for color were plain *Schmucks*. (Prepucelos.) The hero, who was also the narrator and to whom I bore a slight resemblance, had the air of a trapezoid cerebralist. It was his function to keep the merry-go-round turning. Now and then he treated himself to a free ride.

What element there was of the bizarre and the outlandish intrigued Pop no end. He had wondered—openly—how a young woman, the author, in other words, came by such thoughts, such images. It had never occurred to Mona to say: "From another incarnation!" Frankly, I would hardly have known what to say myself. Some of the goofiest images had been stolen from almanacs, others were born of wet dreams. What Pop truly enjoyed, it seemed, was the occasional introduction of a dog or a cat. (He couldn't know, of course, that I was mortally afraid of dogs or that I loathed cats.) But I could make a dog talk. And it was doggy talk, no mistake about it. My true reason for inserting these creatures of a lower order was to show contempt for certain characters in the book who had gotten out of hand. A dog, properly inspired, can make an ass of a queen. Besides, if I wished to ridicule a current idea which was anathema to me all I had to do was to impersonate a mutt, lift my hind leg and piss on it.

Despite all the foolery, all the shenanigans, I nevertheless managed to create a sort of antique glaze. My purpose was to impart such a finish, such a patina, that every page would gleam like star dust. This was the business of authorship, as I then conceived it. Make mud puddles, if necessary, but see to it that they reflect the galactic varnish. When giving an idiot voice mix the jabberwocky with high-flown allusions to such subjects as paleontology, quadratics, hyperboreanism. A line from one of the mad Caesars was always pertinent. Or a curse from the lips of a scrofulous dwarf. Or just a sly Hamsunesque quip, like "Going for a walk, Froken? The cowslips are dying of thirst." Sly, I say, because the allusion, though far-fetched, was to Froken's habit of spreading her legs, when she thought she was well out of sight, and making water.

These rambles taken to relax or to obtain fresh inspiration—often only to aerate the testicles—had a disturbing effect upon the work in progress. Rounding a corner at a sixty-degree angle, it could happen that a conversation (with a locomotive engineer or a jobless hod-carrier) ended only a few minutes previously would suddenly blossom into a dialogue of such length, such extravagance, that I would find it impossible, on returning to my desk, to resume the thread of my narrative. For every thought that entered my head the hod-carrier or whoever would have some comment to make. No matter what answer I made the conversation continued. It was as if these corky nobodies had made up their minds to derail me.

Occasionally this same sort of bitchery would start up with statues, particularly chipped and dismantled ones. I might be loitering in some backyard gazing absent-mindedly at a marble head with one ear missing and presto! it would be talking to me . . . talking in the language of a proconsul. Some crazy urge would seize me to caress the battered features, whereupon, as if the touch of my hand had restored it to life, it would smile at me. A smile of gratitude, needless to say. Then an even stranger thing might happen. An hour later, say, passing the plate glass window of an empty shop, who would greet me from the murky depths but the same proconsul! Terror-stricken, I would press my nose against the show-window and stare. There he was—an ear missing, the nose bitten off. And his lips moving! "A retinal haemorrhage," I would murmur, and move on. "God help me if he visits me in my sleep!"

Thus, not so strangely, I developed a kind of painter's eye. Often I made it my business to return to a certain spot in order to review "a still life" which I had passed too hurriedly the day before or three days before. The still life, as I term it, might be an artless arrangement of objects which no one in his senses would have bothered to look at twice. For example—a few playing cards lying face up on the sidewalk and next to them a toy

pistol or the head of a missing chicken. Or an open parasol torn
to shreds sticking out of a lumberjack's boot, and beside the boot
a tattered copy of *The Golden Ass* pierced with a rusty jack-
knife. Wondering what so fascinated me in these chance arrange-
ments, it would suddenly dawn on me that I had detected similar
configurations in the painter's world. Then it would be an all-
night task to recall which painting, which painter, and where
I had first stumbled upon it. Extraordinary, when one takes up
the pursuit of such chimeras, to discover what amazing trivia,
what sheer insanity, infests some of the great masterpieces of art.

But the most distinctive feature associated with these jaunts,
rambles, forays and reconnoiterings was the realm, panoramic in
recollection, of gesture. Human gestures. All borrowed from the
animal and insect worlds. Even those of "refined" individuals, or
pseudo-refined, such as morticians, lackeys, ministers of the gos-
pel, major-domos. The way a certain nobody, when taken by
surprise, threw back his head and whinnied, would stick in my
crop long after I had ceased to remember his words and deeds.
There were novelists, I discovered, who made a specialty of exploiting such idiosyncrasies, who thought nothing of resorting to
a little trick like the whinnying of a horse when they wished to
remind the reader of a character mentioned sixty pages back.
Craftsmen, the critics called them. Crafty, certainly.

Yes, in my stumbling, bumbling way I was making all manner
of discoveries. One of them was that one cannot hide his identity
under cover of the third person, nor establish his identity solely
through the use of the first person singular. Another was: not
to think before a blank page. *Ce n'est pas moi, le roi, c'est
l'autonome*. Not I, but the Father within me, in other words.

Quite a discipline, to get words to trickle without fanning
them with a feather or stirring them with a silver spoon. To
learn to wait, wait patiently, like a bird of prey, even though the
flies were biting like mad and the birds chirping insanely. Before
Abraham was . . . Yes, before the Olympian Goethe, before the
great Shakespeare, before the divine Dante or the immortal
Homer, there was the Voice and the Voice was with every man.

Man has never lacked for words. The difficulty arose only when man forced the words to do his bidding. *Be still, and wait the coming of the Lord!* Erase all thought, observe the still movement of the heavens! All is flow and movement, light and shadow. What is more still than a mirror, the frozen glassiness of glass—yet what frenzy, what fury, its still surface can yield.

"I wish that you would kindly have the men of the Park Department prune, trim and pare off all the dead wood, twigs, sprigs, stumps, stickers, shooters, sucker-pieces, dirty and shaggy pieces, low, extra low and overhanging boughs and branches from the good trees and to prune them extra close to the bark, and to have all the good trees thoroughly and properly sprayed from the base to the very top parts and all through along by all parts of each street, avenue, place, court, lane, boulevard and so on . . . and thereby give a great deal more light, more natural light, more air, more beauty to all the surrounding areas."

That was the sort of message I should like to have dispatched at intervals to the god of the literary realm so that I might be delivered from confusion, rescued from chaos, freed of obsessive admiration for authors living and dead whose words, phrases, images barricaded my way.

And what was it prevented my own unique thoughts from breaking out and flooding the page? For many a year now I had been scurrying to and fro like a pack-rat, borrowing this and that from the beloved masters, hiding them away, my treasures, forgetting where I had stored them, and always searching for more, more, more. In some deep, forgotten pit were buried all the thoughts and experiences which I might properly call my own, and which were certainly unique, but which I lacked the courage to resuscitate. Had someone cast a spell over me that I should labor with arthritic stumps instead of two bold fists? Had someone stood over me in my sleep and whispered: "You will never do it, never do it!" (Not Stanley certainly, for he would disdain to whisper. Could he not hiss like a snake?) Who then? Or was it that I was still in the cocoon stage, a worm not yet sufficiently intoxicated with the splendor and magnificence of life?

How does one know that one day he will take wing, that like the humming bird he will quiver in mid-air and dazzle with iridescent sheen? One doesn't. One hopes and prays and bashes his head against the wall. But "it" knows. *It* can bide its time. *It* knows that all the errors, all the detours, all the failures and frustrations will be turned to account. To be born an eagle one must get accustomed to high places; to be born a writer one must learn to like privation, suffering, humiliation. Above all, one must learn to live apart. Like the sloth, the writer clings to his limb while beneath him life surges by steady, persistent, tumultuous. When ready plop! he falls into the stream and battles for life. Is it not something like that? Or is there a fair, smiling land where at an early age the budding writer is taken aside, instructed in his art, guided by loving masters and, instead of falling thwack into mid-stream he glides like an eel through sludge, mire and ooze?

I had time unending for such vagaries in the course of my daily routine; like poplars they sprang up beside me as I labored in thought, as I walked the streets for inspiration, or as I put my head on the pillow to drown myself in sleep. What a wonderful life, the literary life! I would sometimes say to myself. Meaning this in-between realm crowded with interlacing, intertwining boughs, branches, leaves, stickers, suckers and what not. The mild activity associated with my "work" not only failed to drain my energy but stimulated it. I was forever buzzing, buzzing. If now and then I complained of exhaustion it was from not being able to write, never from writing too much. Did I fear, unconsciously, that if I succeeded in letting myself go I would be speaking with my own voice? Did I fear that once I found that buried treasure which I had hidden away I would never again know peace, never know surcease from toil?

The very thought of creation—how absolutely unapproachable it is! Or its opposite, chaos. Impossible ever to posit such a thing as the un-created. The more deeply we gaze the more we discover of order in disorder, the more of law in lawlessness, the more of light in darkness. Negation—the absence of things—is unthinkable; it is the ghost of a thought. Everything is humming, pushing, waxing, waning, changing—has been so since eternity. And all according to inscrutable urges, forces, which, when we recognize them, we call laws. *Chaos!* We know nothing of chaos. *Silence!* Only the dead know it. *Nothingness!* Blow as hard as you like, something always remains.

When and where does creation cease? And what can a mere writer create that has not already been created? Nothing. The writer rearranges the gray matter in his noodle. He makes a beginning and an end—the very opposite of creation!—and in between, where he shuffles around, or more properly is shuffled around, there is born the imitation of reality: a book. Some books have altered the face of the world. Re-arrangement, nothing more. The problems of life remain. A face may be lifted, but one's age is indelible. Books have no effect. Authors have no effect. The effect was given in the first Cause. *Where wert thou when I created the world?* Answer that and you have solved the riddle of creation!

We write, knowing we are licked before we start. Every day we beg for fresh torment. The more we itch and scratch the better we feel. And when our readers also begin to itch and scratch we feel sublime. Let no one die of inanition! The airs must ever swarm with arrows of thought delivered by *les hommes de lettres*. Letters, mind you. How well put! Letters strung together with invisible wires charged with imponderable magnetic currents. All this travail forced upon a brain that was intended to work like a charm, to work without working. Is it a person coming towards you or a mind? A mind divided into books, pages, sentences replete with commas, periods, semi-colons, dashes and asterisks. One author receives a prize or a seat in the Academy for his efforts, another a worm-eaten bone. The names of some are lent to streets and boulevards, of others to gallows and almshouses. And when all these "creations" have been finally read and digested men will still be buggering one another. No author, not even the greatest, has been able to get round that hard, cold fact.

A grand life just the same. The literary life, I mean. Who wants to alter the world? (Let it rot, let it die, let it fade away!)

Tetrazzini practising her trills, Caruso shattering the chandeliers, Cortot waltzing like a blind mouse, the great Vladimir horrorizing the keyboard—was it of creation or salvation they were thinking? Perhaps not even of constipation. . . . The road smokes under your horses' hooves, the bridges rumble, the heavens fall backwards. *What is the meaning of it all?* The air, torn to shreds, rushes by. Everything is flying by, bells, collar buttons, moustachios, pomegranates, hand grenades. We draw aside to make way for you, you fiery steeds. And for you, dear Jascha Heifetz, dear Joseph Szigeti, dear Yehudi Menuhin. We draw aside, humbly—do you hear? No answer. Only the sound of their collar bells.

Nights when everything is going whish whoosh! when all the unearthed characters slink out of their hiding places to perform on the roof-top of my brain, arguing, screaming, yodeling, cart-wheeling, whinnying too—what horses!—I know that this is the only life, this life of the writer, and the world may stay put, get worse, sicken and die, all one, because I no longer belong to the world, a world that sickens and dies, that stabs itself over and over, that wobbles like an amputated crab. . . . I have my own world, a *Graben* of a world, cluttered with Vespasiennes, Mirós and Heideggers, bidets, a lone Yeshiva Bocher, cantors who sink like clarinets, divas who swim in their own fat, bugle busters and troikas that rush like the wind. . . . Napoleon has no place here, nor Goethe, nor even those gentle souls with power over birds, such as St. Francis, Milosz the Lithuanian, and Wittgenstein. Even lying on my back, pinned down by dwarves and gremlins, my power is vast and unyielding. My minions obey me; they pop like corn on the griddle, they whirl into line to form sentences, paragraphs, pages. And in some far-off place, in some heavenly day to come, others geared to the music of words will respond to the message and storm heaven itself to spread unbounded delirium. Who knows why these things should be, or why cantatas and oratorios? We know only that their magic is law, and that by observing them, heeding them, reverencing them, we add joy to joy, misery to misery, death to death.

Nothing is so creative as creation itself. Abel begot Bogul, and Bogul begot Mogul, and Mogul begot Zobel. Catheter, blatherer, shatterer. One letter added to another makes for a word; one word added to another makes for a phrase; phrase upon phrase, sentence upon sentence, paragraph upon paragraph; chapter after chapter, book after book, epic after epic: a Tower of Babel stretching almost, but not quite, to the lips of the Great I Am. "Humility is the word!" Or, as my dear, beloved Master explains: "We must remember our close connection with things like insects, pterodactyls, saurians, slow-worms, moles, skunks, and those little flying squirrels called polatouches." But let us also not forget, when creation drags us by the hair, that every atom, every molecule, every single element of the universe is in league with us, egging us on and trimming us down, all to remind us that we must never think of dirt as dirt or God as God but ever of all combined, making us to race like comets after our own tails, and thereby giving the lie to motion, matter, energy and all the other conceptual flub-dub clinging to the asshole of creation like bleeding piles.

("My straw hat mingles with the straw hats of the rice-planters.")

It is unnecessary, in this beamish realm, to feast on human dung or copulate with the dead, after the manner of certain disciplined souls, nor is it necessary to abstain from food, alcohol, sex and drugs, after the manner of anchorites. Neither is it incumbent upon anyone to practice hour after hour the major and minor scales, the arpeggios, pizzicati or cadenzas, as did the progeny of Liszt, Czerny and other pyrotechnical virtuosi. Nor should one slave to make words explode like firecrackers, in conformance to the ballistic regulations of inebriated semanticists. It is enough and more to stretch, yawn, wheeze, fart and whinny. Rules are for barbarians, technic for the troglodytes. Away with the Minnesinger, even those of Cappadocia!

Thus, whilst sedulously and slavishly imitating the ways of the masters—tools and technic, in other words—my instincts were rising up in revolt. If I craved magical powers it was not to rear new structures, not to add to the Tower of Babel, but to destroy, to undermine. The novel I *had* to write. *Point d'honneur.* But after that . . . ? After that, vengeance! Ravage, lay waste the land: make of Culture an open sewer, so that the stench of it would remain forever in the nostrils of memory. All my idols— and I possessed a veritable pantheon—I would offer up as sacri- fices. What powers of utterance they had given me I would use to curse and blaspheme. Had not the prophets of old promised destruction? Had they ever hesitated to befoul their speech, in order to awaken the dead? If for companions I had never aught but derelicts and wastrels, was there not a purpose in it? Were not my idols also derelicts and wastrels—in a profound sense? Did they not float on the tide of culture, were they not tossed hither and thither like the unlettered wretches of the workaday world? Were their daemons not as heartless and ruthless as any slave driver? Did not everything conspire—the grand, the noble, the perfect works as well as the low, the sordid, the mean—to render life more unlivable each day? Of what use the poems of death, the maxims and counsels of the sage ones, the codes and tablets of the law-givers, of what use leaders, thinkers, men of art, if the very elements that made up the fabric of life were incapable of being transformed?

Only to one who has not yet found his way is it permitted to ask all the wrong questions, to tread all the wrong paths, to hope and pray for the destruction of all existent modes and forms. Puzzled and perplexed, yanked this way and that, muddled and befuddled, striving and cursing, sneering and jeering, small wonder that in the midst of a thought, a perfect jewel of a thought, I sometimes caught myself staring straight ahead, mind blank, like a chimpanzee in the act of mounting another chim- panzee. It was in this wise that Abel begot Bogul and Bogul begot Mogul. I was the last of the line, a dog of a Zobel with a bone be- tween my jaws which I could neither chew nor grind, which I teased and worried, and spat on and shat on. Soon I would piss on it and bury it. And the name of the bone was Babel.

A grand life, the literary life. Never would I have it better. Such tools! Such technic! How could anyone, unless he hugged me like a shadow, know the myriads of waste places I frequented in my search for ore? Or the varieties of birds that sang for me as I dug my pits and shafts? Or the cackling, chortling gnomes and elves who waited on me as I labored, who faithfully tickled my balls, rehearsed my lines, or revealed to me the mysteries hidden in pebbles, twigs, fleas, lice and pollen? Who could possibly know the confidences revealed by my idols who were ever sending me night messages, or the secret codes imparted to me whereby I learned to read between the lines, to correct false biographical data and make light of gnostic commentaries? Never was there a more solid terra firma beneath my feet than when grappling with this shifting, floating world created by the vandals of culture on whom I finally learned to turn my ass.

And who, I ask, who but a "master of reality" could imagine that the first step into the world of creation must be accompanied with a loud, evil-smelling fart, as if experiencing for the first time the significance of shellfire? *Advance always!* The generals of literature sleep soundly in their cosy bunks. We, the hairy ones, do the fighting. From that trench which must be taken there is no returning. Get thee behind us, ye laureates of Satan! If it be cleavers we must fight with, let us use them to full advantage. *Faugh a balla!* Get those greasy ducks! *Avanti, avanti!*

The battle is endless. It had no beginning, nor will it know an end. We who babble and froth at the mouth have been at it since eternity. Spare us further instruction! Are we to make green lawns as we advance from trench to trench? Are we landscape artists as well as butchers? Must we storm to victory perfumed like whores? For whom are we mopping up?

How fortunate that I had only one reader! Such an indulgent one, too. Every time I sat down to write a page for him I readjusted my skirt, primped my hair-do and powdered my nose. If only he could see me at work, dear Pop! If only he knew the pains I took to give his novel the proper literary cast. What a Marius he had in me! What an Epicurean!

Somewhere Paul Valéry has said: "What is of value to us alone (meaning the poets of literature) has no value. This is the law of literature." Iss dot so now? Tsch, tsch! True, our Valéry was discussing the art of poetry, discussing the poet's task and purpose, his *raison d'être*. Myself, I have never understood poetry as poetry. For me the mark of the poet is everywhere, in everything. To distill thought until it hangs in the alembic of a poem, revealing not a speck, not a shadow, not a vaporous breath of the "impurities" from which it was decocted, that for me is a meaningless, worthless pursuit, even though it be the sworn and solemn function of those midwives who toil in the name of Beauty, Form, Intelligence, and so on.

I speak of the poet because I was then, in my blissful embryonic state, more nearly that than ever since. I never thought, as did Diderot, that "my ideas are my whores." Why would I want whores? No, my ideas were a garden of delights. An absentminded gardener I was, who, though tender and observing, did not attach too much importance to the presence of weeds, thorns, nettles, but craved only the joy of frequenting this place apart, this intimate domain peopled with shrubs, blossoms, flowers, bees, birds, bugs of every variety. I never walked the garden as a pimp, nor even in a fornicating frame of mind. Neither did I invest it as a botanist, an entomologist or a horticulturist. I studied nothing, not even my own wonder. Nor did I christen any blessed thing. The look of a flower was enough, or its perfume. How did the flower come to be? How did *anything* come to be? If I questioned, it was to ask, *"Are you there, little friend? Are the dewdrops still clinging to your petals?"*

What could be more considerate—better manners!—than to treat thoughts, ideas, inspirational flashes, as flowers of delight? What better work habits than to greet them with a smile each day or walk among them musing on their evanescent glory? True, now and then I might make so bold as to pluck one for my buttonhole. But to exploit it, to send it out to work like a whore or a stockbroker—unthinkable. For me it was enough to have been inspired, not to be perpetually inspired. I was neither a poet nor a drudge. I was simply out of step. *Heimatlos.*

My only reader . . .Later I will exchange him for the ideal reader, that intimate rascal, that beloved scamp, to whom I may speak as if nothing had any value but to him—and to me. Why add—*to me?* Can he be any other, this ideal reader, than my alter

ego? Why create a world of one's own if it must also make sense
to every Tom, Dick and Harry? Have not the others this world
of everyday, which they profess to despise yet cling to like
drowning rats? Is it not strange how they who refuse, or are too
lazy, to create a world of their own insist on invading ours? Who
is it tramples the flower beds at night? Who is it leaves cigarette stubs in the bird bath? Who is it pees on the blushing violets
and wilts their bloom? We know how you ravage the pages of
literature in search of what pleases you. We discover the foot-
prints of your blundering spirit everywhere. It is you who kill
genius, you who cripple the giants. *You, you*, whether through
love and adoration or through envy, spite and hatred. Who
writes for you writes his own death warrant.

> *Little sparrow,*
> *Mind, mind out of the way,*
> *Mr. Horse is coming.*

Issa-San wrote that. Tell me its value!

II Finding His Own Voice

The Inhuman Ones
—*Tropic of Cancer*

Once I thought that to be human was the highest aim a man could have, but I see now that it was meant to destroy me. Today I am proud to say that I am *inhuman*, that I belong not to men and governments, that I have nothing to do with creeds and principles. I have nothing to do with the creaking machinery of humanity—I belong to the earth! I say that lying on my pillow and I can feel the horns sprouting from my temples. I can see about me all those cracked forbears of mine dancing around the bed, consoling me, egging me on, lashing me with their serpent tongues, grinning and leering at me with their skulking skulls. *I am inhuman!* I say it with a mad, hallucinated grin, and I will keep on saying it though it rains crocodiles. Behind my words are all those grinning, leering, skulking skulls, some dead and grinning a long time, some grinning as if they had lock-jaw, some grinning with the grimace of a grin, the foretaste and aftermath of what is always going on. Clearer than all, I see my own grinning skull, see the skeleton dancing in the wind, serpents issuing from the rotted tongue and the bloated pages of ecstasy slimed with excrement. And I join my slime, my excrement, my madness, my ecstasy to the great circuit which flows through the subterranean vaults of the flesh. All this unbidden, unwanted, drunken vomit will flow on endlessly through the minds of those to come in the inexhaustible vessel that contains the history of the race. Side by side with the human race there runs another race of beings, the inhuman ones, the race of artists who, goaded by unknown impulses, take the lifeless mass of humanity and by the fever and ferment with which they imbue it turn this soggy dough into bread and the bread into wine and the wine into song. Out of the dead compost and the inert slag they breed a song that contaminates. I see this other race of individuals ransacking the universe, turning everything upside down, their feet always moving in blood and tears, their hands always empty, always clutching and grasping for the beyond, for the god out of reach: slaying everything within reach in order to quiet the monster that gnaws at their vitals. I see that when they tear their hair with the effort to comprehend, to seize this forever unattainable, I see that when they bellow like crazed beasts and rip and gore, I see that this is right, that there is no other path to pursue. A man who belongs to this race must stand up on the high place with gibberish in his mouth and rip out his entrails. It is right and just, because he must! And anything that falls short of this frightening spectacle, anything less shuddering, less terrifying, less mad, less intoxicated, less contaminating, is not art. The rest is counterfeit. The rest is human. The rest belongs to life and lifelessness.

When I think of Stavrogin for example, I think of some divine monster standing on a high place and flinging to us his torn bowels. In *The Possessed* the earth quakes: it is not the catastrophe that befalls the imaginative individual, but a cataclysm in which a large portion of humanity is buried, wiped out forever. Stavrogin was Dostoievski and Dostoievski was the sum of all those contradictions which either paralyze a man or lead him to the heights. There was no world too low for him to enter, no place too high for him to fear to ascend. He went the whole gamut, from the abyss to the stars. It is a pity that we shall never again have the opportunity to see a man placed at the very core of mystery and, by his flashes, illuminating for us the depth and immensity of the darkness.

Today I am aware of my lineage. I have no need to consult

my horoscope or my genealogical chart. What is written in the stars, or in my blood, I know nothing of. I know that I spring from the mythological founders of the race. The man who raises the holy bottle to his lips, the criminal who kneels in the market-place, the innocent one who discovers that *all* corpses stink, the madman who dances with lightning in his hands, the friar who lifts his skirts to pee over the world, the fanatic who ransacks libraries in order to find the Word—all these are fused in me, all these make my confusion, my ecstasy. If I am inhuman it is because my world has slopped over its human bounds, because to be human seems like a poor, sorry, miserable affair, limited by the senses, restricted by moralities and codes, defined by platitudes and isms. I am pouring the juice of the grape down my gullet and I find wisdom in it, but my wisdom is not born of the grape, my intoxication owes nothing to wine. . . .

I want to make a detour of those lofty arid mountain ranges where one dies of thirst and cold, that "extra-temporal" history, that absolute of time and space where there exists neither man, beast nor vegetation, where one goes crazy with loneliness, with language that is mere words, where everything is unhooked, ungeared, out of joint with the times. I want a world of men and women, of trees that do not talk (because there is too much talk in the world as it is!), of rivers that carry you to places, not rivers that are legends, but rivers that put you in touch with other men and women, with architecture, religion, plants, animals—rivers that have boats on them and in which men drown, drown not in myth and legend and books and dust of the past, but in time and space and history. I want rivers that make oceans such as Shakespeare and Dante, rivers which do not dry up in the void of the past. Oceans, yes! Let us have more oceans, new oceans that blot out the past, oceans that create new geological formations, new topographical vistas and strange, terrifying continents, oceans that destroy and preserve at the same time, oceans that we can sail on, take off to new discoveries, new horizons. Let us have more oceans, more upheavals, more wars, more holocausts. Let us have a world of men and women with dynamos between their legs, a world of natural fury, of passion, action, drama, dreams, madness, a world that produces ecstasy and not dry farts. I believe that today more than ever a book should be sought after even if it has only *one* great page in it: we must search for fragments, splinters, toe-nails, anything that has ore in it, anything that is capable of resuscitating the body and soul.

It may be that we are doomed, that there is no hope for us, *any of us,* but if that is so then let us set up a last agonizing, blood-curdling howl, a screech of defiance, a war-whoop! Away with lamentation! Away with elegies and dirges! Away with biographies and histories, and libraries and museums! Let the dead eat the dead. Let us living ones dance about the rim of the crater, a last expiring dance. But a dance!

"I love everything that flows," said the great blind Milton of our times. I was thinking of him this morning when I awoke with a great bloody shout of joy: I was thinking of his rivers and trees and all that world of night which he is exploring. Yes, I said to myself, I too love everything that flows: rivers, sewers, lava, semen, blood, bile, words, sentences. I love the amniotic fluid when it spills out of the bag. I love the kidney with its painful gallstones, its gravel and what not; I love the urine that pours out scalding and the clap that runs endlessly; I love the words of hysterics and the sentences that flow on like dysentery and mirror all the sick images of the soul; I love the great rivers like the Amazon and the Orinoco, where crazy men like Mora-vagine float on through dream and legend in an open boat and drown in the blind mouths of the river. I love everything that flows, even the menstrual flow that carries away the seed un-fecund. I love scripts that flow, be they hieratic, esoteric, per-verse, polymorph or unilateral. I love everything that flows, everything that has time in it and becoming, that brings us back to the beginning where there is never end: the violence of the prophets, the obscenity that is ecstasy, the wisdom of the fanatic, the priest with his rubber litany, the foul words of the whore, the spittle that floats away in the gutter, the milk of the breast and the bitter honey that pours from the womb, all that is fluid, melting, dissolute and dissolvent, all the pus and dirt that in flowing is purified, that loses its sense of origin, that makes the great circuit towards death and dissolution. The great incestuous wish is to flow on, one with time, to merge the great image of the beyond with the here and now. A fatuous, suicidal wish that is constipated by words and paralyzed by thought.

I Am Chancre, the Crab
—Black Spring

I am thinking of that age to come when God is born again, when men will fight and kill for God as now and for a long time to come men are going to fight for food. I am thinking of that age when work will be forgotten and books assume their true place in life, when perhaps there will be no more books, just one great big book—a Bible. For me the book is the man and my book is the man I am, the confused man, the negligent man, the reckless man, the lusty, obscene, boisterous, thoughtful, scrupulous, lying, diabolically truthful man that I am. I am thinking that in that age to come I shall not be overlooked. Then my history will become important and the scar which I leave upon the face of the world will have significance. I can not forget that I am making history, a history on the side which, like a chancre, will eat away the other meaningless history. I regard myself not as a book, a record, a document, but as a history of our time—a history of *all* time.

If I was unhappy in America, if I craved more room, more adventure, more freedom of expression, it was because I needed these things. I am grateful to America for having made me realize my needs. I served my sentence there. At present I have no needs. I am a man without a past and without a future. *I am—* that is all. I am not concerned with your likes and dislikes; it doesn't matter to me whether you are convinced that what I say is so or not. It is all the same to me if you drop me here and now. I am not an atomizer from which you can squeeze a thin spray of hope. I see America spreading disaster. I see America as a black curse upon the world. I see a long night settling in and that mushroom which has poisoned the world withering at the roots.

And so it is with a premonition of the end—be it tomorrow or three hundred years hence—that I feverishly write this book. So it is too that my thoughts sputter out now and then, that I am obliged to rekindle the flame again and again, not with courage alone, but with desperation—for there is no one I can trust to say these things for me. My faltering and groping, my search for any and every means of expression, is a sort of divine stuttering. *I am dazzled by the glorious collapse of the world!*

Every evening, after dinner, I take the garbage down to the court-yard. Coming up I stand with empty pail at the staircase window gazing at the Sacré Cœur high up on the hill of Montmartre. Every evening, when I take the garbage down, I think of myself standing out on a high hill in resplendent whiteness. It is no sacred heart that inspires me, no Christ I am thinking of. Something better than a Christ, something bigger than a heart, something beyond God Almighty I think of—MYSELF. *I am a man.* That seems to me sufficient.

I am a man of God and a man of the Devil. To each his due. Nothing eternal, nothing absolute. Before me always the image of the body, our triune god of penis and testicles. On the right God the Father; on the left and hanging a little lower, God the Son; and between and above them the Holy Ghost. I can never forget that this holy trinity is man-made, that it will undergo infinite changes—but as long as we come out of wombs with arms and legs, as long as there are stars above us to drive us mad and grass under our feet to cushion the wonder in us, just so long will this body serve for all the tunes that we may whistle.

Today it is the third or fourth day of spring and I am sitting at the Place Clichy in full sunshine. Today, sitting here in the sun, I tell you it doesn't matter a damn whether the world is going to the dogs or not; it doesn't matter whether the world is right or wrong, good or bad. *It is*—and that suffices. The world is what it is and I am what I am. I say it not like a squatting Buddha with legs crossed, but out of a gay, hard wisdom, out of an inner security. This out there and this in me, all this, *every thing*, the resultant of inexplicable forces. A chaos whose order is beyond comprehension. Beyond *human* comprehension.

As a human being walking around at twilight, at dawn, at strange hours, unearthly hours, the sense of being alone and unique fortifies me to such a degree that when I walk with the multitude and seem no longer to be a human being but a mere speck, a gob of spit, I begin to think of myself alone in space, a single being surrounded by the most magnificent empty streets, a human biped walking between the skyscrapers when all the inhabitants have fled and I am alone walking, singing, commanding the earth. I do not have to look in my vest pocket to find my soul; it is there all the time, bumping against my ribs, swelling, inflated with song. If I just left a gathering where it was agreed that all is dead, now as I walk the streets, alone and identical with God, I know that this is a lie. The evidence of death is before my eyes constantly; but this death of the world, a death constantly going on, does not move from the periphery in, to engulf me, this death is at my very feet, moving from me outward, my own death a step in advance of me always. The world is the mirror of myself dying, the world not dying any more than I die, I more alive a thousand years from now than this moment and this world in which I am now dying also more alive then than now though dead a thousand years. When each thing is lived through to the end there is no death and no regrets, neither is there a false spring time; each moment lived pushes open a greater, wider horizon from which there is no escape save living.

The dreamers dream from the neck up, their bodies securely strapped to the electric chair. To imagine a new world is to live it daily, each thought, each glance, each step, each gesture killing and re-creating, death always a step in advance. To spit on the past is not enough. To proclaim the future is not enough. One must act *as if* the past were dead and the future unrealizable. One must act *as if* the next step were the last, which it is. Each step forward is the last, and with it a world dies, one's self included. We are here of the earth never to end, the past never ceasing, the future never beginning, the present never ending.

The never-never world which we hold in our hands and see and yet is not ourselves. We are that which is never concluded, never shaped to be recognized, all there is and yet not the whole, the parts so much greater than the whole that only God the mathematician can figure it out.

Laughter! counseled Rabelais. For all your ills *laughter!* Jesus but it's hard to take his sane, gay wisdom after all the quack medicines we've poured down our throats. How can one laugh when the lining is worn off his stomach? How can one laugh after all the misery they've poisoned us with, the whey-faced, lantern-jawed, sad, suffering, solemn, serious, seraphic spirits? I understand the treachery that inspired them. I forgive them their genius. But it's hard to free oneself from all the sorrow they've created.

When I think of all the fanatics who were crucified, and those who were not fanatics, but simple idiots, all slaughtered for the sake of ideas, I begin to draw a simile. Bottle up every avenue of escape, I say. Bring the lid down hard on the New Jerusalem! Let's feel each other belly to belly, *without hope!* Washed and unwashed, murderer and evangelist, the whey-faced guys and the three-quarter moons, the weather-vanes and the bullet-heads —let them only get closer together, let them stew for a few centuries in this cul-de-sac!

Either the world is too slack or I am not taut enough. If I became unintelligible I would be understood immediately. The difference between understanding and non-understanding is as fine as a hair, *finer*, the difference of a millimeter, a thread of space between China and Neptune. No matter how far out of whack I get the ratio remains the same; it has nothing to do with clarity, precision, et cetera. (The et cetera is important!) The mind blunders because it is too precise an instrument; the threads break against the mahogany knots, against the cedar and ebony of alien matter. We talk about reality as if it were something commensurable, a piano exercise, or a lesson in physics. The Black Death came with the return of the Crusaders. Syphilis came with the return of Columbus. *Reality will come too!*

Reality prime, says my friend Cronstadt. From a poem written on the ocean floor . . .

To prognosticate this reality is to be off either by a millimeter or by a million light years. The difference is a quantum formed by the intersection of streets. A quantum is a functional disorder created by trying to squeeze oneself into a frame of reference. A reference is a discharge from an old employer, that is to say, a muco-pus from an old disease.

These are thoughts born of the street, *genus epileptoid.* You walk out with the guitar and the strings snap—because the idea is not embedded morphologically. To recall the dream one must keep the eyes closed and not budge. The slightest stir and the whole fabric falls apart. In the street I expose myself to the destructive, disintegrating elements that surround me. I let everything wreak its own havoc with me. I bend over to spy on the secret processes, *to obey* rather than to command.

There are huge blocks of my life which are gone forever. Huge blocks gone, scattered, wasted in talk, action, reminiscence, dream. There was never any time when I was living *one* life, the life of a husband, a lover, a friend. Wherever I was, whatever I was engaged in, I was leading multiple lives. Thus, whatever it is that I choose to regard as *my* story is lost, drowned, indissolubly fused with the lives, the drama, the stories of others.

I am a man of the old world, a seed that was transplanted by the wind, a seed which failed to blossom in the mushroom oasis of America. I belong on the heavy tree of the past. My allegiance, physical and spiritual, is with the men of Europe, those who were once Franks, Gauls, Vikings, Huns, Tartars, what not. The climate for my body and soul is here where there is quickness and corruption. I am proud *not* to belong to this century.

For those star-gazers who are unable to follow the act of revelation I append herewith a few horoscopic brush-strokes in the margin of my *Universe of Death.* . . .

I am Chancre, the crab, which moves sideways and backwards and forwards at will. I move in strange tropics and deal in high explosives, embalming fluid, jasper, myrrh, smaragd, fluted snot and porcupines' toes. Because of Uranus which crosses my longitudinal I am inordinately fond of cunt, hot chitterlings, and water bottles. Neptune dominates my ascendant. That means I am composed of a watery fluid, that I am volatile, quixotic, unreliable, independent and evanescent. Also quarrelsome. With a hot pad under my ass I can play the braggart or the buffoon as good as any man, no matter what sign he be born under. This is a self-portrait which yields only the missing parts—an anchor, a dinner bell, the remains of a beard, the hind part of a cow. In short, I am an idle fellow who pisses his time away. I have absolutely nothing to show for my labors except my genius. But there comes a time, even in the life of an idle genius, when he has to go to the window and vomit up the excess baggage. If you are a genius you have to do that—if for no other reason than to build a little comprehensible world of your own which will not run down like an eight-day clock! And the more ballast you throw overboard the easier you rise above the esteem of your neighbors. Until you find yourself all alone in the stratosphere. Then you tie a stone around your neck and you jump feet first. That brings about the complete destruction of anagogic dream interpretation, together with mercurial stomatitis brought about by inunctions. You have the dream for night time and the horse laugh for day time.

And so, when I stand at the bar of Little Tom Thumb and see these men with three-quarter faces coming up through the trapdoors of hell with pulleys and braces, dragging locomotives and pianos and cuspidors, I say to myself: "Grand! Grand! All this bric-a-brac, all this machinery coming to me on a silver platter! It's grand! It's marvelous! It's a poem created while I was asleep."

What little I have learned about writing amounts to this: *it is not what people think it is*. It is an absolutely new thing each time with each individual. Valparaiso, for example. Valparaiso, when I say it, means something totally different from anything it ever meant before. It may mean an English cunt with all her front teeth gone and the bartender standing in the middle of the street searching for customers. It may mean an angel in a silk shirt running his lacy fingers over a black harp. It may mean an odalisque with a mosquito netting around her ass. It may mean any of these things, or none, but whatever it may mean you can be sure it will be something different, something new. Valparaiso is always five minutes before the end, a little this side of Peru, or maybe three inches nearer. It's the accidental square inch that you do with fever because you've got a hot pad under your ass and the Holy Ghost in your bowels—orthopaedic mistakes included. It means "to piss warm and drink cold," as Trimalchio says, "because our mother the earth is in the middle, made round like an egg, and has all good things in herself, like a honeycomb."

And now, ladies and gentlemen, with this little universal can-opener which I hold in my hands I am about to open a can of sardines. With this little can-opener which I hold in my hands it's all the same—whether you want to open a box of sardines or a drug store. It's the third or fourth day of spring, as I've told you several times already, and even though it's a poor, shabby, reminiscent spring, the thermometer is driving me crazy as a bedbug. You thought I was sitting at the Place Clichy all the time, drinking an *apéritif* perhaps. As a matter of fact I *was* sitting at the Place Clichy, but that was two or three years ago. And I *did* stand at the bar of Little Tom Thumb, but that was a long time ago and since then a crab has been gnawing at my vitals. All this began in the Métro (first-class) with the phrase "*l'homme que j'étais, je ne le suis plus.*"

Walking past the railroad yards I was plagued by two fears—one, that if I lifted my eyes a little higher they would dart out of my head; two, that my bung-hole was dropping out. A tension so strong that all ideation became instantly rhombohedral. Imagined the whole world declaring a holiday to think about static. On that day so many suicides that there would not be wagons enough to collect the dead. Passing the railroad yards at the Porte I catch the sickening stench from the cattle trains. It's like this: all day today and all day yesterday—three or four years ago, of course—they have been standing there body to body in fear and sweat. Their bodies are saturated with doom. Passing them my mind is terribly lucid, my thoughts crystal clear. I'm in such a hurry to spill out my thoughts that I am running past them in the dark. I too am in great fear. I too am sweating and panting, thirsty, saturated with doom. I'm going by them like a letter through the post. Or not I, but certain ideas of which I am the harbinger. And these ideas are already labeled and docketed, already sealed, stamped and water-marked. They run in series, my ideas, like electric coils. To live *beyond* illusion, or *with* it? that's the question. Inside me a terrifying gem which will not wear away, a gem which scratches the windowpanes as I flee through the night. The cattle are lowing and bleating. They stand there in the warm stench of their own dung. I hear again now the music of the A Minor Quartet, the agonized flurries of the strings. There's a madman inside me and he's hacking away, hacking and hacking until he strikes the final discord. *Pure annihilation*, as distinguished from lesser, muddier annihilations. Nothing to be mopped up afterwards. A wheel of light rolling up to the precipice—and over into the bottomless pit. I, Beethoven, I created it! I, Beethoven, I destroy it!

From now on, ladies and gentlemen, you are entering Mexico. From now on everything will be wonderful and beautiful, marvelously beautiful, marvelously wonderful. Increasingly marvelously beautiful and wonderful. From now on no more washlines, no suspenders, no flannel underwear. Always summer and everything true to pattern. If it's a horse it's a horse for all time. If it's apoplexy it's apoplexy, and not St. Vitus' Dance. No early morning whores, no gardenias. No dead cats in the gutter, no sweat and perspiration. If it be a lip it must be a lip that trembles eternally. For in Mexico, ladies and gentlemen, it's always high noon and what glows is fuchsia and what's dead is dead and no feather-dusters. You lie on a cement bed and you sleep like an acetylene torch. When you strike it rich it's a bonanza. When you don't strike it rich it's misery, *worse than misery*. No arpeggios, no grace notes, no cadenzas. Either you hold the clue or you don't hold the clue. Either you start with pure melody or you start with listerine. But no Purgatory—and no elixir. It's Fourth Eclogue or Thirteenth Arrondissement!

Peace! It's Wonderful!
   —*The Cosmological Eye*

It was only the other night while entertaining an American writer who had come to visit France after a long absence that I realized poignantly what has happened to me since I left my native land. Like all my compatriots who come to see me he asked quite naturally what it was that had kept me here so long. (It is seven years since I am living in Paris.) I felt that it was useless to answer him in words. I suggested instead that we take a stroll through the streets. We started out from the corner of the Rue de la Gaîté and the Avenue du Maine where we had been sitting; I walked him down the Rue de l'Ouest to the Rue du Château, then over the railroad bridge back of the Gare Montparnasse down the Boulevard Pasteur to the Avenue de Breteuil and thence to a little café facing the Invalides where we sat in silence for a long while. Perhaps that silence which one finds in the streets of Paris at night, perhaps that alone was a sufficient answer to his query. It is something difficult to find in a big American city.

At any rate, it was not chance which had directed my footsteps. Walking with my friend through the deserted streets I was reliving my first days in Paris, for it was in the Rue de Vanves that my new life really began. Night after night without money, without friends, without a language I had walked these streets in despair and anguish. The streets were everything to me, as they must be to every man who is lost in a big city. Walking through them again with my countryman I congratulated myself silently that I had begun my life in Paris behind the scenes, as it were. If I *had* led a Bohemian life, as some imagine, it was through bitter necessity. *A Bohemian life!* What a strange phrase that is when you think of it! There is so little that is Bohemian about it. In any case, the important thing is that in the Rue de Vanves I touched bottom. Like it or not, I was obliged to create a new life for myself. And this new life I feel is mine, absolutely mine, to use or to smash, as I see fit. In this life I am God, and like God I am indifferent to my own fate. I am everything there is—so why worry?

Just as a piece of matter detaches itself from the sun to live as a wholly new creation so I have come to feel about my detachment from America. Once the separation is made a new orbit is established, and there is no turning back. For me the sun had ceased to exist; I had myself become a blazing sun. And like all the other suns of the universe I had to nourish myself *from within*. I speak in cosmological terms because it seems to me that is the only possible way to think if one is truly alive. I think this way also because it is just the opposite of the way I thought a few years back when I had what is called hopes. Hope is a bad thing. It means that you are not what you want to be. It means that part of you is dead, if not *all* of you. It means that you entertain illusions. It's a sort of spiritual clap, I should say.

Before this inward change came about I used to think that we were living in extraordinarily difficult times. Like most men I thought that *our* time was the worst possible time. And no doubt it is—for those, I mean, who still say "our time." As for myself, I've thrown away the calendar by which one reckons the lean and the fat years. For me it is all gravy, one continuous, marvelous stream of time without beginning or end. Yes, the times are bad, permanently bad—unless one becomes immune, *becomes God*. Since I have become God I go the whole hog always. I am absolutely indifferent to the fate of the world: I have my own world and my own private fate. I make no reservations and no compromises. I accept. *I am*—and that is all.

That is why, perhaps, when I sit at my typewriter I always face East. No backward glances over the shoulder. The orbit over which I am traveling leads me farther and farther away from the dead sun which gave me birth. Once I was confronted with a choice—either to remain a satellite of that dead thing or create a new world of my own, with my own satellites. I made my choice. Having made it there is no standing still. One becomes more and more alive, or more and more dead. To get a *piqûre* is useless; a blood transfusion is useless. A new man is made out of the whole cloth, by a change of heart which alters every living cell of the body. Anything less than a change of heart is sure catastrophe. Which, if you follow the reasoning, explains why the times are always bad. For, unless there be a change of heart there can be no act of will. There may be a show of will, with tremendous activity accompanying it (wars, revolutions, etc.), but that will not change the times. Things are apt to grow worse, in fact.

Over many centuries of time a few men have appeared who, to my way of thinking, really understood why the times are permanently bad. They proved, through their own unique way of living, that this sad "fact" is one of man's delusions. But nobody, apparently, understands them. And it is eminently right that it should be thus. If we want to lead a creative life it is absolutely just that we should be responsible for our own destiny. To imagine a way of life that could be patched is to think of the cosmos as a vast plumbing affair. To expect others to do what we are unable to do ourselves is truly to believe in miracles, miracles that no Christ would dream of performing. The whole social-political scheme of existence is crazy—because it is based on vicarious living. A real man has no need of governments, of laws, of moral or ethical codes, to say nothing of battleships, police clubs, high-powered bombers and such things. Of course a real man is hard to find, but that's the only kind of man worth talking about. Why talk about trash? It is the great mass of mankind, the mob, the people, who create the permanently bad times. The world is only the mirror of ourselves. If it's something to make one puke, why then puke, me lads, it's your own sick mugs you're looking at!

Sometimes it almost seems that the writer takes a perverse delight in finding the times out of joint, finding everything awrack and awry. Perhaps the artist is nothing more than the personification of this universal maladjustment, this universal disequilibrium. Perhaps that explains why in the neutral, sterilized countries (Scandinavia, Holland, Switzerland), so little art is forthcoming, or why in the countries undergoing profound

social and political changes (Russia, Germany, Italy), the art
products are of negligible value. But, whether there is little art
or bad art, art, it should be understood, is only a makeshift, a
substitute for the real thing. There is only one art which, if we
practiced it, would destroy what is called "art." With every line
I write I kill off the "artist" in me. With every line it is either
murder in the first degree or suicide. I do not want to give hope
to others, nor to inspire others. If we knew what it meant to be
inspired we would not inspire. We would simply *be*. As it is we
neither inspire nor aid one another: we deal out cold justice. For
myself I want none of this stinking cold justice; I want either
warm-hearted magnanimity or absolute neglect. To be honest, I
want something more than any man can give me. I want everything! I want everything—or nothing. It's crazy, I know, but
that's what I mean.

Is it good here in France? It's wonderful. Marvelous. For *me*
it's marvelous, because it's the only place in the world I know of
where I can go on with my murder-and-suicide business—until I
strike a new zodiacal realm. For a French writer it may be bad
here, but then I am not a French writer. I should hate to be a
French or a German or a Russian or an American writer. It must
be hell. I am a cosmological writer, and when I open my trap I
broadcast to the whole world at once. (Like Father Divine:
Peace! It's Wonderful!) Acting as I do I am apt to get it in the
neck. I am apt to get fucked good and proper, and I know it.
But that's my temperament, and I'll stand or fall by it. Eventually
I shan't even bother to be a cosmological writer: *I shall be just a
man*. But first there's a lot of slaughtering to be done.

Every man who aspires to be a good French writer (or a bad
one), or a (good or bad) German writer, or a (good or bad)
Russian writer, any man, I mean, who hopes to make a living
by giving regular doses of medicine to his sick countrymen
helps to perpetuate a farce which has been going on since the
beginning of history. Such writers, and they are practically all
we have, it seems, are the lice which keep us from knowing
Paradise or Hell. They keep us in a perpetual Purgatory where
we scratch without let. Whereas even the earth wobbles on

its axis, or will change its axis from time to time, these blokes keep us forever on an even keel. In every great figure who has flashed across the horizon there is, or was, a large element of treachery, or hatred, or love, or disgust. We have had traitors to race, country, religion, but we have not yet bred any real traitors, *traitors to the human race*, which is what we need. The chances are slim, I know. I mention it merely to show how the wind blows.

As I say, one needs either a heaven or a hell in which to flourish —until one arrives at that Paradise of his own creation, that middle realm which is not a bread-and-butter Utopia of which the masses dream but an interstellar realm in which one rolls along his orbit with sublime indifference. Dante was the best cartographer of the soul which Europe ever produced, everything clear as a whistle and etched in black and white; but since his time not only Europe, but the whole universe, has moved into new spiritual dimensions. Man is still the center of the cosmos, but having stretched the cosmos almost to the bursting point—the scientists actually predict that the universe will explode!—man himself is practically invisible. Artificial wings won't help, nor artificial eyes, nor escalators, nor pemmican. The whole damned universe has to be taken apart, brick by brick, and reconstructed. Every atom has to be rearranged. Perhaps just to sit quiet and take deep breathing exercises would be better than popping one another off with slugs of dynamite. Because the strange thing is that just doing nothing, just taking it easy, loafing, meditating, things tend to right themselves. As it is we are all terrified by the thought of losing our freedom. And yet it is freedom, *the idea of freedom*, which is what we dread most. Freedom means the strict inner precision of a Swiss watch—combined with absolute recklessness. Whence gayety and indifference, at present non-existent. Of course only lunatics dream of such a condition. And so we all remain sane and bite into one another like lice. And the lousier it gets the more progress we make. *Peace! It's Wonderful!*

I should say that ever since the dawn of history—all through the great civilizations, that is to say—we have been living like lice. Once every thousand years or so a man arises who is not a louse—and then there is even more hell to pay. When a MAN appears he seems to get a stranglehold on the world which it takes centuries to break. The sane people are cunning enough to find these men "psychopathic." These sane ones seem to be more interested in the technique of the stranglehold than in applying it. That's a curious phenomenon, one that puzzles me, to be frank. It's like learning the art of wrestling in order to have the pleasure of letting someone pin you to the mat.

What do I mean to infer? Just this—that art, the art of living, involves the act of creation. The work of art is nothing. It is only the tangible, visible evidence of a way of life, which, if it is not crazy is certainly *different* from the accepted way of life. The difference lies in the act, in the assertion of a will, and individuality. For the artist to attach himself to his work, or identify himself with it, is suicidal. An artist should be able not only to spit on his predecessor's art, or on all works of art, but on his own too. He should be able to be an artist all the time, and finally not be an artist at all, but a piece of art.

In addition to the deep breathing exercises perhaps mercurial inunctions ought also to be recommended—*for the time being*.

A Turning Point in My Life
—*The Cosmological Eye*

I feel that I have some right to speak about the difficulty of establishing communication with the world since my books are banned in the only countries where I can be read in my own tongue. I have enough faith in myself, however, to know that I eventually will make myself heard, if not understood. Everything I write is loaded with the dynamite which will one day destroy the barriers erected about me. If I fail it will be because I did not put enough dynamite into my words. And so, while I have the strength and the gusto I will load my words with dynamite. I know that the timid, crawling ones who are my real enemies are not going to meet me face to face in fair combat. *I know these birds!* I know that the only way to get at them is to reach up inside them, through the scrotum; one has to get up inside and twist their sacred entrails for them. That's what Rimbaud did. That's what Lautréamont did. Unfortunately, those who call themselves their successors have never learned this technique. They give us a lot of piffle about the revolution —first the revolution of the word, now the revolution in the street. How are they going to make themselves heard and understood if they are going to use a language which is emasculated? Are they writing their beautiful poems for the angels above? Is it communication with the dead which they are trying to establish?

You want to communicate. All right, communicate! Use any and every means! If you expect the world to fall for your lingo because it is the right lingo, or even the *left* lingo, you are going to be cruelly deceived. It's like the "pug" who goes into the ring expecting to get it over with quickly. Generally he gets flattened stiff as a board. He thinks he'll deliver an uppercut or a swift one to the solar plexus. He forgets to defend himself. He lays himself wide open. Everybody who's gone out to fight has had to first learn something about the strategy of the ring. The man who refuses to learn how to box becomes what is called, in the language of the ring, "a glutton for punishment." Speaking for myself, I'll say that I've taken all the punishment I could assimilate. From now on I use my head, my bean, as they say. I watch for an opening. I do a little fancy stepping. I duck. I feint. I spar a bit, I bide my time. When the moment comes I let go with all my might.

I am against revolutions because they always involve a return to *status quo*. I am against the *status quo* both *before* and *after* revolutions. I don't want to wear a black shirt or a red shirt. I want to wear the shirt that suits my taste. And I don't want to salute like an automaton either. I prefer to shake hands when I meet someone I like. The fact is, to put it simply, I am positively against all this crap which is carried on first in the name of this thing, then in the name of that. I believe only in what is active, immediate and personal.

I was writing Surrealistically in America before I had ever heard the word. Of course I got a good kick in the pants for it. I wrote for seven years in America without once having a manuscript accepted. I had to beg, borrow and steal in order to get by. Finally I got out of the country. As a foreigner in Paris, without friends, I went through an even worse ordeal, though in another sense it was a thousand times better than the American experience. I grew so desperate that finally I decided to explode—and I did explode. The naive English critics, in their polite, asinine way, talk about the "hero" of my book (*Tropic of Cancer*) as though he were a character I had invented. I made it as plain as could be that I was talking in that book about myself. I used my own name throughout. I didn't write a piece of fiction: I wrote an autobiographical document, a *human* book.

I mention this only because this book marks a turning point in my literary career—I should say, *in my life*. At a certain point in my life I decided that henceforth I would write about myself, my friends, my experiences, what I knew and what I had seen with my own eyes. Anything else, in my opinion, is literature, and *I am not interested in literature*. I realized also that I should have to learn to content myself with what was within my grasp, my scope, my personal ken. I learned not to be ashamed of myself, to talk freely about myself, to advertise myself, to elbow my way in here and there when necessary. The greatest man America ever produced was not ashamed to peddle his own book from door to door. He had faith in himself and he has given tremendous faith to others. Goethe too was not ashamed to beg a friend to put in a good word for him with the critics. Gide and Proust were not ashamed to publish their first books at their own expense. Joyce had the courage to search for years for the person who would publish his *Ulysses*. Was the world better then? Were people more kind, more intelligent, more sympathetic, more understanding? Did Milton get a reasonable price for his *Paradise Lost?* I could go on multiplying instance after instance. What's the use?

Writing Is Its Own Reward
—*Hamlet*

Jan. 26, 1938

Dear Michael Fraenkel of the myth. . . .

And now to talk about myself a little more intimately I will tell you how I feel about the future—*my future*. Every day I live in three times—the past, the present and the future. The past is the springboard, the present the melting pot, and the future the delectation. I participate in all three simultaneously. For instance, when I write something I like extra well I smack my lips and look over my own shoulder. I am already with the man of 2500 A.D. or 5000 A.D., enjoying this great guy Henry Miller who lived in the 20th century. There are certain things I do which while doing them I know beforehand will be appreciated later on. I am sure of it—dead sure. I gloat over the past, I revel in the present and I make merry in the future. What it takes the ordinary man a number of incarnations—supposing there are such things—to live out, I live out in a lifetime. I have the accelebrated rhythm which goes with genius. I make no bones about it—it's a fact. I am gay inside all the time, even when I am depressed. I never doubt for a minute. Never. I am dead certain of everything. I do not even sign contracts with my publisher any more. What for? What have I to fear, what have I to lose? I am inexhaustible. And to date nobody has ever yet done me a dirty turn. Nobody has ever cheated me, that I can say. Now and then I may do a little cheating myself—but as for the others, no, not one ever does me a dirty turn. The longer I live the less protection I demand. As I explained it to Reichel one night, if you are an artist, that means that you are denuding yourself more and more, that by the time you die you are stark naked and your bowels turned inside out. If you are an artist it is quite legitimate to talk about "the man of the record," because there is no other man and there is nothing but the record. Everything is gravy to you and everything turns back into gravy—it slops over and runs right out into the backyard. And that is why, my dear Fraenkel, after having digested Oswald Spengler, D. H. Lawrence, Elie Faure, Friedrich Nietzsche and all the others, I feel very happy about the bad times we are living through and always have lived through. I am glad to be a maggot in the corpse which is the world. I feast on death. The more death there is the stronger I become. Bigger, fatter corpses, is what I say! I am on my way to Godhood, a little angle worm now, but eating my way through and leaving no dirt behind. I am helping the world along with my fine digestive apparatus. Sometimes I begin to munch before the corpse is cold. A friend is talking to me, for example, and not realizing that he has not yet turned cold, I begin to bite into him. You should try that some time. It's like eating cold turkey with a hot sauce.

Anyway, this is the point. Somewhere you talk about words, words, words. I say fine! Words are never just words, even when they seem just words. For the hand that writes there is the mind that reads, the soul that deciphers. Some write syllabically, some cabalistically, some esoterically, some epigrammatically, some just ooze out like fat cabbages or weeds. I write without thought or let. I take down the dictation, as it were. If there are flaws and contradictions they iron themselves out eventually. If I am wrong today I am right tomorrow. Writing is not a game played according to rules. Writing is a compulsive, and delectable thing. Writing is its own reward. *The men of 2500 A.D. will enjoy reading this little passage, I am sure*. For, don't forget it, there will be Fraenkels and Millers then as now, and there will be the same debate, the same problems, only different. I know when I am giving the man of the future pleasure; I share the pleasure with him in advance. You don't settle anything; I don't settle anything. Everything remains unsettled forever, depend on it. But when we say something by which they recognize us that brings pleasure. I tell you, I feel very close to the man of the future. It doesn't matter to me whether the West declines to the point of death and extinction or not. In the same West there will be men who understand what I am saying and who approve, no matter what the fashion may be, no matter who the emperor may be. I pity the emperor as I pity the slave under him. I know they will both enjoy my work, regardless of their circumstance or position in life. I wonder do you ever feel that way about the future?

And then there is another little thing I want to touch on before closing this letter. About growing soft, as you put it. Right you are, my lad. I am growing soft as a jellyfish and with a will. I dote on it. Poke a stick into me and see what happens. Roll me over and step on me a bit. You see, I am not very much bruised. Maybe a tentacle or two lopped off—but tomorrow I will grow others. I am turning into water, did you know it? I am volatilizing. At 98½ I turn into steam and vapor. I reintegrate when it rains. Did you notice yesterday, when it was so cold, that I became completely frozen? Today I'm thawed out again. Fluid.

So it goes. The other night, passing Ecole Militaire, I noticed the café where I thought out the first Hamlet letter. I sat down with Fred and Edgar and we talked about "evil." Very fitting, I thought. Edgar did most of the talking. He's keen now about the elimination of evil. When he had his say I thought to myself, fine! I'll retain a little evil just the same. In fact, I'll swap evil for good, if you like. Evil! What's evil to me? What's good? I see one plasm, protozooic or divine, whichever you choose. Give it all the names you like, that doesn't deceive me. *What it is I have it, and I don't give a fuck by what name you call it.* Nature is with me, and God too, and so are all my brothers in the flesh, though they don't all know it yet. I am just as much for the assassin as I am for the saint. Some see the facets or the poles: I see the whole body of man all the time. And that's why it doesn't matter so much to me whether you agree with me or not. When you write to me you are my meat: alive or dead I welcome you, I devour you.

And now, Brother Ambrose, I will leave off, wishing you the best of health and the elixir of life eternal!

Henry Lin Yutang Miller
of the Villa Seurat Library, Paris, 1938.

Reflections on Writing
—The Wisdom of the Heart

Knut Hamsun once said, in response to a questionnaire, that he wrote to kill time. I think that even if he were sincere in stating it thus he was deluding himself. Writing, like life itself, is a voyage of discovery. The adventure is a metaphysical one: it is a way of approaching life indirectly, of acquiring a total rather than a partial view of the universe. The writer lives between the upper and lower worlds: he takes the path in order eventually to become that path himself.

I began in absolute chaos and darkness, in a bog or swamp of ideas and emotions and experiences. Even now I do not consider myself a writer, in the ordinary sense of the word. I am a man telling the story of his life, a process which appears more and more inexhaustible as I go on. Like the world-evolution, it is endless. It is a turning inside out, a voyaging through X dimensions, with the result that somewhere along the way one discovers that what one has to tell is not nearly so important as the telling itself. It is this quality about all art which gives it a metaphysical hue, which lifts it out of time and space and centers or integrates it to the whole cosmic process. It is this about art which is "therapeutic": significance, purposelessness, infinitude.

From the very beginning almost I was deeply aware that there is no goal. I never hope to embrace the whole, but merely to give in each separate fragment, each work, the feeling of the whole as I go on, because I am digging deeper and deeper into life, digging deeper and deeper into past and future. With the endless burrowing a certitude develops which is greater than faith or belief. I become more and more indifferent to my fate, as writer, and more and more certain of my destiny as man.

I began assiduously examining the style and technique of those whom I once admired and worshipped: Nietzsche, Dostoievski, Hamsun, even Thomas Mann, whom today I discard as being a skillful fabricator, a brick-maker, an inspired jackass or draught-horse. I imitated every style in the hope of finding the clue to the gnawing secret of how to write. Finally I came to a dead end, to a despair and desperation which few men have known, because there was no divorce between myself as writer and myself as man: to fail as a writer meant to fail as a man. And I failed. I realized that I was nothing—less than nothing—a minus quantity. It was at this point, in the midst of the dead Sargasso Sea, so to speak, that I really began to write. I began from scratch, throwing everything overboard, even those whom I most loved. Immediately I heard my own voice I was enchanted: the fact that it was a separate, distinct, unique voice sustained me. It didn't matter to me if what I wrote should be considered bad. Good and bad dropped out of my vocabulary. I jumped with two feet into the realm of aesthetics, the non-moral, non-ethical, non-utilitarian realm of art. My life itself became a work of art. I had found a voice, I was whole again. The experience was very much like what we read of in connection with the lives of Zen initiates. My huge failure was like the recapitulation of the experience of the race: I had to grow foul with knowledge, realize the futility of everything, smash everything, grow desperate, then humble, then sponge myself off the slate, as it were, in order to recover my authenticity. I had to arrive at the brink and then take a leap in the dark.

I talk now about Reality, but I know there is no getting at it, leastwise by writing. I learn less and realize more: I learn in some different, more subterranean way. I acquire more and more the gift of immediacy. I am developing the ability to perceive, apprehend, analyze, synthesize, categorize, inform, articulate—all at once. The structural element of things reveals itself more readily to my eye. I eschew all clear cut interpretations: with increasing simplification the mystery heightens. What I know tends to become more and more unsteable. I live in certitude, a certitude which is not dependent upon proofs or faith. I live completely for myself, without the least egotism or selfishness. I am living out my share of life and thus abetting the scheme of things. I further the development, the enrichment, the evolution and the devolution of the cosmos, every day in every way. I give all I have to give, voluntarily, and take as much as I can possibly ingest. I am a prince and a pirate at the same time. I am the equals sign, the spiritual counterpart of the sign Libra which was wedged into the original Zodiac by separating Virgo from Scorpio. I find that there is plenty of room in the world for everybody—great interspatial depths, great ego universes, great islands of repair, for whoever attains to individuality. On the surface, where the historical battles rage, where everything is interpreted in terms of money and power, there may be crowding, but life only begins when one drops below the surface, when one gives up the struggle, sinks and disappears from sight. Now I can as easily not write as write: there is no longer any compulsion, no longer any therapeutic aspect to it. Whatever I do is done out of sheer joy: I drop my fruits like a ripe tree. What the general reader or the critic makes of it is not my concern. I am not establishing values: I defecate and nourish. There is nothing more to it.

This condition of sublime indifference is a logical development of the egocentric life. I lived out the social problem by dying: the real problem is not one of getting on with one's neighbor or of contributing to the development of one's country, but of discovering one's destiny, of making a life in accord with the deep-centered rhythm of the cosmos. To be able to use the word cosmos boldly, to use the word soul, to deal in things "spiritual"—and to shun definitions, alibis, proofs, duties. Paradise is everywhere and every road, if one continues along it far enough, leads to it. One can only go forward by going backward and then sideways and then up and then down. There is no progress: there is perpetual movement, displacement, which is circular, spiral, endless. Every man has his own destiny: the only imperative is to follow it, to accept it, no matter where it lead him.

I haven't the slightest idea what my future books will be like, even the one immediately to follow. My charts and plans are the slenderest sort of guides: I scrap them at will, I invent, distort, deform, lie, inflate, exaggerate, confound and confuse as the mood seizes me. I obey only my own instincts and intuitions. I know nothing in advance. Often I put down things which I do not understand myself, secure in the knowledge that later they will become clear and meaningful to me. I have faith in the man who is writing, who is myself, the writer. I do not believe in words, no matter if strung together by the most skillful man: I believe in language, which is something beyond words, something which words give only an inadequate illusion of. Words do not exist separately, except in the minds of scholars, etymologists, philologists, etc. Words divorced from language are dead things, and yield no secrets. A man is revealed in his style, the language which he has created for himself. To the man who is pure at heart I believe that everything is as clear as a bell, even the most esoteric scripts. For such a man there is always mystery, but the mystery is not mysterious, it is logical, natural, ordained, and implicitly accepted. Understanding is not a piercing of the mystery, but an acceptance of it, a living blissfully with it, in it, through and by it. I would like my words to flow along in the same way that the world flows along, a serpentine movement through incalculable dimensions, axes, latitudes, climates, conditions. I accept *a priori* my inability to realize such an ideal. It does not bother me in the least. In the ultimate sense, the world itself is pregnant with failure, is the perfect manifestation of imperfection, of the consciousness of failure. In the realization of this, failure is itself eliminated. Like the primal spirit of the universe, like the unshakable Absolute, the One, the All, the creator, i.e., the artist, expresses himself by and through imperfection. It is the stuff of life, the very sign of livingness. One gets nearer to the heart of truth, which I suppose is the ultimate aim of the writer, in the measure that he ceases to struggle, in the measure that he abandons the will. The great writer is the very symbol of life, of the non-perfect. He moves effortlessly, giving the illusion of perfection, from some unknown center which is certainly not the brain center but which is definitely a center, a center connected with the rhythm of the whole universe and consequently as sound, solid, unshakable, as durable, defiant, anarchic, purposeless, as the universe itself. Art teaches nothing,

except the significance of life. The great work must inevitably
be obscure, except to the very few, to those who like the author
himself are initiated into the mysteries. Communication then is
secondary: it is perpetuation which is important. For this only
one good reader is necessary.

If I am a revolutionary, as has been said, it is unconsciously. I
am not in revolt against the world order. "I revolutionize," as
Blaise Cendrars said of himself. There is a difference. I can as
well live on the minus side of the fence as on the plus side.
Actually I believe myself to be just above these two signs, pro-
viding a ratio between them which expresses itself plastically,
non-ethically, in writing. I believe that one has to pass beyond
the sphere and influence of art. Art is only a means to life, to the
life more abundant. It is not in itself the life more abundant. It
merely points the way, something which is overlooked not only
by the public, but very often by the artist himself. In becoming
an end it defeats itself. Most artists are defeating life by their
very attempt to grapple with it. They have split the egg in two.
All art, I firmly believe, will one day disappear. But the artist
will remain, and life itself will become not "an art," but *art*, i.e.,
will definitely and for all time usurp the field. In any true sense
we are certainly not yet alive. We are no longer animals, but we
are certainly not yet *men*. Since the dawn of art every great
artist has been dinning that into us, but few are they who have
understood it. Once art is really accepted it will cease to be. It
is only a substitute, a symbol-language, for something which can
be seized directly. But for that to become possible man must become thoroughly religious, not a believer, but a prime mover, a
god in fact and deed. He will become that inevitably. And of
all the detours along this path art is the most glorious, the most
fecund, the most instructive. The artist who becomes thoroughly
aware consequently ceases to be one. And the trend is towards
awareness, towards that blinding consciousness in which no present form of life can possibly flourish, not even art.

To some this will sound like mystification, but it is an honest
statement of my present convictions. It should be borne in mind,
of course, that there is an inevitable discrepancy between the

truth of the matter and what one thinks, even about himself: but it should also be borne in mind that there exists an equal discrepancy between the judgment of another and this same truth. Between subjective and objective there is no vital difference. Everything is illusive and more or less transparent. All phenomena, including man and his thoughts about himself, are nothing more than a movable, changeable alphabet. There are no solid facts to get hold of. Thus, in writing, even if my distortions and deformations be deliberate, they are not necessarily less near to the truth of things. One can be absolutely truthful and sincere even though admittedly the most outrageous liar. Fiction and invention are of the very fabric of life. The truth is in no way disturbed by the violent perturbations of the spirit.

Thus, whatever effects I may obtain by technical device are never the mere results of technique, but the very accurate registering by my seismographic needle of the tumultuous, manifold, mysterious and incomprehensible experiences which I have lived through and which, in the process of writing, are lived through again, differently, perhaps even more tumultuously, more mysteriously, more incomprehensibly. The so-called core of solid fact, which forms the point of departure as well as repair, is deeply embedded in me: I could not possibly lose it, alter it, disguise it, try as I may. And yet it *is* altered, just as the face of the world is altered, with each moment that we breathe. To record it then, one must give a double illusion—one of arrestation and one of flow. It is this dual trick, so to speak, which gives the illusion of falsity: it is this lie, this fleeting, metamorphic mask, which is of the very essence of art. One anchors oneself in the flow: one adopts the lying mask in order to reveal the truth.

I have often thought that I should like one day to write a book explaining how I wrote certain passages in my books, or perhaps just one passage. I believe I could write a good-sized book on just one small paragraph selected at random from my work. A book about its inception, its genesis, its metamorphosis, its accouchement, of the time which elapsed between the birth of the idea and its recording, the time it took to write it, the thoughts I had between times while writing it, the day of the week, the state of my health, the condition of my nerves, the interruptions that occurred, those of my own volition and those which were forced upon me, the multifarious varieties of expression which occurred to me in the process of writing, the alterations, the point where I left off and, in returning, completely altered the original trend, or the point where I skillfully left off, like a surgeon making the best of a bad job, intending to return and resume some time later, but never doing so, or else returning and continuing the trend unconsciously some few books later when the memory of it had completely vanished. Or I might take one passage against another, passages which the cold eye of the critic seizes on as examples of this or that, and utterly confound them, the analytical-minded critics, by demonstrating how a seemingly effortless piece of writing was achieved under great duress whereas another difficult, labyrinthian passage was written like a breeze, like a geyser erupting. Or I could show how a passage originally shaped itself when in bed, how it became transformed upon arising, and again transformed at the moment of sitting down to record it. Or I could produce my scratch pad to show how the most remote, the most artificial stimulus produced a warm, life-like human flower. I could produce certain words discovered by hazard while riffling the pages of a book, show how they set me off—but who on earth could ever guess how, in what manner, they were to set me off? All that the critics write about a work of art, even at the best, even when most sound, convincing, plausible, even when done with love, which is seldom, is as nothing compared to the actual mechanics, the real genetics of a work of art. I remember my work, not word for word, to be sure, but in some more accurate, trustworthy way; my whole work has come to resemble a terrain of which I have made a thorough, geodetic survey, not from a desk, with pen and ruler, but by touch, by getting down on all fours, on my stomach, and crawling over the ground inch by inch, and this over an endless period of time in all conditions of weather. In short, I am as close to the work now as when I was in the act of executing it—closer perhaps. The conclusion of a book was never anything more than a shift of bodily position. It might have ended in a thousand different ways. No single part of it is finished off: I could resume the narrative at any point, carry on, lay canals, tunnels, bridges, houses, factories, stud it with other inhabitants, other fauna and flora, all equally true to fact. I have no beginning and no ending, actually. Just as life begins at any moment, through an act of realization, so the work. But each beginning, whether of book, page, paragraph, sentence or phrase, marks a vital connection, and it is in the vitality, the durability, the timelessness and changelessness of the thoughts and events that I plunge anew each time. Every line and word is vitally connected with *my* life, my life only, be it in the form of deed, event, fact, thought, emotion, desire, evasion, frustration, dream, revery, vagary, even the unfinished nothings which float listlessly in the brain like the snapped filaments of a spider's web. There is nothing really vague or tenuous —even the nothingnesses are sharp, tough, definite, durable. Like the spider I return again and again to the task, conscious that the web I am spinning is made of my own substance, that it will never fail me, never run dry.

In the beginning I had dreams of rivaling Dostoievski. I hoped to give to the world huge, labyrinthian soul struggles which would devastate the world. But before very far along I realized that we had evolved to a point far beyond that of Dostoievski— *beyond* in the sense of degeneration. With us the soul problem has disappeared, or rather presents itself in some strangely distorted chemical guise. We are dealing with crystalline elements of the dispersed and shattered soul. The modern painters express this state or condition perhaps even more forcibly than the writer: Picasso is the perfect example of what I mean. It was quite impossible for me, therefore, to think of writing novels; equally unthinkable to follow the various blind alleys represented by the various literary movements in England, France and America. I felt compelled, in all honesty, to take the disparate and dispersed elements of our life—the *soul* life, not the cultural life—and manipulate them through my own personal mode, using my own shattered and dispersed ego as heartlessly and recklessly as I would the flotsam and jetsam of the surrounding phenomenal world. I have never felt any antagonism for or anxiety over the anarchy represented by the prevailing forms of art; on the contrary, I have always welcomed the dissolving influences. In an age marked by dissolution, liquidation seems to me a virtue, nay a moral imperative. Not only have I never felt the least desire to conserve, bolster up or buttress anything, but I might say that I have always looked upon decay as being just as wonderful and rich an expression of life as growth.

I think I should also confess that I was driven to write because it proved to be the only outlet open to me, the only task worthy of my powers. I had honestly tried all the other roads to freedom. I was a self-willed failure in the so-called world of reality, not a failure because of lack of ability. Writing was not an "escape," a means of evading the everyday reality: on the contrary, it meant a still deeper plunge into the brackish pool—a plunge to the source where the waters were constantly being renewed, where there was perpetual movement and stir. Looking back upon my career, I see myself as a person capable of undertaking almost any task, any vocation. It was the monotony and sterility of the other outlets which drove me to desperation. I demanded a realm in which I should be both master and slave at the same time: the world of art is the only such realm. I entered it without any apparent talent, a thorough novice, incapable, awkward, tongue-tied, almost paralyzed by fear and apprehensiveness. I had to lay one brick on another, set millions of words to paper before writing one real, authentic word dragged up from my own guts. The facility of speech which I possessed was a handicap; I had all the vices of the educated man. I had to learn to think, feel and see in a totally new fashion, in an uneducated way, *in my own way*, which is the hardest thing in the world. I had to throw myself into the current, knowing that I would probably sink. THE GREAT MAJORITY OF ARTISTS ARE THROWING THEMSELVES IN WITH LIFE-PRESERVERS AROUND THEIR NECKS, AND MORE OFTEN THAN NOT IT IS THE LIFE-PRESERVER WHICH SINKS THEM. Nobody can drown in the ocean of reality who voluntarily gives himself up to the experience. Whatever there be of progress in life comes not through adaptation but through daring, through obeying the blind urge. "No daring is fatal," said René Crevel, a phrase which I shall never forget. The whole logic of the universe is contained in daring, i.e., in creating from the flimsiest, slenderest support. In the beginning this daring is mistaken for will, but with time the will drops away and the automatic process takes its place, which again has to be broken or dropped and a new certitude established which has nothing to do with knowledge, skill, technique or faith. By daring one arrives at this mysterious X position of the artist, and it is this anchorage which no one can describe in words but yet subsists and exudes from every line that is written.

My Two Beginnings
—The World of Sex

The readers of my books fall usually into two distinct classes —those who are disgusted by the strong element of sexuality and those who rejoice in discovering that this element forms such a large ingredient. Many of those who comprise the former group find my critical writing, the essays and studies, not only highly satisfactory but superbly to their liking and are at a loss to explain to themselves how one and the same man could write such vastly dissimilar things. In the latter group are some who have no patience at all with what they choose to call my "classic" side, rejecting it either as unworthy of my talent or as sheer piffle and mysticism. Only a few discerning souls seem able to reconcile the so-called contradictory aspects of my being as revealed through my writing. On the other hand I have observed that, no matter what the reaction to my work, when the reader has a chance to meet me in the flesh he usually accepts me wholeheartedly. In the living man, so I suppose it to be, all questions are silenced. This fact has impressed me so forcibly as to become finally the criterion of my own powers of realization. It gives me to believe that when my writing becomes absolutely truthful there will be no discrepancy between the man and the writer, between what I am and what I do or say. This, I say it without hesitation, is the highest goal a man can set himself; it is the goal of all religious teachers. It goes then without saying that I am essentially a religious person, and always have been. The question might arise, in the minds of some, as to whether there is a conflict between the sexual and the religious. In my opinion there is none. Conflict there is, but only because life is essentially that. Every aspect or element of life is necessary and inevitable, and capable of conversion to different levels. But it is not possible to eliminate, which is the hobby of the moralists. One may succeed in repressing, but the results, as we know, are disastrous. To live out one's desires, and in doing so to subtly alter the quality of desire, is, it seems to me, the great purpose of living. But desire is paramount and ineradicable, even when, according to Buddhist thought, it passes over into its opposite. Because, in order to free oneself from all desire, one has to *desire* to do so.

This subject of desire is one which has interested me profoundly, first when I was coming out of adolescence, and again recently, after I had found myself and was confronted with the great problem of freedom and choice. As a youth I was whipped into a tumultuous life by great urges entirely beyond my control. In the last few years, after a prolonged period of intense creativity, I found myself mystified by all the metaphysical problems centering about this notion of desire. In the midst of my struggles the book *Seraphita* by Balzac was thrust into my hands by a friend who was an occultist. *Seraphita* remains the high peak of my experience in the world of books. From it I quickly passed to a deep study of that other memorable work of Balzac's, *Louis Lambert*, and then to an examination of Balzac's life. With the result that in an essay called "Balzac and His Double," which is to be published shortly in an American review, I gave full expression to the problem and resolved the conflict which had been raging in me.

Few people realize, I imagine, how greatly Balzac wrestled with the problem of the angel in man. If I mention this at all it is only to admit that something of this same problem—the angel in man—has also been my own life-long obsession. In a sense I believe it has always been the problem of the creative being, pre-eminently, almost exclusively his. And the artist, who is one type of creative being—not the highest, by any means—is obsessed, admittedly or not, with the idea of re-creating the world in order, as I see it, to re-establish man's innocence. This innocence, he knows, is achieved only through freedom. It is based primarily on the idea of liberation through one's own effort and involves, necessarily, the complete defeat of the automatic processes. The artist is continually warring against death in whatever form or shape it presents itself. He is not against dying, because to him dying and living are synonymous: he is against stagnation, crystallization, immobility. He is against civilization, because civilization is the supreme expression of the forces of death.

In one of his essays D. H. Lawrence pointed out that there were two great modes of life, the religious and the sexual—the former taking precedence over the latter. The sexual was the lesser way towards salvation, he said. I would not even say there were two ways. To me it seems that there is only one great way and that is the way of truth. However different one civilization may be from another, however varied the laws, customs, religions of man from one period to another, from one type or race of man to another, I perceive in the lives of the great leaders of mankind a singular and simple concordance of behavior, an example of truth and wholeness which even a child can grasp.

It may seem strange for the author of *Tropic of Cancer* to be talking thus. Actually it is not in the least. Liberally dosed with a sexual content as was that book the problem of the author was never one of sex, nor even of religion, but of self-liberation. The violence and rebellion which cropped out in the writing was only a manifestation of this selfsame struggle. Because in his sexual life the man of today is almost dead, the use of obscenity came about automatically, i.e., instinctively. In the *Tropic of Capricorn* the obscenity is used even more nakedly, and more purely, incidentally. It marks the development of awareness in

the author, and with awareness an ever-increasing appreciation
of the medium through which he is obliged to express himself.
The Interlude called "The Land of Fuck," in this latter book,
is in the author's opinion the highwater mark of realization in
the use of the medium of language today. I would almost go so
far as to say that it is for today what Ecclesiastes was for another
time. In this long passage, serving as a breakwater, practically
every line was written with great effort, written blindly, dog-
gedly, without conscious realization of the meaning but with
absolute certitude that it had significance. It was an achievement
almost tantamount to jumping out of one's skin. When a century
has rolled around, it will perhaps be realized what precisely was
the nature of the author's struggle with the world. To hazard a
guess now, I would say that the clue to that struggle lies in the
meaning of the word "polarity." To be more specific I would add
that between the word and the response there is today such an
inert resistance as to almost kill the artist. The mass of writers
are dimly aware of it, but are confused because they attribute it
to social, political and economic disturbances.

But the real reason lies deeper and is scarcely explicable in
words. A new world is being born, a new type of man is in the
bud. The great mass of men, destined now to suffer more cruelly
perhaps than man has ever suffered before, have become paralyzed with fear, have withdrawn into their own shell-shocked
souls, and neither hear, see nor feel, except in relation to the
daily needs of the body. The body, which was once the temple,
has become a living tomb. The body has lost its relation to the
world in which it moves. It is in this way that a world dies. The
form dies first. But, though few perceive it, are aware of it,
the form could not have died unless the spirit had already been
killed. Whilst the deterioration of the body takes place—a process which may require centuries—life loses its significance. An
unheard-of activity, manifesting itself as much in the pursuits of
peaceful scientific men as in wars, screens the complete absence
of life. But this abnormal activity is in itself the symbol of the
death which has taken place. And our country, which seems to

be on the side of peace, for the time being at least, is gripped by a feverish activity. It is here that the death I speak of is taking place most rapidly and effectively, proof for the occult-minded of the fact that here the new germ of man will sprout and bear fruit.

Of all that I hint at in the foregoing I naturally knew or understood very little when I began writing. I had two beginnings really, one here in America, which was abortive, and the other in Europe. How was I able to begin again, one may well ask? I should answer truthfully—by dying. In that first year or so in Paris I literally died, was literally annihilated—and resurrected as a new man. The *Tropic of Cancer* is a sort of human document, written in blood, recording the struggle in the womb of death. The strong sexual odor is, if anything, the aroma of birth, disagreeable, repulsive even, when dissociated from its significance. The *Tropic of Capricorn* represents another death and birth, the transition, if I may say so, from the conscious artist to the budding spiritual being which is the last phase of evolution. In between I have known many births and deaths, but they were minor ones. But from this point on, my feeling is that whatever metamorphoses are to occur will manifest themselves in the realm of action, in conduct and example rather than in writing. There is in process, then, a gigantic conflict between the artist resolved to finish his task and the man who knows in himself that he is no longer obliged to express his conquests in the medium of language. There is a battle going on, more or less conscious, between Duty and Desire. The part of me which belongs to the world wishes to do its duty: the part of me which belongs to God wishes simply to fulfill what is required and which is unstateable. I am obliged to adapt myself to a struggle in a realm wherein I see nothing to sustain me but my own powers. I have to write retrospectively and act forwardly. If I slip I go down into an abyss from which no man can rescue me. The struggle is on all fronts, ceaselessly and remorselessly. Like every man I am my own worst enemy, but unlike most men I know too that I am my own saviour. I know something of freedom and respon-

sibility. I realize how easily desire is transformed into reality. I
have to be careful even of what I dream, since for me between
dream and reality there is only the thinnest veil.

The One Book I Always Wanted to Write
—*The World of Sex*

In reading my books which are purely autobiographical one
should bear in mind that I am writing of things which happened
a considerable time ago. The *Tropic of Capricorn*, for example,
which will run to several volumes, deals chiefly with a period of
about seven years' duration, my life with a woman called Mona
in *Tropic of Cancer*. In telling this story I am not following a strict
chronological sequence but have chosen to adopt a circular or
spiral form of time development which enables me to expand
freely in any direction at any given moment. The ordinary
chronological development seems to me wooden and artificial,
a synthetic reconstitution of the facts of life. The facts and
events of life are for me only the starting points on the way towards the discovery of truth. I am trying to get at the inner
pattern of events, trying to follow the potential being who was
deflected from his course here and there, who circled around
himself, so to speak, who was becalmed for long stretches or who
sank to the bottom of the sea or suddenly flew to the loftiest
peaks. I am trying to seize the quintessential moments in which
things happened, things which altered me profoundly. The man
who tells the story is not the one who experienced the events
recorded. There is distortion and deformation, but only for the
purpose of capturing the true inner reality. Thus, for no apparent reason, I may often lapse back into a period anterior to
the one I am talking about. The reader may find himself puzzled,
he may wonder about the relevancy of such lapses. But they are
dictated by necessity. A sudden switch, a long parenthetical detour, a monologue, a remembrance which suddenly crops up, all
these, without conscious effort on my part, serve to bind the

loose threads together and augment the whole emotional trend. A man does not go forward through life along a straight, horizontal path; often he does not stop at the stations indicated on the time table; sometimes he goes off the track completely; sometimes he dives below and is lost for a time, or he takes to the air and is flung against the side of a steep cliff. Tremendous voyages sometimes occur without the person moving from the spot. In five minutes some men have lived out the span of an ordinary man's life. Some men use up numbers of lives in the course of their stay on earth. Some develop like mushrooms, while others slip back, retrogress. What goes on at every moment in the life of each and every man is something forever unfathomable and inexhaustible to relate. No man can possibly relate the whole story, no matter how limited a fragment of his life he chooses to dwell on.

It is this mysterious aura in which we live and struggle which interests me profoundly. If I tell of facts, events, relationships, something strung along like beads on a string, it is only to bring to the reader's consciousness the all-pervasiveness of the dark, mysterious realm without the existence of which nothing could happen. Years ago, when I first began to write, I was aware of what I now hint at, but in a vague, confused way. I knew that my life was interesting and that the telling of it was of importance to others. But I could not make progress except along a flat, horizontal surface and *that* I soon realized was not progress at all. I produced several abortions which fortunately were never published. Meanwhile events piled up with such speed and in such number that I was literally submerged, as a writer. Everything I wrote up to *Capricorn* was, as I see it now, an effort to get started, to begin the real confession. Each book was just so much ice-breaking.

There was just one book I always wanted to write. This book *(Capricorn)* I planned out long ago in a moment of extreme anguish. Through all my journeying I managed to keep the notes for this book with me. It was a miracle, really, for time and again I have been stripped of everything. But even had I lost the notes the contents of this book were burned into my brain and

blood. In my head I have been writing the book these last fifteen
years, I might say. One volume has thus far appeared, a preface
or vestibule to the vast edifice, so to speak. I say the contents are
with me, in me, part of me, and yet I can also say that I do not
know what the final outcome will be like. I have to live through
it again, discover and rediscover. What I remember like a fiend
are "moments"—not facts. Moments and places, and often looks,
expressions on the human countenance which are unforgettable.
But the chronological record is for me very much like history
itself—confused and confounded. Every man keeps his own historical ledger of world events. If we could compare these individual registers it would make a fabulation so grotesque, so
monstrous, as to make all the myths and legends ever created
seem like the fantasies of a child. With our own lives the personal record is very much the same. It is a labyrinth which each
one interprets differently. Few ever get to the heart of the
labyrinth. Most of us crawl about the entrance, or else venture
timidly a few paces within only to retreat in panic.

He who goes the whole way of course is slain. I have gone the
whole way, I have offered myself up as a sacrifice. That is why
I can live on now and record it fully with no suffering involved.
I can recount the most heartbreaking events almost joyously. I
am telling about another man in another life. I do not need to
tell it any more—I do it gratuitously. I could now lead a life
entirely apart from books, from writing, from this sort of self-
expression. I could lead a life without sex, if need be. I could live
without human companionship. I can live with myself alone, that
is what I mean.

And yet I am going to write this book, and perhaps other
books too. It seems like a contradiction, and undoubtedly it is. I
leave it at that. At the same time it is also true that I am going to
write still more about sex. I am describing my life in the world
of sex. I am recording the death of that world, just as certain
mystics have recorded the disappearance of continents and races
of men. People will draw conflicting conclusions from my work.
That is none of my affair. I too have drawn conflicting conclusions from the experiences I have had. At one and the same mo-

ment in time men are living on a thousand different planes. We speak of evolution, as if it were continuous and all-embracing. But in reality we are each of us absolutely isolate and moving within different orbits and developing within definite, unique frames or spheres. Sex galvanizes the individual spheres of being which clash and conflict. It makes the external world in which we are wrapped shed its death-like folds. It affords us glimpses of that stark, durable reality which is neither beneficent nor cruel.

We go along thinking the world to be thus and so. We are not thinking, of course, or the picture would be different every moment. When we go along thus we are merely preserving a dead image of a live moment in the past. However . . . let us say we meet a woman. We enter into her. Everything is changed. *What* changed? We do not know precisely. It seems as if *everything* had changed. It might be that we never see the woman again, or it might be that we never separate. She may lead us to hell or she may open the doors of the world for us. Or she may give us the itch to know other women, thousands of women, millions of women. In rare cases she can stop us dead, make us live in her and wish to never look at another woman. Once I saw a picture of Rubens as he looked when he married his young wife. They were portrayed together, he standing beside or behind her as she sat for the portrait. I shall never forget the emotion it inspired in me. I had one long deep look into the world of contentment, a world of mutual understanding, of love, of mature bliss. I felt the vigor of Rubens, then in the prime of his life; I felt the confidence which he breathed in the presence of his very young wife. I felt that some great event had occurred and had been fixed on canvas for eternity. I do not know the story of his life, whether he lived happily ever afterwards with her or not. I don't care what happened subsequently. I care about that moment which was true and inspiring. I saw it only a few seconds, but it will remain with me, imperishable.

And so I know that certain things which I have painted in words are true and imperishable, and what happened to me the man or to her the woman in actuality, is of little importance. Something felt, something stated—something recorded in truth for eternity, that is what matters. Sometimes in the recording of a bald sexual incident great significance adheres. Sometimes the sexual becomes a writhing, pulsating façade such as we see on Indian temples. Sometimes it is a fresco hidden in a sacred cave where one may sit and contemplate on things of the spirit. There is nothing I can possibly prohibit myself from doing in this realm of sex. It is a world unto itself and a morsel of it may be just as destructive or beneficent as a ton of it. It is a cold fire which burns in us like a sun. It is never dead, even though the sun may become a moon. There are no dead things in the universe—it is only our way of thinking which makes death. When we look to find life we discover it in even the most inanimate object. Even the mineral is now said to possess sensitivity. As for the corpse, does it not distribute itself among the greedy elements of the earth from which it sprang? The sexual life of the corpse—there would be a theme! How the corpse gives itself to nourish and propagate.

If men would stop to think about this great activity which animates the earth and all the heavens, would they give themselves to thoughts of death? Would a man withhold himself in any way if he realized that alive or dead this frenzied activity goes on ceaselessly and remorselessly? If death is nothing, what fear then should we have of sex? The gods came down from above to fornicate with human kind and with animals and trees, with the earth itself. Why are we so particular? Why can we not love—and do all the other things which give us pleasure too? Why can we not give ourselves in all directions at once. What is it we fear? We fear to lose ourselves. And yet, until we lose ourselves there can be no hope of finding ourselves. We are the world, and to enter fully into the world, we must first abandon it. It doesn't matter what road we take so long as we are giving of ourselves, so long as we are not holding on.

The Supreme Subject — Liberation
—The Books in My Life

Where the specific influences commence is at the brink of manhood, that is, from the time I first dreamed that I too might one day become "a writer." The names which follow may be regarded then as the names of authors who influenced me as a man and as a writer, the two becoming more and more inseparable as time went on. From early manhood on my whole activity revolved about, or was motivated by, the fact that I thought of myself, first potentially, then embryonically, and finally manifestly, as a writer. And so, if my memory serves me right, here is my genealogical line: Boccaccio, Petronius, Rabelais, Whitman, Emerson, Thoreau, Maeterlinck, Romain Rolland, Plotinus, Heraclitus, Nietzsche, Dostoievski (and other Russian writers of the nineteenth century), the ancient Greek dramatists, the Elizabethan dramatists (excluding Shakespeare), Theodore Dreiser, Knut Hamsun, D. H. Lawrence, James Joyce, Thomas Mann, Élie Faure, Oswald Spengler, Marcel Proust, van Gogh, the Dadaists and Surrealists, Balzac, Lewis Carroll, Nijinsky, Rimbaud, Blaise Cendrars, Jean Giono, Céline, everything I read on Zen Buddhism, everything I read about China, India, Tibet, Arabia, Africa, and of course the Bible, the men who wrote it and especially the men who made the King James version, for it was the language of the Bible rather than its "message" which I got first and which I will never shake off.

What were the subjects which made me seek the authors I love, which permitted me to be influenced, which formed my style, my character, my approach to life? Broadly these: the love of life itself, the pursuit of truth, wisdom and understanding, mystery, the power of language, the antiquity and the glory of man, eternality, the purpose of existence, the oneness of everything, self-liberation, the brotherhood of man, the meaning of love, the relation of sex to love, the enjoyment of sex, humor, oddities and eccentricities in all life's aspects, travel, adventure, discovery, prophecy, magic (white and black), art, games, confessions, revelations, mysticism, more particularly the mystics themselves, the varieties of faith and worship, the marvelous in all realms and under all aspects, for "there is only the marvelous and nothing but the marvelous."

Have I left out some items? Fill them in yourself! I was, and still am, interested in everything. Even in politics—when regarded from "the perspective of the bird." But the struggle of the human being to emancipate himself, that is, to liberate himself from the prison of his own making, that is for me the supreme subject. That is why I fail, perhaps, to be completely "the writer." Perhaps that is why, in my works, I have given so much space to sheer experience of life. Perhaps too, though the critics so often fail to perceive it, that is why I am powerfully drawn to the men of wisdom, the men who have experienced life to the full and who give life—artists, religious figures, pathfinders, innovators and iconoclasts of all sorts. And perhaps—why not say it?—that is why I have so little respect for literature, so little regard for the accredited authors, so little appreciation of the transitory revolutionaries. For me the only true revolutionaries are the inspirers and activators, figures like Jesus, Lao-tse, Gautama the Buddha, Akhnaton, Ramakrishna, Krishnamurti. The yardstick I employ is life: how men stand in relation to life. Not whether they succeeded in overthrowing a government, a social order, a religious form, a moral code, a system of education, an economic tyranny. Rather, how did they affect life itself? For, what distinguishes the men I have in mind is that they did not impose their authority on man; on the contrary, they sought to destroy authority. Their aim and purpose was to open up life, to make man hungry for life, to exalt life—and to refer all questions back to life. They exhorted man to realize that he had all freedom in himself, that he was not to concern himself with the fate of the world (which is not his problem) but to solve his own individual problem, which is a question of liberation, nothing else.

And now for "the living books" . . . Several times I have said that there were men and women who came into my experience, at various times, whom I regard as "living books." I have explained why I refer to them in this fashion. I shall be even more explicit now. They stay with me, these individuals, as do the good books. I can open them up at will, as I would a book. When I glance at a page of their being, so to speak, they talk to me as eloquently as they did when I met them in the flesh. The books they left me are their lives, their thoughts, their deeds. It was the fusion of thought, being and act which made each of these lives singular and inspiring to me. Here they are, then, and I doubt that I have forgotten a single one: Benjamin Fay Mills, Emma Goldman, W. E. Burghardt Du Bois, Hubert Harrison, Elizabeth Gurley Flynn, Jim Larkin, John Cowper Powys, Lou Jacobs, Blaise Cendrars. A curious assemblage indeed. All but one are, or were, known figures. There are others, of course, who without knowing it played an important role in my life, who helped to open the book of life for me. But the names I have cited are the ones I shall always revere, the ones I feel forever indebted to.

This Unilateral, Multilingual, Sesquipedalian Activity
—The Books in My Life

From eighteen to twenty-one or twenty-two, the period when the Xerxes Society flourished, it was a continuous round of feasting, drinking, play-acting, music-making ("I am a fine musician, I travel round the world!"), broad farce and tall horseplay. There wasn't a foreign restaurant in New York which we did not patronize. Chez Bousquet, a French restaurant in the roaring Forties, we were so well liked, the twelve of us, that when they closed the doors the place was ours. (O fiddledee, O fiddledee, O fiddledum-dum-dee!) And all the while I was reading my head off. I can still recall the titles of those books I used to carry about under my arm, no matter where I was headed: *Anathema*, Chekov's *Short Stories*, *The Devil's Dictionary*, the complete

Rabelais, the *Satyricon*, Lecky's *History of European Morals*,
With Walt in Camden, Westermarck's *History of Human Mar-
riage*, *The Scientific Bases of Optimism*, *The Riddle of the Uni-
verse*, *The Conquest of Bread*, Draper's *History of the Intellectual
Development of Europe*, the *Song of Songs* by Sudermann,
Volpone, and such-like. Shedding tears over the "convulsive
beauty" of *Francesca da Rimini*, memorizing bits of *Minna von
Barnhelm* (just as later, in Paris, I will memorize the whole of
Strindberg's famous letter to Gauguin, as given in *Avant et
Après*), struggling with *Hermann und Dorothea* (a gratuitous
struggle, because I had wrestled with it for a whole year in
school), marveling over the exploits of Benvenuto Cellini, bored
with Marco Polo, dazed by Herbert Spencer's *First Principles*,
fascinated by everything from the hand of Henri Fabre, plugging away at Max Müller's "philologistica," moved by the quiet,
lyrical charm of Tagore's poetic prose, studying the great Fin-
nish epic, trying to get through the Mahabharata, dreaming with
Olive Schreiner in South Africa, reveling in Shaw's prefaces,
flirting with Molière, Sardou, Scribe, de Maupassant, fighting
my way through the Rougon-Macquart series, wading through
that useless book of Voltaire's—*Zadig* . . . What a life! Small
wonder I never became a merchant tailor. (Yet thrilled to discover that *The Merchant Tailor* was the title of a well-known
Elizabethan play.) At the same time—and is this not more wonderful, more bizarre?—carrying on a kind of "vermouth duck-
bill" talk with such cronies as George Wright, Bill Dewar, Al
Burger, Connie Grimm, Bob Haase, Charlie Sullivan, Bill Wardrop, Georgie Gifford, Becker, Steve Hill, Frank Carroll—all
good members of the Xerxes Society. Ah, what was that atro-
ciously naughty play we all went to see one Saturday afternoon
in a famous little theatre on Broadway? What a great good time
we had, we big boobies! A French play it was, *of course*, and all
the rage. So daring! So risqué! And what a night we made of it
afterwards at Bousquet's!

Those were the days, drunk or sober, I always rose at 5 A.M.
sharp to take a spin on my Bohemian racing wheel to Coney Island and back. Sometimes, skeetering over the thin ice of a dark

winter morning, the fierce wind carrying me along like an ice-boat, I would be shaking with laughter over the events of the night before—just a few hours before, to be exact. This, the Spartan regime, combined with the feasts and festivities, the one-man study course, the pleasure reading, the argument and dis-cussions, the clowning and buffoonery, the fights and wrestling bouts, the hockey games, the six-day races at the Garden, the low dance halls, the piano-playing and piano teaching, the dis-astrous love affairs, the perpetual lack of money, the contempt for work, the goings-on in the tailor shop, the solitary prome-nades to the reservoir, to the cemetery (Chinese), to the duck pond where, if the ice were thick enough, I would try out my racing skates—this unilateral, multilingual, sesquipedalian activ-ity night and day, morning, noon and night, in season and out, drunk or sober, or drunk *and* sober, always in the crowd, always milling around, always searching, struggling, prying, peeping, hoping, trying, one foot forward, two feet backward, but on, on, on, completely gregarious yet utterly solitary, the good sport and at the same time thoroughly secretive and lonely, the good pal who never had a cent but could always borrow somehow to give to others, a gambler but never gambling for money, a poet at heart and a wastrel on the surface, a mixer and a clinker, a man not above panhandling, the friend of all yet really nobody's friend, well . . . there it was, a sort of caricature of Elizabethan times, all gathered up and played out in the shabby purlieus of Brook-lyn, Manhattan and the Bronx, the foulest city in the world, this place I sprang from*—a cheese-box of funeral parlors, museums, opera houses, concert halls, armories, churches, saloons, stadiums, carnivals, circuses, arenas, markets Gansevoort and Wallabout, stinking Gowanus canal, Arabian ice cream parlors, ferry houses,

* "Ah! blissful and never-to-be-forgotten age! when everything was better than it has ever been since, or ever will be again—when Buttermilk Channel was quite dry at low water—when the shad in the Hudson were all salmon, and when the moon shone with a pure and resplendent white-ness, instead of that melancholy yellow light which is the consequence of her sickening at the abominations she every night witnesses in this degen-erate city!" (Washington Irving)

dry docks, sugar refineries, Navy Yard, suspension bridges, roller
skating rinks, Bowery flophouses, opium dens, gambling joints,
Chinatown, Rumanian cabarets, yellow journals, open trolley
cars, aquariums, Saengerbunds, turnvereins, newsboys' homes,
Mills' hotels, Peacock Alley lobbies, the Zoo, the Tombs, the
Ziegfeld Follies, the Hippodrome, the Greenwich Village dives,
the hot spots of Harlem, the private homes of my friends, of the
girls I loved, of the men I revered—in Greenpoint, Williamsburg,
Columbia Heights, Erie Basin—the endless gloomy streets, the
gaslights, the fat gas tanks, the throbbing, colorful ghetto, the
docks and wharves, the big ocean liners, the banana freighters,
the gun boats, the old abandoned forts, the old desolate Dutch
streets, Pomander Walk, Patchin Place, United States Street,
the curb market, Perry's drug store (hard by the Brooklyn
Bridge—such frothy, milky ice cream sodas!), the open trolley to
Sheepshead Bay, the gay Rockaways, the smell of crabs, lobsters,
clams, baked bluefish, fried scallops, the schooner of beer for five
cents, the free lunch counters, and somewhere, anywhere, every
old where, always one of Andrew Carnegie's "public" libraries,
the books you so passionately wanted always "out" or not listed,
or labeled, like Hennessy's whiskies and brandies, with three
stars. No, they were not the days of old Athens, nor the days
and nights of Rome, nor the murderous, frolicsome days of
Elizabethan England, nor were they even the "good old 'Nine-
ties"—but it was "little ole Manhattan" just the same, and the
name of that little old theatre I'm trying so hard to remember is
just as familiar to me as the Breslin Bar or Peacock Alley, but it
won't come back, not now. But it was there *once*, all the theatres
were there, all the grand old actors and actresses, including the
hams such as Corse Payton, David Warfield, Robert Mantell, as
well as the man my father loathed, his namesake, Henry Miller.
They still stand, in memory at least, and with them the days long
past, the plays long since digested, the books, some of them, still
unread, the critics still to be heard from. (*"Turn back the universe and give me yesterday!"*)

And now, just as I am closing shop for the day, it comes to me,
the name of the theatre! *Wallack's!* Do you remember it? You

see, if you give up struggling (memoria-technica) it always comes back to you. Ah, but I see it again now, just as it once was, the dingy old temple façade of the theatre. And with it I see the poster outside. Shure, and if it wasn't—*The Girl from Rector's!* So naughty! So daring! So risqué!

A sentimental note to close, but what matter? I was going to speak of the plays I had read, and I see I have hardly touched on them. They seemed so important to me once, and important they undoubtedly were. But the plays I laughed through, wept through, lived through, are more important still, though they were of lesser caliber. For then I was with others, with my friends, my pals, my buddies. Stand up, O ancient members of the Xerxes Society! Stand up, even if your feet are in the grave! I must give you a parting salute. I must tell you one and all how much I loved you, how often I have thought of you since. May we all be reunited in the beyond!

We were all such fine musicians. O fiddledee, O fiddledee, O fiddledum-dum-dee!

And now I take leave of that young man sitting alone upstairs in the lugubrious parlor reading the Classics. What a dismal picture! What could he have done with the Classics, had he succeeded in swallowing them? The Classics! Slowly, slowly, I am coming to them—not by reading them, but by making them. Where I join with the ancestors, with my, your, our glorious predecessors, is on the field of the cloth of gold. *Bref*, daily life . . . Voltaire, though you are not precisely a classic, you gave me nothing, neither with your *Zadig*, nor with your *Candide*. And why pick on that miserable, vinegar-bitten skeleton, Monsieur Arouet? Because it suits me at this moment. I could name twelve hundred different duds and dunderheads who likewise gave me nothing. I could let out a *pétarade*. *To what end?* To indicate, to signify, to asseverate and adjudicate that, whether drunk or sober, whether with roller skates or without, whether with bare fists or six-ounce gloves, life comes first. *Oui, en terminant ce fatras d'événements de ma pure jeunesse, je pense de nouveau à Cendrars. De la musique avant toute chose! Mais, que donne mieux la musique de la vie que la vie elle-même?*

The Voice

—Big Sur and the Oranges of
Hieronymus Bosch

Here I must interrupt to relate what happened a few minutes
ago when I was taking a nap. I say "taking a nap," but more
truthfully I mean—when I was *trying* to take a nap. In lieu of
sleep I got messages. This business has been going on ever since
I got the happy thought about the oranges of Hieronymus Bosch.
This noon it was bad, very bad. I could hardly taste the delicious
lunch my wife Eve had prepared for me. As soon as I had
finished lunch, I threw a few sticks of wood on the fire, rolled
myself up in a blanket and prepared to take my usual snooze before resuming work. (The more snoozes I take the more work I
do. It pays off.) I closed my eyes, but the messages kept on
coming. When they became too insistent, too clamorous, I
would open my eyes and call out, "Eve, jot this down on the
pad for me, will you? Just say 'abundance' . . . 'pilfering' . . .
'Sandy Hook.'" I thought that in tabbing a few key words I
could turn off the current. But it didn't work. Whole sentences
poured in on me. Then paragraphs. Then pages. . . . It's a
phenomenon that always astounds me, no matter how often it
happens. Try to bring it about and you fail miserably. Try to
squelch it and you become more victimized.

Forgive me, but I must go into it further. . . . The last time it
happened was while I was writing *Plexus*. During the year or so
that I was occupied with this work—one of the worst periods, in
other respects, that I have ever lived through—the inundation
was almost continuous. Huge blocks—particularly the dream
parts—came to me just as they appear in print and without any
effort on my part, except that of equating my own rhythm with
that of the mysterious dictator who had me in his thrall. In
retrospect I wonder about this period, for the reason that every
morning on entering my little studio I had first to quell the surge

of anger, disgust and loathing which the daily drama inevitably aroused. Quieting myself as best I could, reproving and admonishing myself aloud, I would sit before the machine—and strike the tuning fork. Bang! Like a sack of coal it would spill out. I could keep it up for three or four hours at a stretch, interrupted only by the arrival of the mailman. At lunch more wrangling. Just sufficient to bring me to the boil. Then back to my desk, where I would again tune in and race on until the next interruption.

When I had finished the book, a rather long one, I was so keyed up that I confidently expected to write two more books—*pronto*. However, nothing worked out as I had expected. The world went to smash about me. My own little world, I mean.

For three years thereafter I was unable to advance more than a page at a time, with long intervals between these spurts. The book which I was endeavoring to write—getting up the courage to write, would be better!—I had been thinking and dreaming about for over twenty-five years. My despair reached such a point that I was almost convinced my writing days were over. To make matters worse, my intimate friends seemed to take pleasure in insinuating that I could write only when things were bad for me. It was true that seemingly I had no longer anything to fight. I was only fighting myself, fighting the venom which I had unconsciously stored up.

To come back to the Voice. . . . There was *The World of Lawrence*, to take another instance. Begun at Clichy, continued in Passy and abandoned after the writing of some seven to eight hundred pages. A missfire. A flop. Yet what a grand affair it was! Never had I been so possessed. In addition to the finished pages, I piled up a mountain of notes and a staggering heap of citations, taken not only from Lawrence's writings but from dozens of other writers, all of which I strove unsuccessfully to weave into the book. Then there were the charts and diagrams—the ground plan—with which I decorated the doors and walls of the studio (Villa Seurat), waiting for inspiration to continue the task and praying for a solution to the dilemma in which I found myself.

It was the "dictation" which got me down. It was like a fire which refused to be extinguished. For months it went on, without let-up. I couldn't take a drink, even standing at a bar, without being forced to whip out pad and pencil. If I ate out, and I usually did, I would fill a small notebook during the course of a meal. If I climbed into bed and made the mistake of switching off the light, it would begin all over again, like the itch. I was that frazzled I could scarcely type a few coherent pages a day. The situation reached the height of the ludicrous when I suddenly realized one day that of everything I had written about the man I could just as well have said the opposite. I had indubitably reached that dead end which lies so artfully hidden in the phrase "the meaning of meaning."

That voice! It was while writing the *Tropic of Capricorn* (in the Villa Seurat) that the real shenanigans took place. My life being rather hectic then—I was living on six levels at once—there would come dry spells lasting for weeks sometimes. They didn't bother me, these lulls, because I had a firm grip on the book and an inner certainty that nothing could scotch it. One day, for no accountable reason, unless it was an overdose of riotous living, the dictation commenced. Overjoyed, and also more wary this time (especially about making notes), I would go straight to the black desk which a friend had made for me, and, plugging in all the wires, together with amplifier and callbox, I would yell: *"Je t'écoute . . . vas-y!"* (I'm listening . . . go to it!) And how it would come! I didn't have to think up so much as a comma or a semicolon; it was all given, straight from the celestial recording room. Weary, I would beg for a break, an intermission, time enough, let's say, to go to the toilet or take a breath of fresh air on the balcony. Nothing doing! I had to take it in one fell swoop or risk the penalty: excommunication. The most that was permitted me was the time it took to swallow an aspirin. The john could wait, "it" seemed to think. So could lunch, dinner or whatever it was I thought necessary or important.

I could almost *see* the Voice, so close, so impelling, so authoritative it was, and withal bearing such ecumenical import. At times it sounded like a lark, at other times like a nightingale, and sometimes—really eerie, this!—like that bird of Thoreau's fancy which sings with the same luscious tones night and day.

When I began the Interlude called "The Land of Fuck"—meaning "Cockaigne"—I couldn't believe my ears. "*What's that?*" I cried, never dreaming of what I was being led into. "Don't ask me to put *that* down, please. You're only creating more trouble for me." But my pleas were ignored. Sentence by sentence I wrote it down, having not the slightest idea what was to come next. Reading copy the following day—it came in installments—I would shake my head and mutter like a lost one. Either it was sheer drivel and hogwash or it was sublime. In any case, I was the one who had to sign his name to it. How could I possibly imagine then that some few years later a judicial triumvirate, eager to prove me a sinner, would accuse me of having written such passages "for gain." Here I was begging the Muse *not* to get me into trouble with the powers that be, *not* to make me write out all those "filthy" words, all those scandalous, scabrous lines, pointing out in that deaf and dumb language which I employed when dealing with the Voice that soon, like Marco Polo, Cervantes, Bunyan *et alii*, I would have to write my books in jail or at the foot of the gallows . . . and these holy cows deep in clover, failing to recognize dross from gold, render a verdict of guilty, guilty of dreaming it up "to make money"!

It takes courage to put one's signature to a piece of pure ore which is handed you on a platter straight from the mint. . . .

And only yesterday—what a coincidence—coming from a walk in the hills, a thin, transparent fog touching everything with quicksilver fingers, only yesterday, I say, coming in view of our grounds, I suddenly recognized it to be "the wild park "which I had described myself to be in in this same *Capricorn*. There it was, swimming in an underwater light, the trees spaced just right, the willow in front bowing to the willow in back, the roses in full bloom, the pampas grass just beginning to don its plumes of gold, the hollyhocks standing out like starved sentinels with big, bright buttons, the birds darting from tree to tree, calling to one another imperiously, and Eve standing barefoot in her Garden of Eden with a grub hoe in her hand, while Dante

Alighieri, pale as alabaster and with only his head showing above
the rim, was making to slake his awesome thirst in the bird bath
under the elm.

My Aims and Intentions
—*Art and Outrage*

From Henry Miller to Lawrence Durrell

Dear Larry,

Your two letters to Fred, of which you so thoughtfully sent
me carbons, excite me no end. Not because it's about *me*, but
because of the nature of the project. What a task! Of course, you
won't really get anywhere, you know. Take that for granted
immediately—and you'll travel far and enjoy it.

There are many, many things come to my mind at the outset.
Helpful hints and clues, for the most part. Though I trust you
understand that I too have difficulty putting my finger on "it,"
making the right, eternal statement. But I can offer some cor-
rectives and some new tacks, perhaps.

One of the first things that hits me between the eyes is this
effort you are making to discover the "intention." You speak of
the difficulty of explaining or placing me with the younger
generation. And with it you couple this business of morality and
iconoclasm. As the recipient of thousands of letters, most of
them from young people, I get such a different picture. (Could
it be that there is this difference in comprehension between the
British and the American youth?) At any rate, the young who
write me do "get" me to an amazing extent. Naturally, they
"identify" with me, particularly those who are trying to express themselves. But how interesting it is that the same situations are at work eternally and eternally molding new artists.
One could almost sum it up, like Lawrence, and say our troubles
are largely, almost exclusively, societal. The social pattern remains the same, fundamentally, despite all the dazzling changes

we have witnessed. It gets more thwarting all the time—for the born individualist. And, as you know, I am interested—like God —only in the individual.

One of the things which irks me most, with the critics, is the statement you throw out—about being unlike myself.

This is simply impossible. I don't care who the artist is, if you study him deeply, sincerely, detachedly, you will find that he and his work are one. If it were otherwise the planets would be capable of leaving their orbits. I think your trouble may lie here, that the part of me you don't know from direct experience —I mean the me of youth, of long before we met—you tend to idealize. The man you met in the Villa Seurat was a kind of monster, in a way, in that he was in the process of transformation. He had become partially civilized, so to speak. The tensions had eased up, he could be himself, and his own, natural self was, at the risk of being immodest, what you always sense and respect in me. (To myself I always think I was born "ultra civilized." Another way of saying it, a more invidious way, would of course be to say that I was oversensitive.) And I suppose it is always the oversensitive creatures who, if they are bent on surviving, grow the toughest hides. This tough hide revealed itself in my case, more in what I passively permitted to be done for me and to me than by what I did of my own volition—vindictively, outrageously, and so on. The coward in me always concealed himself in that thick armor of dull passivity. I only grew truly sensitive again when I had attained a certain measure of liberation.

I don't want to embark on another autobiographical fragment! Stop me, for God's sake. If I let myself go it is only because with the years I get new visions of myself, new vistas, and their one value to me is that they are more inclusive pictures of the parts that go to make the whole—the enigmatic whole.

Here I digress a moment to mention a noticeable difference in the reactions of Europeans to my work. Seldom do they, for instance, speak of these "discrepancies." Perhaps they have had too much contact with discordant authors all their lives. They seem to realize, without mentioning it, that all the contrarieties of make-up and attitude are the leaven necessary to the making of the bread. When they are shocked, to take another example, it is because of the language itself, what has been done to it and with it by the author, not by the moral or immoral implications of this language. There is a difference, do you see? And when I say shocked, I mean in a healthy, agreeable way. It is an aesthetic shock, if you like, but one which vibrates throughout their whole being.

And here, all the young, and often the old too, are unanimous in writing of the therapeutic value of my work. They were altered. They thank me, bless me, bless me for "just being," as they often say.

But to come back to "intentions." It is almost classic what I have to say on this score. I know it all by heart, and when you read again, if you read with this in mind, you too will see it very clearly.

(Oh, yes, but before I forget—one important thing! Remember always that, with the exception of *Cancer*, I am writing counter-clockwise. My starting point will be my end point—the arrival in Paris—or, in another way of speaking, the breakthrough. So what I am telling about is the story of a man you never met, never knew; he is mostly of a definite period, from the time he met June (Mona-Mara) until he leaves for Paris. Naturally, some of what he is at the time of writing comes to the fore. Inevitable. But the attempt is—I am talking only of the auto-novels, of course—to be and act the man I was during this seven-year period. From this segment of time I am able to look backward and forward. Very much as our own time is described —the Janus period, the turning point, where both avenues become clear and recognizable—at least to those who see and think. Oof!)

I wanted so much, so much, to be a writer (maybe not to write so much as to *be* a writer). And I doubt that I ever would have become one had it not been for the tragedy with June. Even then, even when I knew I would and could, my intention was to do nothing more than tell the story of those years with her, what it had done to me, to my soul, if you like. Because it was the damage to the soul, I must tell you, that was the all. (And I doubt if I have made that at all clear in my writing!) And so, on the fateful day, in the Park Department of Queens County, N.Y., I mapped out the whole autobiographical romance—in one sitting. And I have stuck to it amazingly well, considering the pressures this way and that. (The hardest part is coming—*Nexus* —where I must reveal myself for what I was—something less than zero, something worse than the lowest knave.)

With June I could not begin this magnum opus which, as you know, I thought would be just one enormous, endless tome—perhaps bigger than the Bible. My suffering was so great—and my ego too, no doubt—that I imagined it needed a canvas of that scope.

Note: *My* suffering I say. For *then* I was concerned with what had been done *to me*. As I wrote, of course, I began to perceive that what I had done to others was far more heinous. Whoever greatly suffers must be, I suppose, a sublime combination of sadist and masochist. Fred easily perceived the masochist that I was. But neither you nor he see so easily the sadist. Fred has touched on it in a subtly diabolical way—really too exalted to suit my case, I think. It was plainer, coarser than that. (But here you are up against the dilemma of not being privy to the facts of my life; it is my word as a man and a writer, against the apperceptions of readers and critics and psychologists. I admit that I have the power to warp what I honestly think may be the truth about my thoughts and actions. But I do believe I am nearer the mark than the outsider.)

So, as you hint, I coined this word Truth. The key to my whole work to be the utter truth. And, as you realize, I found it easier to give the truth about the ugly side of my nature than the good. The good in me I only know as it is reflected back to me in the eyes and voices of those I talk to.

Whether I *then* knew what later I have come to know absolutely is a question, namely, the words of Jesus, that the truth shall set ye free. If I had only set myself to tell the truth about myself, that would have been fine. But I also wanted to tell the

truth about others, about the world. And that's the greatest
snare of all: it sets you above the others if not precisely above
the world. Time and again I try to cut myself down. You all
know how I rant and rave. There's always some truth in these
outbursts, to be sure, but how caricatural!

Yet I do feel that truth is linked to violence. Truth is the
naked sword; it cuts clean through. And what is it we are fighting, who love truth so much? The lie of the world. A perpetual
lie. But I'm going off again. . . .

Let me tell you something more simple and yet revealing. I
said I wanted nothing more of God than the power to write.
Yes, this began in my late teens, I imagine. In my early twenties,
confined to my father's shop, a slave to the most idiotic kind of
routine imaginable, I broke out—inside. Inwardly I was a perpetual volcano. I will never forget the walks to and from my
father's shop every day: the tremendous dialogues I had with
my "characters," the scenes I portrayed, and so on. And never
a line of any of this ever put to paper. Where would you begin
if you were a smothered volcano?

And then, after the first attempt at a book—when with the
Western Union and married to that woman B——, my first wife
—I dream of making my entry into the lists—by the back door.
To write something that will sell, that people will read, that will
permit me to say—"There is my name signed to it, you see."
Proof.

And then the break, thanks to June, the plunge. And I am
free, spoon-fed, have leisure, paper, everything, but can't do it.
Oh yes, I do write, but how painfully, and how poorly, how
imitatively. And then when June left for France with her friend
Jean Kronski, then I broke, then I mapped out my whole career.
And even then, think of it, even after leaving for France, three
years later, I still do not begin that great work. I write *Tropic of
Cancer*, which was not in the schema—but of the moment. I suppose one could liken it to the volcano's eruption, or the breaking
of the crust. (Only, let me say it as knows, it was such a feeble
eruption compared to those imaginary street-walking ones I had
every day, inwardly, walking to and from my father's shop!)

How well I know the tremendous *décalage* between what one wishes to do and what one does! Nowhere in my work have I come anywhere near to expressing what I meant to express. Now, if you can believe this, and I am sure you must because you must also suffer it, then imagine what sort of beast it is that a woman, any woman, has to live with who marries a writer. Imagine what happens to one who never says all, never does all, who smiles and nods his head in that civilized way and is all the while a raging bull. Well, what happens is that either the writer gains the upper hand eventually, or the man. One or the other must take the lead. My effort has been to give the lead to the man in me. (With what success others know best.) But there is no war involved, you must understand. It is rather a matter of leaning more this way than that, of shifting the emphasis and so forth.

And I do not want to be a saint! Morality, in fact, drops out of the picture. Maybe the writer will drop out too. Or the man. Never the ego, rest assured. Nor do I give a damn about that.

I certainly do not hope to alter the world. Perhaps I can put it best by saying that I hope to alter my own vision of the world. I want to be more and more myself, ridiculous as that may sound.

Where the writing is concerned, I did nothing consciously. I followed my nose. I blew with every wind. I accepted every influence, good or bad. My intention was, as I said, merely to write. Or, *to be a writer*, more justly. Well, I've been it. Now I just want—to be. Remember, I beg you, that this infinitive is "transitive" in Chinese. And I am nothing if not Chinese.

Does this help? If not, walk on—and over me.

Henry

Next day—April 2nd

It's pouring and I feel like saying a bit more. . . .

Those fan letters I spoke of. If someone had the courage to publish these, volume after volume, what a broadside that would be. And how revealing! Here are the books which readers say have influenced them, enlarged their outlook on life, altered their being: *The Colossus, Capricorn, Cancer, Wisdom of the Heart*—primarily. But there are others in which *I* believe I have given most revelatory passages: *The Books in My Life, Rimbaud,* the *Hamlet* letters, even *Aller Retour New York.* And in "The Brooklyn Bridge"—where is that?—I am astounded each time I read it by what I have said "unknowingly."

There is another too, quite important: *The World of Sex.* No one has ever written me *against* this book—or *The Colossus.* Curious, what! When I speak of *Books in My Life* and the *Rimbaud,* I mean the passages about youth, as in the Rider Haggard chapter and the last chapter, called "The Theatre," where I dwell on the Xerxes Society days.

Myself I like *Plexus* very much, not for the revelatory this time, but for the fantastic bits—about Stanley, about Mimi Aguglia and what follows, about John Brown, and Picodiribibi. Enough. . . .

What I can never write enough about are the "influences"—both men, haphazard meetings, books, places. Places have affected me as much or more than people, I think. (I find it the same with you here.) Think of my repeated journeys to Toulouse, or of the returns to the old neighborhood (the 14th Ward), or to the places where as a boy I spent my summer vacations, or to the regions in America where I dreamed things my own way, only to find them so otherwise. Strange that I never think of the afterlife this way! Dear old Devachan, which Fred and Edgar and I spoke of so often. All I see there is a breathing spell, another "open" womb, so to speak, where all the senses and the intellect are intensified, clarified, unobstructed—and one learns just by looking, looking back at one's meager, pitiable self in action.

But this business of youth—rebellion, longing for freedom—and the business of vision are two very cardinal points in my orientation. At sixty-six I am more rebellious than I was at sixteen. Now I *know* the whole structure must topple, must be razed. Now I am positive that youth is right—or the child in its innocence. Nothing less will do, will satisfy. The only purpose of knowledge must be certitude, and this certitude must be established through purity, through innocence. Fred can tell you of the unknown man from Pekin who hangs above my doorway here. When I look at him I know he knows and is all that I expect a human being to be. (The photo of him is on the back of the Penguin edition of *The Colossus*. Study it. That is the person or being I would like to be, if I wanted to be someone else than I am.)

*Influence*s . . . It should have been an eye-opener for you to read that chapter in *The Books in My Life*. At various times you have credited me with a live interest in certain writers and thinkers, who to tell the truth, were only passing fancies. My loyalty and adoration have been constant—for the same men, all throughout my life: Whitman, Emerson, Thoreau, Rabelais, above all. I still think that no one has ever had a larger, freer, healthier view of man and his universe than Walt Whitman. And the passage from one of his prose works which I cited in my essay on him (originally published in some French anthology, now in English in the *Colorado Review*) comes close to expressing my own view of how man may live and function in this world with joy and meaning and purpose. (Look it up!)

And there was always Lao-tse, even before I had read him. He stands there, at the back of one's head, like the great Ancestor. Old Adam Cadmus. ("What's all the fuss about? Take it easy! Sit down, get quiet, don't think. . . . *Think!*" And from him the line of Zen masters, which I only got wise to from Villa Seurat days on. "When you walk, walk; when you sit, sit; but don't wobble!"

But no one, it seems to me, can honestly put his finger on the real and vital influences which affected his course. That's why I mentioned, along with books and people, trivial things as well—things, happenings (little events), dreams, reveries, places.

In a book, for example—I say in a book and not *the* book, or a certain book—there are lines, just lines page so and so, top left, that stand out like mountain peaks—and they made you what you have become. No one else but you could respond to those lines. They were written *for* you. Just as everything else which

happens to you was intended *for* you, and never mistake it.
Particularly the bad things.

(And this reminds me to say again that perhaps one reason
why I have stressed so much the immoral, the wicked, the ugly,
the cruel in my work is because I wanted others to know how
valuable these are, how equally if not more important than the
good things. Always underneath, you see, this idea of "acceptance"—which is Whitman's great theme, his contribution.)

And then there is this curious business about Knut Hamsun.
The one writer I started out to write like, to be like. How much
time and thought I have given to that man's work—in the past.
How I struggled to phrase my thoughts as he did. And without
the least success. No one has ever remarked on it, after reading
me. How do you explain that? When you look at early Picassos,
early Gauguins, early van Goghs, you can very easily trace
their influences, their idols. They did not begin as Picasso, as
Gauguin, as van Gogh. I sometimes think of those two novels I
wrote before going to Paris: what was I, who was I then? I have
borrowed these scripts from the Library time and again, but I am
never able to read them.

And then I must say another thing—perhaps it bears on the
foregoing, perhaps not. . . . The other day I began reading *A
Glastonbury Romance* by John Cowper Powys. My head began bursting as I read. No, I said to myself, it is impossible that
any man can put all this—so much!—down on paper. It is super-
human. And what was it stirred me so? A description of a man
and a woman in a boat floating down-stream. (I thought of that
marvelous Japanese expression employed, I believe, to describe
a certain genre of painting: "This floating world.") Old John
had caught the world by the throat. And lovingly and surely he
squeezed every bit of beauty, of meaning, of purposeless purpose out of it in a few pages. Utterly phenomenal.

And Old Friar John, as he calls himself, was one of my first
living idols. I was a lad then of about twenty-five and he in his
forties. The first man I beheld who was possessed by his daemon.
Talk such as I have never heard again in my life. Inspired talk.
And now at eighty he is still inspired, still writing masterpieces,

still filled with the joie de vivre, the élan vital. You mentioned Chuang-Tzu. He was old John's great favorite. I too loved him better than Lao-tse, I must admit.

You mentioned Otto Rank. Yes, dear Otto too. But then, you know, after a time it palled. *What?* This seeking for meaning in everything. So Germanic! This urge to make everything profound. What nonsense! If only they could also make everything unimportant at the same time!

Ah yes, only a few years ago it was that I stumbled on Hesse's *Siddhartha*. Nothing since the Tao Teh Ching meant so much to me. A short book, a simple book, profound perhaps, but carrying with it the smile of that old man from Pekin over my doorway. The smile of "above the battle." Overcoming the world. And thus finding it. For we must not only be in it and above it, but of it too. To love it for what it is—how difficult! And yet it's the first, the only task. Evade it, and you are lost. Lose yourself in it and you are free.

How I love the dying words of St. Thomas Aquinas: "All that I have written now seems so much straw!" Finally he saw. At the very last minute. He knew—and he was wordless. If it takes ninety-nine years to attain such a moment, fine! We are all bound up with the Creator in the process. The ninety-eight years are so much sticks of wood to kindle the fire. It's the fire that counts.

To come back. . . . The child is alive with this fire, and we, the adults, smother it as best we can. When we cease throwing the wood of ignorance on the fire, it bursts forth again. Experience is an unlearning, an undoing. We must start from the beginning, not on the backs of dinosaurs—culture, that is, in all its guises. "Lime Twigs and Treachery"—that will be the title of a forthcoming book if I can ever get down to it. The title is borrowed from one of Brahms' "Waltz Songs," so help me God, What matter?

And now to close with a passage from *Les Provinces de France*, which I look at once in a while, nostalgically:

"*L'herbe n'a jamais repoussé sous les pas du cheval de Simon de Montfort, de sinistre mémoire.... Le talent n'a jamais refleuri,*

*le génie est mort à jamais. Il ne reste aux Languedociens, avec
leur austère protestantisme, que des grâces superficielles. Race
à fleur de peau . . .*

"*En somme, pour qui pense que la Haute Garonne est bien
près d'être pyrénéenne, que l'Aude pourrait faire partie du
Roussillon, Nîmes apparaît comme la véritable capitale du
Languedoc, dans le Gard où tout est sobre et ordonné, où rien
n'est plantureux, abondant, insolent, mais où tout . . . (je cherche
le mot qui convient) . . . où tout est* muscat."

*Allez voir Joseph Delteil à Montpellier un de ces jours. Ça
vous fera, vous et Claude, du bien. Il peut vous parler des
Albigeois—et mille autres choses, comme St. François, par
exemple, ou le cimetière à Sète et l'esprit qui y trouve son
sommeil tranquille, Paul Valéry. Salut a Frédéric Temple et au
Pont du Gard. Je l'ai vu pour la première fois en 1928 quand
June et moi ont fait un tour de France avec bicyclettes. Je
n'oublierai jamais ma première vau de la Mediterraneé, des
oliviers, des vignes, de tout un pays ensoleillé et sec et brillant
comme une gemme.*

Ta-ta! Assez pour une séance.

Henry

From Henry Miller to Alfred Perlès

Dear Fred,

Just got your two letters to Larry and once again I can't
restrain myself . . . must add a few words. Of course I wept a
little—*le vieux pleurnicheur!*—but then I began laughing and I
couldn't stop. (Haven't laughed so hard since you left four
years ago!) That same mail brought me the two volumes of
Sexus (in Swedish). Thinking to restore my equanimity, I
opened volume one at random, and then I began really laughing
like a madman. Here is what I read—wouldn't it make any man
laugh his guts out? What a language!

"'*Langa hit den bara,*' *sa jag, och tog honom i armen.* '*Det ar ingenting att sta och dividera om nu.' Vi gick ut i hallen och han stack at mig en sedel. Just som vi var pa vag mot dorren kom Irene ut ur badrummet. 'Ni tanker val inte ga?' . . . 'Jo, han maste skynda sig ivag nu,' sa Ulric, men han har lovat att jomma tillbaka senare."*

(Sweden's greatest poet is now on his way to see me, dispatched by the Cultural Attaché in Washington. Must be serious when he comes.)

How curious it is, this business of who owes whom, of master and disciple. When I added that final letter, from Spain, to our "Aller Retour" correspondence, I tried so hard to explain that it is I who am indebted—to *you*. Do you want to know the secret, or the test of "masterhood"? The master is he who can make you laugh the hardest and longest. And, Joey, that's you! Somewhere there is mention of Rabelais' humor. Yes, there were two great things (aside from the "word lists") which I got from Master Rabelais: one, laughter; two, the holy bottle. The one who understands the meaning of the holy bottle always reaches you—and cures you—through laughter. (And in my peculiar way I connect such austere and democratic figures as Emerson and Whitman with Rabelais because all three knew, as few men do, the origin and the meaning of creation—or creativity. In Zen all this is resynchronized and reoriented: the humor, the leveling off, the annihilation of Buddhas, masters, genuises, and the sure knowledge that creation is endless and inexhaustible.)

When I hear the word Culture I reach for my revolver. Remember that? So, too, when I hear the word Genius. I never felt I had genius, even if I boasted about it in my writings. I always feel that I am "just a Brooklyn boy." (And here I urge you to read again Emil Schnellock's and Knut Merrild's contributions to *The Happy Rock*.) They came very close to sizing me up; they had that human approach which you so rightly stress.

But to return for one moment to the master-disciple business. Each of us is both at once, is he not? Even Jesus and Buddha were disciples—of whom or what we do not know. The only master is life. To be just a master is to be static, dead. As long as we are alive we are growing, stretching out our hands towards God . . . any God. And God is reaching down to us. No end, no conclusion, no completion. Perpetual becoming.

And so pertinent to all the foregoing is what you say about spirit and flesh. They are one, of course. And suddenly I saw myself as the "earnest young man," the youth with a book under his arm, wherever he went. And how is it all the critics, and even my good friends sometimes, forget what I have told about so often—my efforts to find a God, a religion, a belief, a way of life. At a very early age too. New Thought, Ethical Culture, Theosophy, the Bahai movement . . . what didn't I look into? And that evangelist, Benjamin Fay Mills, whom Bob Challacombe introduced me to! How much I owe that man! How much I still revere him! Don't you know that story of how I heard him lecture and, moved to the guts, I went down to speak to him (from the gallery) and I said, as only an "innocent" could: "Dear Sir, I believe that I am one who should hear your (private) lectures. I know what you are thinking about. Couldn't you let me do something for you to pay for those lectures?" (It cost about a hundred dollars for the series.) And I shall never forget the look he gave me, a long, down-slanting look with piercing gimlet eyes, like those of a mage or an old witch. And after reading my very soul, it seemed, he said, breaking into a smile: "Of course you are the man! Certainly you shall hear the lectures." And then he suggested that I pay for them by passing the salver around (for money) after his public lectures. Which I did. (Can you picture me doing that?)

There's another point in your letter which interests me—that of the seemingly perpetual *décalage* between the writer and his work, the man and his product. I can't see why people dwell on this as much as they do, finding disappointment in either the man or his work. In life, it seems so obvious, man has a more limited scope to the play of his many-faceted being. There are exceptions to be sure—in the hero type—men like Alexander, Caesar, Napoleon, artists in action. But how many writers can do or be what they do and are through their characters in books? Exceptions again—Voltaire, Casanova, Cendrars, for example.

But usually where life is exalted the art suffers, and vice versa.

And this brings me, perhaps for the nth time, to the business which you all seem agreed upon and wish to explain away: the slag. Nice that image of the volcano. Flattering. But let me give you a look again at myself as I see myself, that is, see myself writing. What is my weakness? The desire to devour all. Or, and from a Zen view not such a weakness either, the desire to imitate life. Not record or present life, but imitate it, in short, make books live. All this leading to that point I began to make in my writings, and which bothers writers no end, that the highest art is the art of living, that writing is but a prelude or form of initiation for this purpose. From this standpoint most every writer is consequently a rank failure. The fear which writers or artists in general have when confronted with such an issue is that art would disappear. Dear Art! As if anything could destroy it. How do you destroy the cornerstone of life? Why worry? True, we may eliminate the hot-house geniuses—but on the other hand we might, once again, endow everything we see, do, touch or think about with art. We may all become, or re-become, artists! There is the kind of immolation (of the artist) I believe in.

But even from a limited, academic, hidebound point of view, the traditional art view, how silly it is for critics to be disturbed about slag, excrescences, drift and scoriae. How little they understand the role or the value of the so-called non-essential, the commonplace, the ugly, the inartistic. Their desire for perfection is so similar to that false religious attitude which desires only the good. You may think I am trying to justify my weakness. No, I am trying to tell you that I learned as much, or more, from the bad, the wrong, the slipshod, the evil, the misfit, and so on, than the other way round. When we speak of a person getting to grips with himself, accepting himself for what he is, we do not simply mean that he admits and recognizes his weaknesses but that he also discovers how important they were in his evolution. Asked how long a man's legs should be, Lincoln replied: "Just long enough to reach from his waist to the ground."

And then there's another thing about the drift and slag . . . have you ever noticed how, in life, there come these dull, dull

moments when everything drags, everything seems futile, and
you grow into a sort of vegetable . . . and just when you have
reached the nadir, so to speak, of your being, there comes an
awakening from deep down, like a flower opening its petals, and
little by little, as if there were chinks in your armor, the light
seeps in, stirs you gently back to life and awareness. But that
vegetable pause or break was necessary; without it there would
be no wonderful return. I say "wonderful" return to distinguish
it from the usual returns which occur more frequently—because
admit it or not, we are continually on the verge of falling asleep
(mentally, morally, spiritually). In this wonderful return you
dimly, unconsciously perhaps, realize the significance of that
word gamut, that you or "it" (again) are strung along a gamut
of being which is not human only but animal, vegetable, mineral.
These fantasies which I indulge in occasionally (in the books),
are not some of them distinctly mineral, others vegetable, and
so on? Of course, I know you and Larry are not objecting to the
"fantasies" or even the less valid "excursi," but rather to a sort of
everyday writing or thinking which is supposedly a betrayal of
the artist in oneself. Don't worry about it! Don't explain it!
Think of an adorable "haiku." (Here a crazy thought intrudes.
Not one of the faithful disciples ever spoke of Jesus farting or
even blowing his nose. But he must have, what! Would it have
been inartistic, sacrilegious, irreverent to introduce such a note?
There are many still who can't excuse him, who refuse to believe, that in his agony on the cross he cried out: "O Lord, why
hast thou forsaken me!" A saviour shouldn't have spoken such
words, they will tell you. And yet it is this, just this piece of
weakness, of doubt, of complaint, that is the most human thing
about Jesus, that keeps him linked to us human-all-too-human
trash).

And now a final word about "intentions." I think you are
quite right in thinking that my intentions do not matter much.
Or did not. Man proposes, God disposes. How often I think of
Rabelais who, while working for the printer, decided that he
could write just as lusty and humorous works as those he was
printing. And he did. *But* . . . then he got caught in his own

machinery, as it were. He got terribly serious. He employed his Gargantuan humor to awaken us to greater things. He had intended to do something with his left hand, merely. ("The left hand is the dreamer.") He got caught. He had stirred the muddy waters of his own being. He awoke the artist in him, the creator, the imaginator. And so, true to his lights, poor devil that he is, he is driven from pillar to post, always trying to save his skin—and tell the truth.

And now an "excursus." . . . The other day I meant to sit down and tell you lads of the wonderful remembrance which came to me. Suddenly one morning I fell to thinking of that trip abroad in 1953, with Eve. And suddenly it occurred to me how blessed was that trip from one aspect alone: my visits to the homes of certain celebrated men. What a list it is! Rabelais, Da Vinci, Moses Maimonides, El Greco, Ruysbroeck the Admirable, Shakespeare, Proust, van Eyck . . . And throw in the Cathedral of Chartres and the Mosque of Cordova. Each home, each countryside, each atmosphere was so very different. I say "home." Not always. Da Vinci, for example—the Château at Amboise, where he died. Proust, the countryside made famous in the *Côté de Guermantes*. Van Eyck, the famous triptych in the Cathedral at Ghent. But the home of Rabelais, yes! The most idyllic countryside, as I glimpsed it from the window where his cradle once stood, I have ever laid eyes on. Across it had marched Joan of Arc, to meet the king. El Greco, on the other hand—I am thinking of Toledo—inhabited a doll's house. All miniature rooms, and an alcove, off the dining room, where the musicians played for him as he ate. Around and about his dwelling the strongest, grimmest, severest city I have ever stepped into: Toledo. Rock and torture. Superstition, pomp, cruelty, ignorance, intolerance. And then the cloister in the forest outside Brussels, where Ruysbroeck lived. How serene, how ordered, how noble and silent and grave! A forest entirely of beeches, if I remember right. And then Bruges. The most alive of the dead. Saying to myself—I would get lost every time I took a walk—what a pity I never lived here. Here I could have written such a different book!

I forgot Cervantes. . . . Yes, through his country too we passed. Got off to look at the no longer existing windmills. Think of it, though. Oh yes, and even more important than all these . . . With Delteil we made a detour coming out of Spain and passed by that mountain where the last of the Albigensians had been walled in.

And another name still: Nostradamus. Not only my talks with the French doctor, but my talks with the man and wife who maintained Michel Simon's home in La Ciotât. They came from Nostradamus' country. They communed with Petrarch.

I'll reel them off again, and twenty-one salutes to Waremme (of *The Maurizius Case*): Nostradamus, Cervantes, Ruysbroeck, El Greco, Rabelais, Proust, Da Vinci, Moses Maimonides, Shakespeare—and Old Friar John (Powys). And just a stone's throw from Glastonbury—and all Arthur's great realm around us . . . "the matter of Britain," as they say. . . . Joey, I must get back to work. So long. Tootle—oo.

                                                                        Henry

From Henry Miller to Alfred Perlés

Dear Fred,

It's a strange thing but just a few days before I received your Third Letter to Larry I lay awake early one morning asking myself if all these books I have written (about my life, my suffering, my sins) were really as important, as necessary, as I once thought. I was reading them over from beyond the grave, as it were. I wasn't thinking of them critically but rather as one does sometimes with his own life—of what use, of what good, to what end, and so on.

And here is the strange conclusion I came up with: that God had answered my prayers and suffered me to become a writer, but, as the gods often do when responding to human pleas, my request had been answered only literally. What do I mean? I am not quite sure if I can tell you exactly, but it's something like this. . . . I proved to my satisfaction that, like any other mortal, I too could write. But since I wasn't really meant to be a writer all that was permitted me to give expression to was this business of writing and being a writer; in short, my own private struggles with this problem. My grief, in other words. Out of the lack I made my song. Very much as if a warrior, challenged to mortal combat and having no weapons, must first forge them himself. And in the process, one that takes all his life, the purpose of his labors gets forgotten or sidetracked.

Sometimes I say to myself, quite seriously, I mean: "when will you begin to write?" Write like other writers do. Like Larry, for instance, who is definitely what is called "a born writer." Or, to put it another way, like Larry who has respect and reverence for his tools, his material. What I have done all through my work is to repeat: "This is the best I can do; take it or leave it." Or again: "If it isn't literature, call it what you like. I don't give a damn." This, I suppose, is the *"je m'en foutisme"* you refer to. And there is truth in it.

When I said that I only approximated what I wanted to say in writing I meant that I do understand what writers are about when they undertake to give us a book. And that I too am aware of what I am about during the genesis of a book. But I never seem capable of submitting to the discipline demanded of an author. And you are again right when you speak of this day by day business. I would even stretch it and say hour by hour. My whole life is a kind of sparking activity. I spark, I don't glow steadily, like a sun. Hence my adoration for the sages, the masters, the great teachers of life. In a word, my infatuation with "serenity."

It must strike you as quite fatuous, my saying this. Did you ever suspect anything of the sort of me? I seem to hear you laughing, saying to yourself—"he's in another mood today."

But the truth is that from a very early age this thought formed itself and led me to seek out strange individuals, strange books, even strange adventures. When I come into the presence of the serene at heart I am completely myself, thoroughly stilled, at one with the world, and only then living, living in the full sense of the word. All other times, and they may be good, bad or indifferent, I am not myself but another—"*l'autre*." Many others. There's no harm in it, to be sure. It may not be in the least injurious—to the psyche or the immortal soul or what have you. But it's in these rare moments that I know that I know, that I feel complete and realized, that I am free of moods, fears and ambitions, and above all, reach beyond happiness.

Maybe I ought to say a word here about being happy, since you mentioned your suffering. You see, I often tell myself that I was born happy. I never had to reach for it, as so many people do. For me it was the natural state. That may explain, in passing, why I have had to taste so much suffering. I am not sure. I don't want to be facile. It's so easy to make explanations—afterwards.

But here is the strange thing. . . . I was happy with myself and in myself. It was the others who brought misery and unhappiness into my life. Not only women, though they chiefly, but men too, my friends and comrades; sometimes just "the world outside," if you know what I mean. And I don't mean the old hackneyed "Weltschmerz." I mean before and after the Weltschmerz period.

Let us put it another way. People gravitate towards happy souls, but in doing so they tend to make the person unhappy. They *need* happiness. Happy people don't need it, they are it. It isn't produced because of this or that, it just is, and they are blessed though they may know it not. In this country of ours everybody wants to be happy and the result is, as you well know, that we are about as miserable a body of people as the earth has ever spawned. And I loathe my countrymen for dwelling on the subject; they make me most unhappy.

I am floundering a bit but bear with me. The three great periods of anguish I went through were, as you know, with the first girl I fell in love with, then the widow, then June. And in all three periods I was inarticulate. What I needed most desperately was voice with which to express my grief and abandonment. That is how I came to write. My thought was simple and direct. My prayer, I should say, for it virtually took that form. "Give me, O God," is what I kept saying, "the power to express this anguish which afflicts me. Let me tell it to the world, for I can't bear to keep it locked in my own breast."

It was not until I came to the writing of *Capricorn* that I began this story of my suffering. I quoted Abélard in the frontispiece, you remember. My ego must have been enormous, to compare my suffering with his. But it was sincere, my feeling.

Perhaps the book that I botched the most of all was *Black Spring*. I was too happy then. Fate had to remind me of my task. You remember the last appearance of June—in Clichy. It was like sobering up after a long drunk. The time had come to put it down.

All during this Paris period prior to tackling *Capricorn* I had been enjoying, if I might put it that way, the effect of other men's writing. I was open to any and all influences. Especially from the French. I was writing in my head constantly . . . as they might write, I mean. I was a literary man. I might have written books and not the story of my life.

What happened? I suppose you might say that I suffered a kind of dementia. The more I wrote the more I became a human being. The writing may have seemed monstrous (to some), for it was a violation, but I became a more human individual because of it. I was getting the poison out of my system, no doubt. Curiously enough, this poison had a tonic effect for others. It was as if I had given them some kind of immunity.

What was this poison? Not a hatred that I had to work off, for by the time of writing I had no hate for any of my "characters." Indeed, I fell in love with many of them, the ones who lent themselves to ridicule and caricature particularly. All the while puffed up, no doubt, by that vanity which writers are plagued with—the belief that they can enter into the heart and soul of their inventions. And while the writer in me reveled at his prowess the human being had to admit more and more to the annihilating truth that no matter how sincerely, how tenderly, how reverently, he approached the character he was writing about, he could never, never capture him, never enter him, never render back what had been created by God alone. In other words, the truth teller, as I always styled myself, came face to face with the fabricator, or the writer.

Is it any wonder that between whiles, between opera, or between sections of any one book, I gave myself up to the wildest dreams? Oscillating always between the desire to be solely an inventor and the hope to become completely a man of truth? And what was I forging all the while in preparation for that mortal combat? The weapons with which to destroy the warrior who would use them. In short, myself.

No wonder I am full of anomalies, both as writer and as human being. Criticism bounces off me, not because I am vain and self-centered, not because I think I am a great writer . . . oh no! Because, my dear fellow, art has been my life-long preoccupation. The word means nothing to me, nor what it is supposed to stand for. Like God. But I am never fooled by men who pretend they cannot get it past their lips. I don't look for art in art, any more than I look for God in religion. But if you have prayed earnestly for certain powers you recognize them when you witness them, even though you yourself may never have been granted these powers. I wonder if I make myself clear? All I mean is that I am truly humble in the presence of art, whether on a cultural level, a primitive level or a child's level. Spirit can shine through an idiot as well as through a saint, what! I never turned my back on art; I may have been defiant, nothing more. I may only have believed (naively) that art is capable of more than men have dared hope for. In the same way that I might say God is capable of far worse crimes than any we mortals can imagine. Praising Him all the while. But never pretending to *know* Him. "Let me sing thy praises, O Lord!" In that spirit.

But the poison I spoke of. . . . The poison was that anybody or anything could unseat me from my happiness, my deep natural inner happiness. I did not want to be a wobbly, as other men. To sway from joy to despair. The day I came upon that passage in Nijinsky where he says: "I want everyone to be like me," I nearly jumped out of my skin. They could have been my own words. Must one be a complete solipsist or a madman to speak thus? Often I have asked myself the question.

Naturally it wasn't identity that Nijinsky wanted; he didn't want to see ten billion Nijinskys all about him. No. He wanted them to be filled with his divine, radiant, out-going spirit. Is that not it? Was there any harm in that?

All my rebelliousness, all this crazy tampering with the world, the divine set-up, or rather the man-made set-up, for it was the human never the cosmic woes which disturbed me, spring from my failure to comprehend what people meant—and by people I mean parents, sweethearts, friends, counselors—when they urged me to do this or that, become this or that. Let me be, was all I wanted. Be what I am, no matter how I am. Why is it that at this moment, and I have thought it a thousand times to myself, I always summon as proof of the foregoing this image—of myself as a little boy going down into the street to play, having no fixed purpose, no particular direction, no especial friend to seek out, but just divinely content to be going down into the street to meet whatever might come. In the most bitter arguments, with women, something like this thought always crept in. As though I was yelling my head off to put this simple thought into their heads—"I find life so simple, so good, so easy . . . why must you complicate it?" Or if they said, as they often did—"But how do I know you love me?"—I would become tongue-tied. Such a preposterous accusation to make against me. As if I did not love them! Only, I also loved others too. . . . Not in the way they meant, but in a natural wholesome easy way. Like one loves garlic, honey, wild strawberries. One must not love in this wide, indiscriminate way. One must not have friends who also happen to be traitors, thieves or what not. One must not enjoy a bad movie as much as a good movie. And so on. Clear?

Serenity is when you get above all this, when it doesn't matter what they think, say or want, but when you do as you are, and see God and Devil as one. Then you stop writing, of course. You don't need to play at God or Devil any longer. You've seen through, and the world is always at the level of your vision, of the stuff of your vision. It's when you discover that light is not a manifestation of some physical law but one of the infinite aspects of spirit itself. And there is no light on earth which matches the inner light.

I was going to speak about Homer and the gods, Homer and carnage, Homer and his last-minute introductions, Homer the exoskeletonized psychologist . . . but some other time. I am nearly finished with the *Iliad*. But not with Homer. One thing I am tempted to say in parting . . . at this writing there isn't one character, one god, in the *Iliad* whom I truly like or admire. Certainly not the two magnificent ones—Hector and Achilles. I know no author who has filled his characters with so many faults —unlovable, unforgivable faults. Enough!

Make what you can of all this! And don't wobble, what!

Cheers!

Henry

III   The Author at Work

Work Schedule, 1932–1933
—Henry Miller Miscellanea

COMMANDMENTS

1. Work on one thing at a time until finished.
2. Start no more new books, add no more new material to "Black Spring."
3. Don't be nervous. Work calmly, joyously, recklessly on whatever is in hand.
4. Work according to Program and not according to mood. Stop at the appointed time!
5. When you can't *create* you can *work*.
6. Cement a little every day, rather than add new fertilizers.
7. Keep human! See people, go places, drink if you feel like it.
8. Don't be a draught-horse! Work with pleasure only.
9. Discard the Program when you feel like it—but go back to it next day. *Concentrate. Narrow down. Exclude.*
10. Forget the books you want to write. Think only of the book you *are* writing.
11. Write first and always. Painting, music, friends, cinema, all these come afterwards.

DAILY PROGRAM

MORNINGS:
    If groggy, type notes and allocate, as stimulus.

If in fine fettle, write.

AFTERNOONS:

Work on section in hand, following plan of section scrupulously. No intrusions, no diversions. Write to finish one section at a time, for good and all.

EVENINGS:

See friends. Read in cafés.

Explore unfamiliar sections—on foot if wet, on bicycle, if dry.

Write, if in mood, but only on Minor program.

Paint if empty or tired.

Make Notes. Make Charts, Plans. Make corrections of MS.

Note: Allow sufficient time during daylight to make an occasional visit to museums or an occasional sketch or an occasional bike ride. Sketch in cafés and trains and streets. Cut the movies! Library for references once a week.

MAJOR PROGRAM

1. Finish everything on "Streets."
    a. Urinals (stretching bet. Chicago Exposition & Palais des Papes).
    b. Funerals (Dakar Expedition versus Clichy interments).
    c. Apotheosis: expand infancy theme with view to Paradise.
    d. Obsessional walks: amass all data—Times Square vs. Place Clichy; Broadway against La Fourche.
        Architecture, Language, Whores, Insane, Criminals.
    e. Rewrite Late-City Man (keeping George Grosz) but employing self against a general type.
        Clarify the symbolism still more—mother's womb, hero-wanderer, labyrinth-throngs, neuroses-civilization, disease-insanity. Battleships, aeroplanes, bridges, architecture, cemeteries, tombs, cement.
        Sacre du Printemps counterpointed against Grosz' caricatures. Hiler's mad period. Brassai's photography—Dali's Object.
2. Finish "China." Contrast Cronstadt's statistical China with

own imaginary China representing pure being. Dream-plant as ideal. Not evolution but self-expression, self-development. Employ opium bout as leitmotif. The theatre and the mask. Complete extraversion. The ideograph—Fenollosa. Recast "Trocadero Notes" for China as cosmic theme. China versus Mexico—2 original cultures. The artist's paradise: function of cruelty.

3. Combine Tante Melia and George Insel: Hereditary picture —the ancestral swarm, blood, race, prejudices, taints. Insanity and deaths. (Deaths in horoscope—death as dominant philosophic theme.)

Artist's patriotism—infancy: 14th Ward. The psychic patterns there laid down, recurring in all later relations—marriage, friendship, etc. Predominance of themes in dreams and in unconscious use of symbols in writing. Paint the symbols large.

4. Expand last Cronstadt section to full proportions—see notes. The Poem. Picasso-Structure. Death as fecundity. Creation at the joints, roots, cellular.

5. *France:* the artist's condition—escape, dream. Assemble all notes and weave into tapestry—from good to bad influences. Gare St. Lazare, Louveciennes rides, Place Clichy.

6. *Violence:* Assemble all data, ranging from original "Tropic of Cancer" scene opposite Gaumont to mad thoughts on way to Louveciennes. The post office as starting point for tour of world. Hiler's Anthropological chart: from Magdalenian period to now—finished. New type of man. Kill history, culture, cyclical development. Creative personality—Rank's last chapter and Lawrence's "Apocalypse." Give this section an equal, if not more intense quality, as original "Black Spring." Mars in 9th House! Mars and Venus. Dionysian symbolism extended to whole culture. Germ of idea lies in Brassaï article—"one man can destroy entire city." The individual as against the collectivity.

7. *Tailor Shop:* Recast materials and focus about "origins of writing."

Allocate under various themes: obsessional walks, nuts and influences, deaths, insanity, literature, personality.

8. *Dreams:* Exploit as illustrative of major themes and their source in infancy. Employ Surrealistically always. If unsuccessful, reserve them for scenario uses.

9. Epilogue: Recast "Black Spring" as thing in itself for reproducing process. Ask Hiler to illustrate or make cover design.

10. Finish Lawrence Book.

11. Finish Brochure.

12. Lay out new Plan for "Tropic of Capricorn."

MINOR PROGRAM

1. Write Scenario for Alraune: preferably in one continuous session—during week at Louveciennes. Exploit fundamental ideas laid down in "Palace of Entrails" plan. Cosmic and psychologic cast—anthropology and ethnology. Write as literature of ideas.

2. Rewrite "Extase": "What is Ecstasy," showing Lawrence theme in its ideal presentation—with thesis on possible use of the film. Reproduce a la Nin.

3. Finish microscopic analysis of "Aaron's Rod," "Lady Chatterley," "Apocalypse" and Murry's "Son of Woman."

4. Continue Hiler portrait—as possible brochure—under *"What is Art?"*

5. Draw up comprehensive outline of main divisions for Cinema Book.

6. Finish excerpts from: "Black Death," "Lawrence Letters," "Rabelais," "Challenge to Defeat," "Dance over Fire & Water," "Art & Artist," Jung's "Two Analytical Essays," Zweig's "Freud," "Dostoievski" and "L'Enfer," and "Don Juan." *(Double.)*

7. Write *Fairy Tale,* as for Michael: make study of "Alice in Wonderland" and "Pinocchio," showing psychologic themes. Exploit Analysis and Astrology—satirically.

8. Tackle *Novelettes* on: Bertha, Osborn, Fred, Bald, Bachmann, Cresswell, Paul Kerls, Pauline. (Swift, vigorous, careless, violent, Surrealistic.)

9. Write a *"Double"* story: exploiting possibilities revealed in "L'Homme à la Barbiche" (see 2nd Cronstadt section).

10. Do Humorous book *(An Almanac)* based on clippings and New Instinctivism—*for America!*

PAINTING PROGRAM

1. *Wall Charts:* For Material in Note Books, according to "Scheme and Significance." Find symbols and employ with color scheme. (For purposes of reproduction, Hiler idea.) Symbols for recurring themes: violence, dream, whores, streets, architecture, insanity, death, etc.

2. Treat symbols as picture: The Horse, Battleship, Figure on Garden Wall, Driggs Avenue, Tante Melia, China, Walls.

3. Self-Portraits—many as possible.

4. Dream streets, dream people, dream situations.

5. Paris memoranda: places and objects recorded in notebook, to be done with some degree of realism—Place Vauban, Cinema Vanves, St. Augustin Church, Notre Dame, St. Michel, Rue Mouffetard, Bagnolet, Place de la Réunion, Cemetery Montparnasse, various Impasses, Place des Vosges, Jewish Quarter, etc.

6. Illustrations for books: "Tropic of Cancer" (crazy characters), "Fairy Tales" (Monotype & Pressed Aquarelles), "Black Spring."

7. Try all mediums: gouache, tempera, monotypes, Chinese Ink, Aniline inks, Water Colors (Holty, Reichel).

8. See Zadkine's gouaches again and Halasz' photographs. *Dali.*

Note: Do nothing except it be connected with own books, ideas—always personal and practical. Paintings should supplement and reinforce my literature.

AGENDA

1. READ: "Folkways" (chapter on Cannibalism), Voyage au Bout de la Nuit, Freud's "Pleasure Principle" and the circuitous route towards death, Faure's "Spirit of the Forms," Delteil, Henri Fabre, Jane Harrison: "*The Orphic Myths*," Grobinalour, Chevaux de Diomedes, Medieval Culture (Cossler), Dante, Bouvard et Pecuchet, Japanese Chess (Sho-Go), Wilhelm's China Tamerlane & Genghis Khan, books on the Film. Lafcadio Hearn's "Tales of Old Japan," Weigall on "Akhenaton." Swipe from library books on geology, botany, anatomy, etc.

2. MUSEUMS: See Valentine Prax' work at Salon d'Automne, Dali's work at Surindependent, Chinese Wing of Louvre (Hiler's screens). See Zadkine's gouaches again and Holty's work. See "Tin Soldiers" at Invalides and "Race Types" at Trocadéro. See Tête de Mort, Aztec wing, Trocadéro.

3. Search for tracts on writings and paintings of idiot-savants.

4. Visit Catacombs, Denfert-Rochereau.

5. See Halasz' work and make detailed notes. Visit Dali.

6. See Harvey (Matisse, Brancusi, Delteil, etc.). Get copy of his wife's book on Dreiser.

7. Read Hiler's Costume book and Munsell Color Scheme and and return.

8. Get large loose-leaf sheets for big Note Book. Tracing paper, compass, T square, triangle. Roller. Pane of glass, oils from A.

9. Varnish water colors or use banana oil and get framed for A.

10. When finished with payments, get César Franck's "Quintette" and Beethoven A Minor Quartet (Huxley-Stavrogin). (See list.)

11. Look up "Benno" Greenstein—another technician.
12. Get big table with drawers, and army trunk for manuscripts.
13. Finish Annotations of Lowenfels' "Mental Climate."
14. Collect Accidents in Water Colors—send Emil some things.
15. Get Crevel tract on Dali—send Emil with Grosz album.
16. Go through Osborn's letters & Mss. to complete notes for novelette.

Manuscript Notes for *Plexus* (1947)—"Basic Chart"
  —(previously unpublished)

Manuscript Notes for *Plexus* (1947)–"Materials for Writing"
  —(previously unpublished)

Material for Writing

Bike Races – Press box – Sam + Joe
Prize fights – with Van Norden
Wrestling bouts – O'Regan + Harold H.
Liberty – Words
Chewing Gum Factory – L.I.   Ocean Liners
"Brooklyn's Back Yard"   Tug boats
Coney Island in Winter   * Garbage Disposal
Canarsie   (Cousin Henry D.
Harlem
Old No. 1 — School House!!   First article
Docks + Wharves — flop houses   with Bug?
Under Bridge —   in Jersey   Negro review
Hoboken + weird towns   (re Crisis)
Bowery – old + new
Chinatown   Snappy Stories
Sand St. — B'klyn (Spanish quarter)
Irish section – lower N.Y. (Cherry St.)
Ship Yards   Shoe Factory
Dance Halls – (Harlem!!)
Synagogues   Sherwood Anderson
Old South 3rd St. Church   Triumph of the Egg
Father Carroll's north 6th St. Inn
Russian churches – near Greenpoint D = Eternal Husband
Greenpoint – Polish district
Salvation army   Malloy – W. H.)
Boys' Clubs – N.Y.
Insane Asylums   Pasta – old
Prisons + Jails (giving Carl, + brother! meg. Ed.
* Advertising world (Bruce Barton + old (?)
                     Fantastic day with head)
Ghettos
Ellis Island Immigrants
Governor's Island – military   Prison Book
Statue of Liberty – Bedloe's Island
Sheepshead Bay + Far Rockaway (Reminiscences
Water + Fire Islands
(Blue Point + Peconic Bay – Shelter Island
 Patchogue
Steel Mills
Hitch hiking — for fun of it — hopes!

Manuscript Notes for *Plexus* (1947)—"Scheme"
—(previously unpublished)

Scheme

Loss of job — writing!   borrowing from Henry
Looking for work — defeat!   Bunman
Sixth avenue — alimony racket — child   +
Sessions with Fleres etc.   Joey Imhof
Gold-digging on side — staggering gifts
Drunk with Sam & Kamos at Paul & Joe's — Battling Siki
Café Royal — acte gratuit!
Arcadia Dance Hall — girl from Texas

*) Writing campaign — staggering!
**) in Search of literary material   marvelous!
     First mss.!
Absorption in & study of books
Letter Writing
Encounters with old-time friends — See text
   "   "   cracked vespers — see addenda
throw-backs   (to touch them up)
John Cowper Powys Lectures
June working at Cabarets — after theatre lowdown
Return from Bensonhurst with fabulous story of birth
Dewar's arrival — ride into country
O'Regan's arrival in nick of time — Chess session
                              talks of South
                                   etc.
                              Philippines
                              army life

Visit from Rezmin   Ali Khan
Discussions with Joe & Emil on other writers,
   craft, technique etc. (fantastic)
Peddling MSS. — Visits from Police
Loss of g/s with June
(femme de menage)
     List places lived in: Old German woman — Harcock
                              Old Blue nose Nova Scotian Sp
                              Karstens — beach
                              Clinton avenue — 2 places
                              Clinton street
                              last furnished room — Heil St.
                              Cellar on Henry St.
                              Stanley's house

Manuscript Notes for *Plexus* (1947)—"Don't Forget!"
  —(previously unpublished)

√ Van Gogh — Simple life — make notes! (Books to read!)

√ The Bicycle Path — Bedford Road — the old rider!

Shubulled, Crazy, Driggs etc.
Frank Reilly, Wardrop + Asylum theme — repeat!
Detective with Crucifix (Pleading innocent division)
(Gauguin by Arkansas writer)
Sheaco, Sheldon + Crazy George (Sheaco's girl)
Joe O'Regan and his red fathers.
She Candy Saga — flop up big
Work out with had — etc — old man hr, Clune
George Schindler — short coat — manners, type
certain new German Stock (Schaefer)
(and Uncle Theodore worries)
Annie Rosenbaum, Grillanitz + man who
his wife's mother — Mr. Weyers.
Doc Wanckes — wonky — chess — fights etc.
Dentists — rectal exercises! lamb of friend
Guy from Ridgewood — ___ sure for Haswell + friend "

IV Writing and Obscenity

Obscenity and the Law of Reflection
—Remember to Remember

To discuss the nature and meaning of obscenity is almost as difficult as to talk about God. Until I began delving into the literature which has grown up about the subject I never realized what a morass I was wading into. If one begins with etymology one is immediately aware that lexicographers are bamboozlers every bit as much as jurists, moralists and politicians. To begin with, those who have seriously attempted to track down the meaning of the term are obliged to confess that they have arrived nowhere. In their book, *To the Pure*, Ernst and Seagle state that "no two persons agree on the definitions of the six deadly adjectives: obscene, lewd, lascivious, filthy, indecent, disgusting." The League of Nations was also stumped when it attempted to define what constituted obscenity. D. H. Lawrence was probably right when he said that "nobody knows what the word obscene means." As for Theodore Schroeder, who has devoted his whole life to fighting for freedom of speech,* his opinion is that "obscenity does not exist in any book or picture, but is wholly a quality of the reading or viewing mind." "No argument for the suppression of obscene literature," he states, "has ever been offered which by unavoidable implications will

* See his *A Challenge to Sex Censors* and other works.

not justify, and which has not already justified, every other limitation that has ever been put upon mental freedom."

As someone has well said, to name all the masterpieces which have been labeled obscene would make a tedious catalogue. Most of our choice writers, from Plato to Havelock Ellis, from Aristophanes to Shaw, from Catullus and Ovid to Shakespeare, Shelley and Swinburne, together with the Bible, to be sure, have been the target of those who are forever in search of what is impure, indecent and immoral. In an article called "Freedom of Expression in Literature,"* Huntington Cairns, one of the most broad-minded and clear-sighted of all the censors, stresses the need for the re-education of officials charged with law enforcement. "In general," he states, "such men have had little or no contact with science or art, have had no knowledge of the liberty of expression tacitly granted to men of letters since the beginnings of English literature, and have been, from the point of view of expert opinion, altogether incompetent to handle the subject. Administrative officials, not the populace who in the main have only a negligible contact with art, stand first in need of re-education."

Perhaps it should be noted here, in passing, that though our Federal government exercises no censorship over works of art originating in the country, it does permit the Treasury Department to pass judgments upon importations from abroad. In 1930, the Tariff Act was revised to permit the Secretary of the Treasury, in his discretion, to admit the classics or books of recognized and established literary or scientific merit, even if obscene. What is meant by "books of recognized and established literary merit?" Mr. Cairns gives us the following interpretation: "books which have behind them a substantial and reputable body of American critical opinion indicating that the works are of meritorious quality." This would seem to represent a fairly liberal attitude, but when it comes to a test, when a book or other work of art is capable of creating a

* From the *Annals of the American Academy of Political and Social Science*, Philadelphia, November, 1938.

furore, this seeming liberality collapses. It has been said with regard to the sonnets of Aretino that they were condemned for
four hundred years. How long we shall have to wait for the ban
to be lifted on certain famous contemporary works no one can
predict. In the article alluded to above, Mr. Cairns admits that
"there is no likelihood whatever that the present obscenity
statutes will be repealed." "None of the statutes," he goes on to
say, "defines the word 'obscenity' and there is thus a wide lati-
tude of discretion in the meaning to be attributed to the term."
Those who imagine that the *Ulysses* decision established a precedent should realize by now that they were overoptimistic.
Nothing has been established where books of a disturbing nature
are concerned. After years of wrestling with prudes, bigots and
other psychopaths who determine what we may or may not
read, Theodore Schroeder is of the opinion that "it is not the
inherent quality of the book which counts, but its hypothetical
influence upon some hypothetical person, who at some problem-
atical time in the future may hypothetically read the book."

In his book called *A Challenge to Sex Censors*, Mr. Schroeder
quotes an anonymous clergyman of a century ago to the
effect that "obscenity exists only in the minds that discover
it and charge others with it." This obscure work contains most
illuminating passages; in it the author attempts to show that, by
a law of reflection in nature, everyone is the performer of acts
similar to those he attributes to others; that self-preservation is
self-destruction, etc. This wholesome and enlightened viewpoint, attainable, it would seem, only by the rare few, comes
nearer to dissipating the fogs which envelop the subject than all
the learned treatises of educators, moralists, scholars and jurists
combined. In Romans xiv: 14 we have it presented to us axiomat-
ically for all time: "I know and am persuaded by the Lord Jesus
that there is nothing unclean of itself, but to him that esteemeth
anything to be unclean, to him it is unclean." How far one
would get in the courts with this attitude, or what the postal
authorities would make of it, surely no sane individual has any
doubts about.

A totally different point of view, and one which deserves attention, since it is not only honest and forthright but expressive of the innate conviction of many, is that voiced by Havelock Ellis, that obscenity is a "permanent element of human social life and corresponds to a deep need of the human mind."* Ellis indeed goes so far as to say that "adults need obscene literature, as much as children need fairy tales, as a relief from the oppressive force of convention." This is the attitude of a cultured individual whose purity and wisdom has been acknowledged by eminent critics everywhere. It is the worldly view which we profess to admire in the Mediterranean peoples. Ellis, being an Englishman, was of course persecuted for his opinions and ideas upon the subject of sex. From the nineteenth century on, all English authors who dared to treat the subject honestly and realistically have been persecuted and humiliated. The prevalent attitude of the English people is, I believe, fairly well presented in such a piece of polished inanity as Viscount Brentford's righteous self-defense—"Do We Need a Censor?" Viscount Brentford is the gentleman who tried to protect the English public from such iniquitous works as *Ulysses* and *The Well of Loneliness*. He is the type, so rampant in the Anglo-Saxon world, to which the words of Dr. Ernest Jones would seem to apply: "It is the people with secret attractions to various temptations who busy themselves with removing these temptations from other people; really they are defending themselves under the pretext of defending others, because at heart they fear their own weakness."

As one accused of employing obscene language more freely and abundantly than any other living writer in the English language, it may be of interest to present my own views on the subject. Since the *Tropic of Cancer* first appeared in Paris, in 1934, I have received many hundreds of letters from readers all over the world: they are from men and women of all ages and all walks of life, and in the main they are congratulatory messages. Many of those who denounced the book because of its

* *More Essays of Love and Virtue.*

gutter language professed admiration for it otherwise; very, very few ever remarked that it was a dull book, or badly written. The book continues to sell steadily "under the counter" and is still written about at intervals although it made its appearance eleven years ago and was promptly banned in all the Anglo-Saxon countries. The only effect which censorship has had upon its circulation is to drive it underground, thus limiting the sales but at the same time insuring for it the best of all publicity—word of mouth recommendation. It is to be found in the libraries of nearly all our important colleges, is often recommended to students by their professors, and has gradually come to take its place beside other celebrated literary works which, once similarly banned and suppressed, are now accepted as classics. It is a book which appeals especially to young people and which, from all that I gather directly and indirectly, not only does not ruin their lives, but increases their morale. The book is a living proof that censorship defeats itself. It also proves once again that the only ones who may be said to be protected by censorship are the censors themselves, and this only because of a law of nature known to all who overindulge. In this connection I feel impelled to mention a curious fact often brought to my attention by booksellers, namely, that the two classes of books which enjoy a steady and ever-increasing sale are the so-called pornographic, or obscene, and the occult. This would seem to corroborate Havelock Ellis's view which I mentioned earlier. Certainly all attempts to regulate the traffic in obscene books, just as all attempts to regulate the traffic in drugs or prostitution, are doomed to failure wherever civilization rears its head. Whether these things are a definite evil or not, whether or not they are definite and ineradicable elements of our social life, it seems indisputable that they are synonymous with what is called civilization. Despite all that has been said and written for and against, it is evident that with regard to these factors of social life men have never come to that agreement which they have about slavery. It is possible, of course, that one day these things may disappear, but it is also possible, despite the now seemingly universal disapproval of it, that slavery may once again be practiced by human beings.

The most insistent question put to the writer of "obscene" literature is: why did you have to use such language? The implication is, of course, that with conventional terms or means the same effect might have been obtained. Nothing, of course, could be further from the truth. Whatever the language employed, no matter how objectionable—I am here thinking of the most extreme examples—one may be certain that there was no other idiom possible. Effects are bound up with intentions, and these in turn are governed by laws of compulsion as rigid as nature's own. That is something which non-creative individuals seldom ever understand. Someone has said that "the literary artist, having attained understanding, communicates that understanding to his readers. That understanding, whether of sexual or other matters, is certain to come into conflict with popular beliefs, fears and taboos, because these are, for the most part, based on error." Whatever extenuating reasons are adduced for the erroneous opinions of the populace, such as lack of education, lack of contact with the arts, and so on, the fact is that there will always be a gulf between the creative artist and the public because the latter is immune to the mystery inherent in and surrounding all creation. The struggle which the artist wages, consciously or unconsciously, with the public, centers almost exclusively about the problem of a necessitous choice. Putting to one side all questions of ego and temperament, and taking the broadest view of the creative process, which makes of the artist nothing more than an instrument, we are nevertheless forced to conclude that the spirit of an age is the crucible in which, through one means or another, certain vital and mysterious forces seek expression. If there is something mysterious about the manifestation of deep and unsuspected forces, which find expression in disturbing movements and ideas from one period to another, there is nevertheless nothing accidental or bizarre about it. The laws governing the spirit are just as readable as those governing nature. But the readings must come from those who are steeped in the mysteries. The very depth of these interpretations naturally makes them unpalatable and unacceptable to the vast body which constitutes the unthinking public.

Parenthetically it is curious to observe that painters, however unapproachable their work may be, are seldom subjected to the same meddling interference as writers. Language, because it also serves as a means of communication, tends to bring about weird obfuscations. Men of high intelligence often display execrable taste when it comes to the arts. Yet even these freaks whom we all recognize, because we are always amazed by their obtuseness, seldom have the cheek to say what elements of a picture had been better left out or what substitutions might have been effected. Take, for example, the early works of George Grosz. Compare the reactions of the intelligent public in his case to the reactions provoked by Joyce when his *Ulysses* appeared. Compare these again with the reactions which Schönberg's later music inspired. In the case of all three the revulsion which their work first induced was equally strong, but in the case of Joyce the public was more articulate, more voluble, more arrogant in its pseudo-certitude. With books even the butcher and the plumber seem to feel that they have a right to an opinion, especially if the book happens to be what is called a filthy or disgusting one.

I have noticed, moreover, that the attitude of the public alters perceptibly when it is the work of primitive peoples which they must grapple with. Here for some obscure reason the element of the "obscene" is treated with more deference. People who would be revolted by the drawings in *Ecce Homo* will gaze unblushingly at African pottery or sculpture no matter how much their taste or morals may be offended. In the same spirit they are inclined to be more tolerant of the obscene works of ancient authors. Why? Because even the dullest are capable of admitting to themselves that other epochs might, justifiably or not, have enjoyed other customs, other morals. As for the creative spirits of their own epoch, however, freedom of expression is always interpreted as license. The artist must conform to the current, and usually hypocritical, attitude of the majority. He must be original, courageous, inspiring and all that—but never too disturbing. He must say Yes while saying No. The larger the art public, the more tyrannical, complex and perverse does this irrational pressure become. There are always exceptions, to be sure, and Picasso is one of them, one of the few artists in our time able to command the respect and attention of a bewildered and largely hostile public. It is the greatest tribute that could be made to his genius.

The chances are that during this transition period of global wars, lasting perhaps a century or two, art will become less and less important. A world torn by indescribable upheavals, a world preoccupied with social and political transformations, will have less time and energy to spare for the creation and appreciation of works of art. The politician, the soldier, the industrialist, the technician, all those in short who cater to immediate needs, to creature comforts, to transitory and illusory passions and prejudices, will take precedence over the artist. The most poetic inventions will be those capable of serving the most destructive ends. Poetry itself will be expressed in terms of block-busters and lethal gases. The obscene will find expression in the most unthinkable techniques of self-destruction which the inventive genius of man will be forced to adopt. The revolt and disgust which the prophetic spirits in the realm of art have inspired, through their vision of a world in the making, will find justification in the years to come as these dreams are acted out.

The growing void between art and life, art becoming ever more sensational and unintelligible, life becoming more dull and hopeless, has been commented on almost ad nauseam. The war, colossal and portentous as it is, has failed to arouse a passion commensurate with its scope or significance. The fervor of the Greeks and the Spaniards was something which astounded the modern world. The admiration and the horror which their ferocious struggles evoked was revelatory. We regarded them as mad and heroic, and we had almost been on the point of believing that such madness, such heroism, no longer existed. But what strikes one as "obscene" and insane rather than mad, is the stupendous machine-like character of the war which the big nations are carrying on. It is a war of materiel, a war of statistical preponderance, a war in which victory is coldly and patiently calculated on the basis of bigger and better resources. In the war which the Spaniards and the Greeks waged there was not only a hopelessness about the immediate outcome but a hopelessness as to the eternal outcome, so to speak. Yet they fought, and with tooth and nail, and they will fight again and again, always hopelessly and always gloriously because always passionately. As for the big powers now locked in a death struggle, one feels that they are only grooming themselves for another chance at it, for a chance to win here and now in a victory that will be everlasting, which is an utter delusion. Whatever the outcome, one senses that life will not be altered radically but to a degree which will only make it more like what it was before the conflict started. This war has all the masturbative qualities of a combat between hopeless recidivists.

If I stress the obscene aspect of modern warfare it is not simply because I am against war but because there is something about the ambivalent emotions it inspires which enables me better to grapple with the nature of the obscene. Nothing would be regarded as obscene, I feel, if men were living out their inmost desires. What man dreads most is to be faced with the manifestation, in word or deed, of that which he has refused to live out, that which he has throttled or stifled, buried, as we say now, in his subconscious mind. The sordid qualities imputed to the enemy are always those which we recognize as our own and therefore rise to slay, because only through projection do we realize the enormity and horror of them. Man tries as in a dream to kill the enemy in himself. This enemy, both within and without, is just as but no more real than the phantoms in his dreams. When awake he is apathetic about this dream self, but asleep he is filled with terror. I say "when awake," but the question is, *when is he awake, if ever?* To those who no longer need to kill, the man who indulges in murder is a sleep walker. He is a man trying to kill himself in his dreams. He is a man who comes face to face with himself *only in the dream.* This man is the man of the modern world, everyman, as much a myth and a legend as the Everyman of the allegory. Our life today is what we dreamed it would be aeons ago. Always it has a double thread

running through it, just as in the age-old dream. Always fear
and wish, fear and wish. Never the pure fountain of desire. And
so we have and we have not, we are and we are not.

In the realm of sex there is a similar kind of sleepwalking and
self-delusion at work; here the bifurcation of pure desire into
fear and wish has resulted in the creation of a phantasmagorical
world in which love plays the role of a chameleon-like scape-
goat. Passion is conspicuous by its absence or by monstrous deformations which render it practically unrecognizable. To trace
the history of man's attitude towards sex is like threading a
labyrinth whose heart is situated in an unknown planet. There
has been so much distortion and suppression, even among primitive peoples, that today it is virtually impossible to say what
constitutes a free and healthy attitude. Certainly the glorification
of sex, in pagan times, represented no solution of the problem.
And, though Christianity ushered in a conception of love superior to any known before, it did not succeed in freeing man
sexually. Perhaps we might say that the tyranny of sex was
broken through sublimation in love, but the nature of this
greater love has been understood and experienced only by a rare
few.

Only where strict bodily discipline is observed, for the purpose of union or communion with God, has the subject of sex
ever been faced squarely. Those who have achieved emancipation by this route have, of course, not only liberated themselves
from the tyranny of sex but from all other tyrannies of the
flesh. With such individuals, the whole body of desire has become so transfigured that the results obtained have had practically no meaning for the man of the world. Spiritual triumphs,
even though they affect the man in the street immediately, concern him little, if at all. He is seeking for a solution of life's problems on the plane of mirage and delusion; his notions of reality
have nothing to do with ultimate effects; he is blind to the permanent changes which take place above and beneath his level
of understanding. If we take such a type of being as the Yogi,
whose sole concern is with reality, as opposed to the world of illusion, we are bound to concede that he has faced every human

problem with the utmost courage and lucidity. Whether he in-
corporates the sexual or transmutes it to the point of transcend-
ence and obliteration, he is at least one who has attained the vast
open spaces of love. If he does not reproduce his kind, he at
least gives new meaning to the word birth. In lieu of copulating
he creates; in the circle of his influence conflict is stilled and
the harmony of a profound peace established. He is able to love
not only individuals of the opposite sex but all individuals, everything that breathes, in fact. This quiet sort of triumph strikes a
chill in the heart of the ordinary man, for not only does it make
him visualize the loss of his meager sex life but the loss of passion itself, passion as he knows it. This sort of liberation, which
smashes his thermometrical gauge of feeling, represents itself to
him as a living death. The attainment of a love which is bound-
less and unfettered terrifies him for the very good reason that it
means the dissolution of his ego. He does not want to be freed
for service, dedication and devotion to all mankind; he wants
comfort, assurance and security, the enjoyment of his very limited powers. Incapable of surrender, he can never know the healing power of faith; and lacking faith he can never begin to
know the meaning of love. He seeks release but not liberation,
which is like saying that he prefers death instead of life.

As civilization progresses it becomes more and more apparent
that war is the greatest release which life offers the ordinary
man. Here he can let go to his heart's content for here crime
no longer has any meaning. Guilt is abolished when the whole
planet swims in blood. The lulls of peacetime seem only to permit him to sink deeper into the bogs of the sadistic-masochistic
complex which has fastened itself into the heart of our civilized
life like a cancer. Fear, guilt and murder—these constitute the
real triumvirate which rules our lives. *What is obscene then?*
The whole fabric of life as we know it today. To speak only
of what is indecent, foul, lewd, filthy, disgusting, etc., in connection with sex, is to deny ourselves the luxury of the great
gamut of revulsion-repulsion which modern life puts at our service. Every department of life is vitiated and corroded with
what is so unthinkingly labeled "obscene." One wonders if

perhaps the insane could not invent a more fitting, more inclusive term for the polluting elements of life which we create and shun and never identify with our behavior. We think of the insane as inhabiting a world completely divorced from reality, but our own everyday behavior, whether in war or peace, if examined from only a slightly higher standpoint, bears all the ear-marks of insanity. "I have said," writes a well-known psychologist, "that this is a mad world; that man is most of the time mad; and I believe that in a way, what we call morality is merely a form of madness, which happens to be a working adaptation to existing circumstances."

———

When obscenity crops out in art, in literature more particularly, it usually functions as a technical device; the element of the deliberate which is there has nothing to do with sexual excitation, as in pornography. If there is an ulterior motive at work it is one which goes far beyond sex. Its purpose is to awaken, to usher in a sense of reality. In a sense, its use by the artist may be compared to the use of the miraculous by the Masters. This last-minute quality, so closely allied to desperation, has been the subject of endless debate. Nothing connected with Christ's life, for example, has been exposed to such withering scrutiny as the miracles attributed to him. The great question is: should the Master indulge himself or should he refrain from employing his extraordinary powers? Of the great Zen masters it has been observed that they never hesitate to resort to any means in order to awaken their disciples; they will even perform what we would call sacrilegious acts. And, according to some familiar interpretations of the Flood, it has been acknowledged that even God grows desperate at times and wipes the slate clean in order to continue the human experiment on another level.

It should be recognized, however, with regard to these questionable displays of power, that only a Master may hazard them. As a matter of fact, the element of risk exists only in the eyes of the uninitiated. The Master is always certain of the result; he never plays his trump card, as it were, except at the psychological moment. His behavior, in such instances, might be compared to that of the chemist pouring a last tiny drop into a prepared solution in order to precipitate certain salts. If it is a push it is also a supreme exhortation which the Master indulges in. Once the moment is passed, moreover, the witness is altered forever. In another sense, the situation might be described as the transition from belief to faith. Once faith has been established, there is no regression; whereas with belief everything is in suspense and capable of fluctuation.

It should also be recognized that those who have real power have no need to demonstrate it for themselves; it is never in their own interests, or for their own glorification, that these performances are made. In fact, there is nothing miraculous, in the vulgar sense, about these acts, unless it be the ability to raise the consciousness of the onlooker to that mysterious level of illumination which is natural to the Master. Men who are ignorant of the source of their powers, on the other hand, men who are regarded as the powers that move the world, usually come to a disastrous end. Of their efforts it is truly said that all comes to nought. On the worldly level nothing endures, because on this level, which is the level of dream and delusion, all is fear and wish vainly cemented by will.

To revert to the artist again. . . . Once he has made use of his extraordinary powers, and I am thinking of the use of obscenity in just such magical terms, he is inevitably caught up in the stream of forces beyond him. He may have begun by assuming that he could awaken his readers, but in the end he himself passes into another dimension of reality wherein he no longer feels the need of forcing an awakening. His rebellion over the prevalent inertia about him becomes transmuted, as his vision increases, into an acceptance and understanding of an order and harmony which is beyond man's conception and approachable only through faith. His vision expands with the growth of his own powers, because creation has its roots in vision and admits of only one realm, the realm of imagination. Ultimately, then, he stands among his own obscene objurgations like the conqueror midst the ruins of a devastated city. He realizes that the real nature of the obscene resides in the lust to convert. He knocked to awaken, but it was himself he awakened. And once awake, he is no longer concerned with the world of sleep; he walks in the light and, like a mirror, reflects his illumination in every act.

Once this vantage point is reached, how trifling and remote seem the accusations of moralists! How senseless the debate as to whether the work in question was of high literary merit or not! How absurd the wrangling over the moral or immoral nature of his creation! Concerning every bold act one may raise the reproach of vulgarity. Everything dramatic is in the nature of an appeal, a frantic appeal for communion. Violence, whether in deed or speech, is an inverted sort of prayer. Initiation itself is a violent process of purification and union. Whatever demands radical treatment demands God, and always through some form of death or annihilation. Whenever the obscene crops out one can smell the imminent death of a form. Those who possess the highest clue are not impatient, even in the presence of death: the artist in words, however, is not of this order, he is only at the vestibule, as it were, of the palace of wisdom. Dealing with the spirit, he nevertheless has recourse to forms. When he fully understands his role as creator he substitutes his own being for the medium of words. But in that process there comes the "dark night of the soul" when, exalted by his vision of things to come and not yet fully conscious of his powers, he resorts to violence. He becomes desperate over his inability to transmit his vision. He resorts to any and every means in his power; this agony, in which creation itself is parodied, prepares him for the solution of his dilemma, but a solution wholly unforeseen and mysterious as creation itself.

All violent manifestations of radiant power have an obscene glow when visualized through the refractive lens of the ego. All conversions occur in the speed of a split second. Liberation implies the sloughing off of chains, the bursting of the cocoon. What is obscene are the preliminary or anticipatory movements of birth, the preconscious writhing in the face of a life to be. It is in the agony of death that the nature of birth is apprehended. For in what consists the struggle if it is not between form and being, between that which was and that which is about to be? In such moments creation itself is at the bar; whoever seeks to unveil the mystery becomes himself a part of the mystery and thus helps to perpetuate it. Thus the lifting of the veil may be interpreted as the ultimate expression of the obscene. It is an attempt to spy on the secret processes of the universe. In this sense the guilt attaching to Prometheus symbolizes the guilt of man-the-creator, of man-the-arrogant-one who ventures to create before being crowned with wisdom.

The pangs of birth relate not to the body but to the spirit. It was demanded of us to know love, experience union and communion, and thus achieve liberation from the wheel of life and death. But we have chosen to remain this side of Paradise and to create through art the illusory substance of our dreams. In a profound sense we are forever delaying the act. We flirt with destiny and lull ourselves to sleep with myth. We die in the throes of our own tragic legends, like spiders caught in their own webs. If there is anything which deserves to be called "obscene" it is this oblique, glancing confrontation with the mysteries, this walking up to the edge of the abyss, enjoying all the ecstasies of vertigo and yet refusing to yield to the spell of the unknown. The obscene has all the qualities of the hidden interval. It is as vast as the Unconscious itself and as amorphous and fluid as the very stuff of the Unconscious. It is what comes to the surface as strange, intoxicating and forbidden, and which therefore arrests and paralyzes, when in the form of Narcissus we bend over our own image in the mirror of our own iniquity. Acknowledged by all, it is nevertheless despised and rejected, wherefore it is constantly emerging in Protean guise at the most unexpected moments. When it is recognized and accepted, whether as a figment of the imagination or as an integral part of human reality, it inspires no more dread or revulsion than could be ascribed to the flowering lotus which sends its roots down into the mud of the stream on which it is borne.

Obscenity in Literature
    —*New Directions 16*

When I think of all I have set down on paper to express my attitude towards life, and the connection between art and life, I

find it difficult to decide what to add, in a few pages, which will
prove illuminating or convincing to those who now wish to pass
judgment upon me. To start with, I think it appropriate to repeat what I have said in numerous ways throughout my works,
namely, that it is from two inexhaustible Gallic sources, Rabelais
and Élie Faure, I have drawn the fullest measure of courage,
inspiration and sense of freedom. Nowhere in the works of these
masters have I ever found excuses or apologies for the curtail-
ment of freedom of expression in art. French to the core, human-
ists above all, these two figures have proved more liberating to
me than the most flaming revolutionaries. There is, of course,
another figure in our history, one still more liberating, still more
passionate in his expression of truth, justice, freedom, and that
is Jesus Christ. Morality, it would seem, never occupied his
thoughts. We know this, however, that he particularly singled
out for scorn and rebuke the true enemies of society, the
Pharisees.

I am only too keenly aware that we are living in the closing
years of the twentieth century. I know too that throughout these
last twenty centuries society has changed its ways, its habits,
customs, laws, its morals as well, innumerable times. Calling itself
a "Christian" society, it has transgressed and violated every
tenet of its belief in a new way of life, the way ordained by the
Saviour.

I am as much a part of the present order as any man alive. I
have been molded and formed by it; I have revolted against it;
and finally I have been forced to accept it or die of a broken
heart. But to accept the condition of life in which I happen to
find myself does not mean that I believe in or approve of it.
I have always endeavored, and I still endeavor, to live my own
life in my own way. I have no desire to kill my fellow-man nor
to rob him of his possessions nor to persecute him for thinking or
behaving other than I do. I am a man of peace whose sole aim is
to enjoy life to the utmost. Simple and banal as it sounds, it has
nevertheless taken me the greater part of a lifetime to make
this a reality.

To become a writer was not easy for me. It was not until my

thirty-third year that I ventured it. Even then I did not really begin. From the year 1924, when I resolved never again to work for any man but to be my own master absolute, from that year when I began practicing the art, as they say, until the year 1934, nothing I wrote was ever published excepting three or four short texts in magazines of no importance. It was in Paris, in the year 1934, that my first published book was brought out by the Obelisk Press: *Tropic of Cancer*. It was in Paris, I may add, that I found myself, as a man and as an artist.

During those ten years in which I was acquiring mastery over my medium I remained unpublished not because my work was larded with pornography or obscenity but, as I am now convinced, because I had yet to discover my own identity. It was in writing the *Tropic of Cancer* that I found my own voice. The critics have coined all sorts of images to reveal the supposed character of this work. It could be described very simply, in my opinion, by saying that it was an attempt to blow off steam. If it was not a pleasant, conventional or decorous piece of literature it was at least normal and natural, given the circumstances which made its birth inevitable. After twenty years the critics, most of them at any rate, have conceded that it is a serious work, even a work of art.

In the intervening years I have written over twenty-five books, all of them published, and most of them translated into various languages. By the end of next year virtually everything I have written will exist in French. It is in France, I should like to point out, that I am most widely read and perhaps most deeply appreciated or esteemed.

I believe it no exaggeration to say that the French reading public has accepted me as a sincere and earnest writer. It is not out of egotism that I state this. I have just returned to my native land after eight months abroad, most of which time was spent in France, many parts of France. Nowhere was I treated as an emissary of the devil. On the contrary, and I say it with a full heart, my reception everywhere was such that I shall never forget it. To put it more accurately, I am tempted to say that I was treated "almost" as if I were a Frenchman myself. By that I mean that I was not looked upon as a freak from some outlandish quarter of the globe. Men spoke to me as if I spoke their own language, the language of free men, which is understood everywhere.

In the year 1927, while still in America, supposing myself like Abélard to have suffered more grievously than any ordinary mortal, I laid out the plan for a huge "book of my life" which I purposed writing one day. It was only in 1938, in Paris, that the first fragment of this work—the beginning of a series of "autobiographical novels"—appeared. It was called *Tropic of Capricorn*. It was this book, together with *Black Spring* and *Tropic of Cancer*, which provided material for the celebrated "affaire Miller." Thanks to the efforts of a group of French writers who had formed a "Comité de Défense," I was eventually *amnistié* by the authorities. I have never understood how I could have been granted an amnesty, first because the case never came to court, and second because I had not been found guilty of committing a crime either against the people or against the government of France. Moreover, throughout this entire period of controversy, the books in question were never withdrawn from sale.

But to go on. . . . With the publication of *Sexus,* the first volume of a trilogy called *The Rosy Crucifixion,* I am accused of offending the morals of the French public. As a consequence I have been requested to explain my position—where do I, as a writer, stand with regard to morality?

To begin with, I should say that my concern has never been with morals but with life, my own life more particularly. In the above named trilogy, of which two volumes have been thus far written and published, I dwell on the ten years preceding my voluntary exile in France. They are the crucial years of my life in more ways than one, and have, in my humble opinion, a significance far beyond the personal. In elaborating on the events of this decade when, it still seems to me, I endured nearly every form of trial and ordeal, I am persuaded that my example will offer hope and encouragement to other desperate souls.

That it has been no easy task to unburden and reveal myself

may be attested by the fact that, twenty-five years since the projection of my plan, I have still to write the final volume, *Nexus*. It was never my intention, incidentally, to make this work a trilogy. My thought originally was to issue the entire work, when completed, under the caption *The Rosy Crucifixion*. But because of its great bulk, as well as the delay involved, this idea proved impracticable from a publishing standpoint.

Meanwhile the second volume, *Plexus*,* has come out both in French and in English, and thus far there has been no question of censorship. Almost simultaneously with the French version of *Plexus* there appeared a short work called *The World of Sex*,** written some ten years ago; in this book I endeavored to make clear my attitude towards sex. In addition there exists a *plaquette* called *Obscenity and the Law of Reflection*, † written expressly for my friend Huntington Cairns, our "unofficial" censor here in America.

In the course of the coming year Gallimard will issue the last book I have written—the first of a series—under the title *The Books in My Life*. This work must also be considered as forming a part of the autobiographical series, inasmuch as the books I have read constitute as important a part of my life as any other factors entering into it. In an Appendix to this work I list *all* the books I can recall ever having read since I first began to read. It may be of interest to observe how very few of the books listed fall into the category of the obscene or pornographic.

The preceding pages are preliminary, intended simply as an aid to those unacquainted with my life and work. To be more direct and explicit, let me begin by stating what I sincerely believe my purpose to be in expressing myself through words. It is this: to reveal myself as openly, nakedly and unashamedly

---

* *Plexus* (version française), Corrêa, Paris, 1952; *Plexus* (English version), Olympia Press, Paris, 1953.

** Olympia Press, Paris, 1957. (Publisher's Note.)

In *Remember to Remember*, New Directions, and *The Intimate Henry Miller*, New American Library. (Publisher's Note.)

as possible. If I be asked why I should want to do this I can only answer—because my nature or my temperament compels me to do so. I am interested in life, all life, and every aspect of it. The one life I know best of all is my own. Examining my own life, describing it in detail, exposing it ruthlessly, I believe that I am rendering back life, enhanced and exalted, to those who read me. This seems to me a worthy task for a writer and one for which I have had illustrious predecessors.

That sex is a vital part of life goes without question. It is also commonly acknowledged that the role of sex, or the importance of it in one's life, varies with the individual. The question seems to be—how much of the truth of life, in so far as it pertains to sexual behavior, may be utilized in literature? Perhaps it is not even a question of this but rather of the manner in which the sexual is introduced. In short, perhaps the question could be formulated thus: Is there a right and a wrong way in which to treat sex in a work of art? Which immediately leads us to the next question: Is the right way the way of the moralist, the censor, the policeman? Or, if you like, is the State through its law-makers the final arbiter of what is right and wrong, good and bad, in questions of art?

To me it seems that the whole assumption on which the restrictive activities of our moral guardians rests is that access to forbidden literature may cause us to behave like animals. But to think thus is to cast a slur upon the animal kingdom. At the same time it makes of passion, man's greatest attribute, a caricature. The gamut of human passion is almost without limits, reaching heights and depths unthinkable. Precisely because it embraces such extremes, passion is the very touchstone of our humanity, and perhaps of our divinity also. Of all the creatures of the earth man is the only one whose behavior is unpredictable. There is in us something of all creation. If we are denied the smallest measure of freedom we are spiritually thwarted and crippled. It is the full awareness of our diverse nature and the integration of the myriad elements of which we are composed that make us whole, make us *human*. Religion may make us saints, or just good citizens; but what makes us men, what makes us human to

he core, is freedom. It is a terrifying word, freedom, for those
who have lived all their lives in mental shackles.

In an essay entitled "On Some Lines of Virgil," Montaigne
writes: "What harm has the genital act, so natural, so necessary,
and so lawful, done to humanity, that we dare not speak of it
without shame, and exclude it from serious and orderly conversation? We boldly utter the words *kill, rob, betray;* and the
other we only dare to utter under our breath. Does this mean
that the less of it we breathe in words, the more we are at liberty
to swell our thoughts with it? For it is amusing that the words
which are least used, least written, and most hushed up, should
be the best known and the most generally understood. There
is no person of any age or morals but knows them as well as he
knows the word *bread....*"

It is my honest conviction that the fear and dread which the
obscene inspires, particularly in modern times, spring from the
language employed rather than the thought. It is very much as
if we were dealing here with primitive taboos. That certain
words, certain expressions, usually though not always connected
with sex, have come to be thought of as "forbidden" is, at
bottom, absolutely mystifying. Those who are shocked, pained,
wounded or horrified by these written symbols are not unfamiliar with them in speech. We all hear these "foul," "coarse,"
"ugly" expressions daily, from the cradle to the grave. How is
it, why is it, that we have not become immune to them? What
magic do they possess against which we have no protection?
Notice that it is particularly against their use in literature that
the righteous ones object. But why should literature be more
sacrosanct than speech? Is not writing another form of speech?
Is youth being *corrupted*—that is the venerable term we are
always trotting out—by obscene language alone? The corrupt-
ers of youth have been indicted throughout the ages on so
many counts, such varied counts, that it is difficult to imagine
how the list of "evils" might be amplified. And always it is
against the life spirit itself that these indictments are aimed.
Life, however, as is demonstrated again and again, refuses to be
restricted or diminished by moral codes, by laws or ukases of any

sort. What rules life is spirit, and the spirit of man, which is in essence divine, remains unassailable.

As illustrative of a sound point of view, even if it be an exceptional one, I should like to cite a passage or two from the book called *Hieroglyphics* by the Welsh writer, Arthur Machen. He is referring to the *Pantagruel* of Rabelais . . . ."It is not in the least a 'pleasant,' or a 'life-like,' or even an 'interesting' book; I think that when one knows of the key—or rather of the keys—one opens the pages almost with a sensation of dread. So it is a book that one consults at long intervals, because it is only at rare moments that a man can bear the spectacle of his own naked soul, and a vision that is splendid, certainly, but awful also, in its constant apposition of the eternal heights and eternal depths." And now, referring to Rabelais' flagrant use of obscenity, Machen makes a point which cuts like a double-edged sword. He has been reminding us "never to forget that the essence of the book is its splendid celebration of ecstasy." He goes on to speak of a symbolism of ecstasy—"in the shape of *gauloiserie*, of gross, exuberant gaiety, expressing itself by outrageous tales, outrageous words, by a very cataract of obscenity, if you please, if only you will notice how the obscenity of Rabelais transcends the obscenity of common life; how grossness is poured out in a sort of mad torrent, in a frenzy, a very passion of the unspeakable . . ." Referring to the "lists" (the word lists) in the *Pantagruel,* he says: "Consider these 'lists,' that more than frankness, that ebullition of grossness, plainly intentional, designed: it is either the merest lunacy, or else it is sublime . . ." Nor does he stop here. As if to clinch the matter once and for all, he adds: "The Persian poet expresses the most transcendental secrets of the Divine Love by the grossest phrases of carnal love; so Rabelais soars above the common life, above the streets and the gutter: he brings before you the highest by positing that which is lower than the lowest, and if you have the prepared, the initiated mind, a Rabelaisian 'list' is the best preface to the angelic song . . ."

Is it not possible, I sometimes ask myself, that there be a deeper reason for the proscribing of "immoral" books? I have observed that more often than not the author of an "obscene" work is a man of truth. Frequently he has employed his objectionable "licentious" language in order to expose the evil of our ways. His truths come as a shock because truth always goes naked. Deceit and hypocrisy, such as are prevalent in our time, have a way of provoking honest men to explosive language, to shocking language. They, however, who welcome truth, who believe in life, find nothing loathsome in such language. To be truthful, I myself find very little in life that may be considered "loathsome," unless it be stark evil, which is rare. It is certainly beyond my comprehension to understand how subject, style or treatment can be condemned of itself or in itself. If our daily life is full of ugliness it is inevitable that men will arise to describe it and reveal it in all its manifold details. The truth about life can no more be throttled than the spread of knowledge. All that censorship may hope to accomplish is to delay the inevitable. For books, like everything else in this universe, are created in answer to our needs, our inner needs. They are part of the time spirit. Thought will out. If it does not find its way to the surface, through the various media of art, it will dig under, follow subterranean channels, and eventually poison the very springs of life. Moreover, it is hardly likely that ideas, however abhorrent, are the product of certain monstrous individuals. Ideas are in the air, as we say, and the artist does but make use of them. It is also a most curious phenomenon that so-called obscene literature is the hardiest of all forms of literature. It has existed from most ancient times, and it endures, without protection, without ballyhoo, despite all that may be said against it. Only one other class of literature is admittedly as durable, and that is the occult. The one obviously corresponds to some vital need which no amount of moralizing or penalizing can eradicate, while the other answers to that sense of mystery in us which no scientific or religious explanations ever satisfy.

Every day in the forest, on the farm, under the ground, in the air, everywhere throughout this planet, the creatures of this earth, as well as men and women, are indulging in the sexual act, and, if we are to believe a writer like Rémy de Gourmont, often in ways that would stagger the imagination. The only permissible word language with which to describe this cosmic state of rut is, at present, scientific language. The cattle breeder may write his pamphlets and treatises; the physician may detail his psychopathic case histories; the anthropologist may describe his researches into the sexual habits of primitive peoples—but the writer who is interested purely in creative literature, the writer who would like to describe the life about him fully and freely, is forbidden to speak. Yet he is the only one who can write passionately and meaningfully, the only one who is truly detached, free in spirit, who sees life in its entirety and can therefore be honest, truthful, gay, and ultimately *therapeutic*.

Though we no longer believe in alchemy, our age is nevertheless *the* one in which the art of transformation manifests itself in every realm. Almost everything we touch, eat, drink, smell has undergone an amazing process of transmutation. Everything we have learned about the "secret processes" derives from a study of nature. From eternity nature has been transforming everything—always in terms of a richer, more complicated life. In studying nature's ways we observe that everything is necessary and indispensable, or, as the mystics put it, that "everything has been given." Man can not alter nature, try as he will. He is not even able to subdue or chasten her. He can merely quicken or retard her processes. Despite himself, despite his petty, vain will, I mean, he is obliged to act in conformity with her laws. The more closely he studies her ways, the more obedient he becomes, the better and speedier his results.

There is a cosmic elasticity, if I may call it such, which is highly deceptive. It gives man the illusion, for a time, that he has the power to alter things. In the end, however, he is always brought back to himself. There, in his own nature, is where transmutation may be practiced, where indeed it *should* be practiced, and nowhere else. And when man perceives the truth of this he becomes reconciled to all apparent evil, ugliness, falsehood and frustration; thenceforth he ceases to impose upon the world his private picture of grief and woe, of sin and corruption.

I could, of course, put it more simply by saying that in the eyes of God all is divine. And when I say all I mean all. Looking at things in this light the word transmutation carries still greater significance: it implies that our welfare is dependent upon our spiritual understanding, on the use we make of the divine vision which we possess. With this as criterion, what could possibly shock us?

This word morality! Whenever it comes up I think of the crimes which have been committed in its name. Almost the entire history of man's persecution of his fellow-man is embraced by the confusion engendered by this term. Aside from the fact that there is not just one morality but many, it is evident that in all countries, whatever the prevailing morality, there exists one morality for peace times and another for war. In times of war everything is permitted, everything condoned. That is to say, everything abominable and infamous committed by the winning side. The vanquished, always the scapegoats, possess "no morality." One would think, if we really worshipped life and not death, if we valued creation and not destruction, if we believed in fecundity and not impotence, that the supreme task we would set ourselves would be the elimination of war. One would think that, sick of butchery, men would get after the butchers, i.e., the men who plan to make war, the men who decide the modes of warfare, the men who command the manufacture of war materials, materials now unspeakably diabolical. I say "butchers," because in the ultimate such men are nothing else. In cold blood, years before any outbreak, they prepare to make others do their bidding; mentally they embrace every conceivable form of horror and destruction, and they set about their business calmly, deliberately, ruthlessly, waiting only for the opportune moment to put their plans into execution. The men who are called to arms, the men who are obliged to put this inhuman machinery into operation, though not entirely innocent, are nevertheless not guilty of planning and preparing the butchery. They are simply the victims who subsequently, according to the hazards of fate, will be dubbed cowards or heroes. Their role is to obey. And, even though their lives should be spared, even though they be not mutilated in the flesh, they who

survive will most certainly be maimed in spirit. Faced with a
new war—for one war breeds another and another—it is unthinkable to expect of these "victims" that they be charitable and
magnanimous. Having suffered unwillingly, it is inevitable that
they will exact the same toll of their sons and daughters. . . . I
say, then, that if this bondage of sacrifice and vengeance is not
immoral, if it is not the last word in immorality, then the word
has no meaning. We are not being destroyed or undermined by
pornographic or obscene writings; we are being destroyed and
damned in every way by making war or planning to make war.

And now to come to the point of this seemingly gratuitous
tirade. Thinking as I do, feeling as I do, about war, I would
nevertheless refuse to destroy books dealing with the manufacture of war materials or war machines, or with the manufacture
of poison gases or the creation of destructive bacteria, or any
other of the fiendish inventions of the military-minded; I would
not destroy books dealing with military strategy or with the
rules and conventions governing "civilized" warfare. On the
contrary, I would wish to see the distribution and circulation of
all such literature increased. I would have children informed as
to these matters as well as grown-ups. I would have every man,
woman and child throughout the land become as familiar with
these words as they are supposed to be with the Holy Bible. I
would go yet further. I would put the Bible on one shelf and
all this homicidal literature on another shelf. I would say: If
you look at the one, then you must look at the other also. I
would make a clean cleavage between the book in which it is
commanded not to kill and all the other books in which human
slaughter, slaughter en masse, is taught, explained, approved and
exemplified. I would divide family against family, brother
against brother, on this single question. Act according to your
conscience, I would urge. Either it is going to be one world or
no world before long. If you are for the world of death, enlist
in it immediately! Do not confound us with your indecision. Do
not speak of morality if your ultimate aim is to collaborate in
the destruction of our world.

Between the Bible and the slaughter-house manuals lies the

world of literature, evolved through human passion, hunger and imagination, and dealing with human thought, deed, dream and aspiration. It is a world drawn from life, concerned only with life, and sustaining life. If there is death in it it is but to the extent that it lacks fire, depth, freedom and choice. If this vast product of creative energy were a celebration of death it would be nothing more than a mockery. We know full well that, whatever its defeats or limitations, this great body of creation represents the triumph of life over death. And so I make bold to say that no matter how vile, filthy, scabrous, scatalogical or obscene a book may be, if it serves life, if it aims at the cancer which is eating out the heart of the world, it is a good book, a righteous book, a holy book. To say of it that it is immoral, to call it pornographic or obscene, is like talking of spittle in connection with the hydrogen bomb. There is no book yet written devastating enough to wipe from the consciousness of living man the horrors to which he is now privy, the horrors which he is being asked to accept in advance in return for the privilege of belonging to a civilization which has virtually converted him into an unthinking, unfeeling monster.

Monster, robot, slave, accursed one—it makes little difference which term one uses to convey the picture of our dehumanized condition. Never was mankind as a whole in a more ignoble condition than ours. We are all bound to one another in a disgraceful master-slave relationship; we are all caught in the same vicious circle of judge and be judged; we all aim to destroy one another if we cannot have our way. Instead of respect, toleration, kindness and consideration, to say nothing of love, we view one another with fear, suspicion, hatred, envy, rivalry and malevolence. Our world is grounded in falsity. In whatever direction you venture, into whatever sphere of human activity you penetrate, you encounter nothing but sham, fraud, deceit, falsehood.

Cognizant of the fact that, no matter how highly placed, men can not, dare not, think freely, independently, I almost despair of making myself heard. And if I speak at all, if I venture to hazard my point of view about matters fundamental, it is because I am convinced that, however black the picture may be, a drastic change is not only possible but inevitable. I feel that it is my right and my duty as a human being to further this change. Without in the least wishing to glorify myself I should like to point out that there is evidence throughout my work that I myself have undergone a change; I say it is evident and obvious that the man who relates the story of his life is not the same as the "hero" who stalks the pages of these autobiographical novels. The man who confesses his sins, his crimes or his misdeeds is never the same as the one who committed them. Is it necessary for me to underline the fact that the author, in exposing his guilt and suffering, his fears and his triumphs, is but announcing his liberation and emancipation? And as to the element of "evil" itself, how can I be more explicit than to say that the narrative is armed with double truth. The seeing eye will perceive in this long narration not only the historical facts of one man's life but a reality going far beyond thought, word and deed. Long before I began this work I was conscious of the justice of the Tibetan view which insists that a man be more severely punished for misdemeanors committed in his dream life than for those committed in waking life. In exposing myself as fully and completely as possible I have pronounced sentence upon myself, and in advance, beyond any that could be meted out by a worldly court. I am living not "this side of Paradise" but in a world of my own making—where punishment and reward seem alike futile. I have still a road to travel, but I see clearly what the goal is. And seeing it clearly, I can only say that I value more than ever truth and freedom.

I would like to go one step farther, in closing. It is to say this: if all that I have set forth herein is not clear from the reading of my books then I have failed utterly. In which case I beg to be condemned not only as an "immoral" writer but as a stupid and impotent one. I had thought to join with this testimony a selection of letters, unsolicited letters, culled from the thousands I have received from my readers all over the world. I no longer believe it worth while to make this effort. I realize that it is too easy to object that all these (largely) unknown individuals are simply "fellow travelers," or, to put it more harshly, emotional cripples. If I knew I were addressing myself to men who believe in the power of truth I would say: "Put my work to the test! Let it be read openly, freely, everywhere, by all classes of men and women. Let them be my judges!"

And this is not my last thought on the subject. Let us look at it in the worst light. Supposing that tomorrow, as a result of reading Henry Miller, everyone began talking freely, talking gutter language, if you will, and acting according to his own beliefs and convictions. What then? My answer is that no matter what took place, it would be as if nothing had occurred, *nothing*, I want to emphasize, in comparison with the effect of a single exploded atom bomb. This, I must confess, is the saddest admission that I, a creative individual, can make. It is my belief that we are now passing through a period of what might be called "cosmic insensitivity," a period when God seems more than ever absent from the world and man doomed to come face to face with the fate which he has created for himself. At such a moment the question of whether a man be guilty of using obscene language in printed books seems to me thoroughly inconsequential. It is almost as if, while taking a walk through a green field, I espied a blade of grass with manure on it, and, bending down to that obscure little blade of grass I said to it scoldingly: "Naughty, naughty!"

First Letter to Trygve Hirsch
—Henry Miller—Between Heaven and Hell

Big Sur, California
September 19, 1957

Mr. Trygve Hirsch
Oslo, Norway

My dear Mr. Hirsch:

I have just received your most interesting letter with enclosures from Peter Rohde and Johan Voght, and take pleasure in responding to your request. Before proceeding, however, let me say that I have just air-mailed you several small books in which you will find texts of mine which may aid you even further. I have also written my Paris publisher, Maurice Girodias, of the Olympia Press, to air-mail you a copy of the revised edition of *The World of Sex* which has just come out. I think you will find some striking references to the subject in hand in this little volume. There were some bad printer's errors in the opening pages which I asked Girodias to correct in your copy; if he has not done so, please write him about it, or write me. Note, please, that the text called "Obscenity in Literature" was originally written for my Paris lawyer, Maître Sev, to be used as testimony in court, when the trial of *Sexus* was to come up. The case against me (personally) was dismissed only a few weeks ago. The text called "Reflections on Writing" was written expressly for my friend Huntington Cairns, our unofficial censor for imported books. I must also point out that in my latest book, *Big Sur and the Oranges of Hieronymus Bosch*, you will find more useful data on pages 126–30. Perhaps Hans Reitzel, Copenhagen, can give you these pages in Danish or Norwegian; I believe the work is now being translated there. (Not positive, however.)

But, to answer your letter. . . . Yes, I *am* rather weary of explaining my position to censors, judges and moralists of all kinds. Particularly since all that I stand for is explicit in my work—and in my life. As I said to the *juge d'instruction* in Paris, when I appeared before him early in 1953, to explain my position, I believe in absolute freedom of expression.

As most everyone who has given any thought to the subject agrees, censorship works like a boomerang. It is ironic but true that it would be better for your countrymen if the Norwegian authorities decided to ban my books. By doing so they would stimulate the public to make more determined efforts to read these books. No matter what barriers are created to prevent the spread of "insidious" ideas, no power on earth can effectively stop the circulation of thought. Men will think and dream, no matter how much their freedom is curtailed. Truth will out, no matter how unpleasant (for those who resist) it may be.

But what is it I am advocating, in the writing of one after another of these censorable books? Nothing more than the right to write as one speaks. In one of the texts I sent you you will find a quotation from an essay by Montaigne which touches on this very point. I think it is in "Obscenity in Literature."

The point of law raised by your attorney-general is familiar to me; it obtains here, in England, and in other Western countries. I mean, whether a book should be condemned in toto because of objectionable passages, or whether the objectionable parts should be regarded from the standpoint of the author's ultimate intention. It is the author's "integrity," it seems to me, which the interpreters of the law seek to establish. Speaking strictly for myself, I would say that it may one day happen that I might question the wisdom of my own point of view, but I could never modify my stand, never compromise. I have staked my whole career on my right as a human being to employ freedom of speech, and I have paid the price for it.

With regard to the work in question, *Sexus*, there is no question but that this book, as the title indicates, is a work freighted with sex. The second book of the trilogy (*Plexus*), on the other hand, is almost free of it; there may be four or five censorable pages—a passage en bloc—in the entire book. As for *Nexus*, which I am still in the process of writing—I have not advanced very far—I am unable to predict at this point how much or how little the sexual content of it will be. In writing I follow my nose: "it" decides, not me.

It may be interesting to note that, as I observed in "Obscenity in Literature," I never set out to write a *trilogy*. Nor did I have in mind, when beginning this work known as *The Rosy Crucifixion*, that I would give to the separate parts the titles of *Sexus*, *Plexus* and *Nexus*. The over-all title was the one which had significance for me. Through being crucified one may be resurrected—or "transformed," if you like. My thought, very simply, was to tell, no matter how many pages it took, the story of the most crucial period of my life, namely, the seven years preceding my voluntary flight to France. A goodly part of the narrative has to do with my struggle to express myself in words—I started late!—my difficulties in earning a living, the fight with my own complex being, my encounters with other men and women as a "roving cultural desperado," and so on. And more than anything, perhaps, my effort to understand the pattern of my life, its purpose and significance.

All my autobiographical novels, as they are sometimes called, starting with *Tropic of Cancer* and continuing through ten other volumes—a sort of modern *Marriage of Heaven and Hell*—bear little resemblance to most autobiographical outpourings. The difference lies primarily in the understanding and the use I have made of "reality." To get at the nature of this reality which pervades all life, and which *is* life, I have had to grapple with the metaphysical aspects of suffering, freedom, experience. As Berdyaev so well puts it, when treating of Dostoievski, "Suffering is not only profoundly inherent in man, but it is the sole cause of the awakening of conscious thought." Or again, in explaining what he means by "eschatology," he says, and this thought underlies my whole work: "The Church is not the Kingdom of God; the Church has appeared in history and it has acted in history; it does not mean the transfiguration of the world, the appearance of a new heaven and a new earth. The Kingdom of God is the transfiguration of the world, not only the transfiguration of the social and the cosmic; and that is the end of this world, of the world of wrong and ugliness, and it is the principle of a new world, a world of right and beauty." Let me quote yet another man, a friend of long standing, who writes under the pseudonym of Dane Rudhyar: "No man can become truly and actually 'human' save by reaching a state of maximum clarity and wakefulness. And this state is symbolized in Asia by the figure of the Buddha, the Awakened, the Illumined, the absolutely Clear One. In him humanity came to a condition of total and unqualified acceptance of all human experience, to a state of undisturbable wakefulness and lucidity, free from illusion, glamour and uncertainty. He dared to face facts, all the facts. He dared to contain all reality known to man—to include in his clear consciousness the experience of hell as well as of heaven. And, in him, every experience a human being ever lived anywhere became significant. He 'shaped' all experiences unto the likeness of his all-inclusive selfhood; for his being had become a vessel, container of all. Thus he overcame suffering."

And so, in a fashion quite other than that of realistic novelists and faithful chroniclers, I have made extensive use throughout these books of irruptive onslaughts of the unconscious, such as dream, fantasy, burlesque, Pantagruelian word play, etc., which lend the narrative a chaotic, whimsical, perplexing character—in the minds of many critics. But these "extravaganza," so to speak, have great significance for me. Especially, need I add, the sexual eruptions. They represent my endeavor, successful or not, to portray the *whole* man. It is my contention, of course, that modern literature suffers precisely because, for one reason or another, writers in general now abstain from giving us man in all the heights and depths of his being. And the public, long inured to this prescribed sort of amputation, no longer deeply cares. Indeed, there is little revolt of any sort left in modern man. He no longer acts, he reacts. He is the victim who at long last has been caught in his own trap.

What I am trying to say by all this is that the question to what extent a writer may be permitted to speak freely and naturally—on any question, any subject—is only part of a greater question, in a word: *what is freedom?* Men will fight and die, apparently, for greater political or economic freedom, perhaps even for religious freedom, but when it comes to education—what and how our children should be taught—or the right to speak and act freely in the domain of sex, or even to write about sex openly, honestly, unashamedly, they display striking little courage. So it seems to me, at any rate. Yet sex and education are of cardinal importance in the creation of any social fabric. Indeed, there are many today who are convinced that most of our woes stem from our reluctance or our inability to cope with these fundamental issues.

To get back to the core of the matter. . . . I repeat that, in

writing *The Rosy Crucifixion*, I had but one thought in mind—
to tell the story of the crucial years which marked a turning
point in my life, and to relate my experiences (good and bad)
as honestly and as faithfully as possible. In short, to expose the
whole man and thus, obliquely, the society which fostered him.
It therefore seems somewhat ridiculous to be asked, as I often
am, whether I could not have written otherwise, meaning—could
I not have rendered my words and thoughts more palatable, less
offensive to public taste. (Who are the arbiters of taste, by the
way?) This same sort of question has been put to every innovator
throughout the ages. I should like to add, moreover, that I very
much question the wisdom, the purity and the understanding of
the so-called guardians of morality who so brashly assume responsibility for the mental, moral and spiritual health of the dear
public. What tests have they undergone to earn the right to
judge and condemn those who do not subscribe to their view of
life? No, the real protectors, not of the "public" but of humanity,
are never moralists but rather men of spirit. These men I revere.
They do not talk good and evil, they talk God. They do not
judge, punish and condemn; they show compassion. And what
is compassion if not understanding tempered by love?

No, I have no fear that those who read my works will become
depraved or demoralized. Indeed, I possess thousands of letters
from readers all over the world which tell the opposite story.
Every day I receive letters from people of all ages, all classes of
society, who thank me for opening their eyes, thank me for giving them the courage to lead their own lives, and so on. Perhaps
it would not be out of order to ask what the defenders of morality
do, for their part, to induce similar responses. The test of a man's
humanity lies in his acceptance of life, all aspects of life, not
just those which correspond with his own limited viewpoint. As
dear old sadly misunderstood Nietzsche said—"The Yea-sayers!"

One last thing . . . In your letter you made reference to Knut
Hamsun. Yes, I am happy to confess that this Norwegian writer,
like his illustrious predecessor, Ibsen, exerted a great influence
upon me in the formative years of my life. I know that to many

of your countrymen his name is now anathema. In my eyes, nevertheless, he remains one of the half-dozen writers whom, as a novice, I tried to emulate. He gave me many, many hours of sheer joy; he opened my eyes to the beauties of nature; he revealed, in ways utterly magical, the souls of men and women caught in the throes of love, and the sorrows and sufferings of his figures had for me a poignant redemptive quality. I tried my best, naive as I then was, to copy him—but I never succeeded. None of our esteemed critics, to show you how obtuse these creatures can be, ever detected the influence, in style and approach, of this, my early, idol. Yet it is there for those who have eyes to see. Though he may have been a traitor to his country, I somehow do not believe that, had he read these questionable books of mine, he would have judged me harshly. Any more than he would have condemned any writer who endeavored to express himself freely and honestly. It was from your Knut Hamsun that I derived much of my love of life, love of nature, love of man. All I have done, or hope I have, in relating the distressing story of my life, is to increase that love of life, nature and all God's creatures in those who read me.

"Praise God from whom all blessings flow!"

Most sincerely yours,
Henry Miller

Second Letter to Trygve Hirsch
—The Henry Miller Reader

Big Sur, California
February 27, 1959

Mr. Trygve Hirsch
Oslo, Norway

Dear Mr. Hirsch:

To answer your letter of January 19th requesting a statement of me which might be used in the Supreme Court trial to be conducted in March or April of this year. . . . It is difficult to be more explicit than I was in my letter of September 19th, 1957, when the case against my book *Sexus* was being tried in the lower courts of Oslo. However, here are some further reflections which I trust will be found à propos.

When I read the decision of the Oslo Town Court, which you sent me some months ago, I did so with mingled feelings. If occasionally I was obliged to roll with laughter—partly because of the inept translation, partly because of the nature and the number of infractions listed—I trust no one will take offense. Taking the world for what it is, and the men who make and execute the laws for what they are, I thought the decision as fair and honest as any theorem of Euclid's. Nor was I unaware of, or indifferent to, the efforts made by the Court to render an interpretation beyond the strict letter of the law. (An impossible task, I would say, for if laws are made for men and not men for laws, it is also true that certain individuals are made for the law and can only see things through the eyes of the law.)

I failed to be impressed, I must confess, by the weighty, often pompous or hypocritical, opinions adduced by scholars, literary pundits, psychologists, medicos and such-like. How could I be when it is precisely such single-minded individuals, so often wholly devoid of humor, at whom I so frequently aim my shafts?

Rereading this lengthy document today, I am more than ever aware of the absurdity of the whole procedure. (How lucky I am not to be indicted as a "pervert" or "degenerate," but simply as one who makes sex pleasurable and innocent!) Why, it is often asked, when he has so much else to give, did he have to introduce these disturbing, controversial scenes dealing with sex? To answer that properly, one would have to go back to the womb—with or without the analyst's guiding hand. Each one—priest, analyst, barrister, judge—has his own answer, usually a ready-made one. But none go far enough, none are deep enough, inclusive enough. The divine answer, of course, is: first remove the mote from your own eye!

If I were there, in the dock, my answer would probably be —"Guilty! Guilty on all ninety-seven counts! To the gallows!"

For when I take the short, myopic view, I realize that I was guilty even before I wrote the book. Guilty, in other words, because I am the way I am. The marvel is that I am walking about as a free man. I should have been condemned the moment I stepped out of my mother's womb.

In that heartrending account of my return to the bosom of the family which is given in "Reunion in Brooklyn,"* I concluded with these words, and I meant them, each and every one of them: "I regard the entire world as my home. I inhabit the earth, not a particular portion of it labeled America, France, Germany, Russia. . . . I owe allegiance to mankind, not to a particular country, race or people. I answer to God, not to the Chief Executive, whoever he may happen to be. I am here on earth to work out my own private destiny. My destiny is linked with that of every other living creature inhabiting this planet —perhaps with those on other planets too, who knows? I refuse to jeopardize my destiny by regarding life within the narrow rules which are laid down to circumscribe it. I dissent from the current view of things, as regards murder, as regards religion, as regards society, as regards our well-being. I will try to live my life in accordance with the vision I have of things eternal. I say "Peace to you all!" and if you don't find it, it's because you haven't looked for it.

It is curious, and not irrelevant, I hope, to mention at this point the reaction I had upon reading Homer recently. At the request of the publisher Gallimard, who is bringing out a new edition of the *Odyssey*, I wrote a short Introduction to this work. I had never read the *Odyssey* before, only the *Iliad*, and that but a few months ago. What I wish to say is that, after waiting sixty-seven years to read these universally esteemed classics, I found much to disparage in them. In the *Iliad*, or "the butchers' manual," as I call it, more than in the *Odyssey*. But it would never occur to me to request that they be banned or burned. Nor did I fear, on finishing them, that I would leap outdoors, axe in hand, and run

---

* In *Sunday After the War*, New Directions, 1944, 1962; and *The Intimate Henry Miller*, New American Library, 1959. (Publisher's Note.)

amok. My boy, who was only nine when he read the *Iliad* (in a child's version), my boy who confesses to "liking murder once in a while," told me he was fed up with Homer, with all the killing and all the nonsense about the gods. But I have never feared that this son of mine, now going on eleven, still an avid reader of our detestable "Comics," a devotee of Walt Disney (who is not to my taste at all), an ardent movie fan, particularly of the "Westerns," I have never feared, I say, that he will grow up to be a killer. (Not even if the Army claims him!) I would rather see his mind absorbed by other interests, and I do my best to provide them, but, like all of us, he is a product of the age. No need, I trust, for me to elaborate on the dangers which confront us all, youth especially, in *this* age. The point is that with each age the menace varies. Whether it be witchcraft, idolatry, leprosy, cancer, schizophrenia, communism, fascism, or what, we have ever to do battle. Seldom do we really vanquish the enemy, in whatever guise he presents himself. At best we become immunized. But we never know, nor are we able to prevent in advance, the dangers which lurk around the corner. No matter how knowlegeable, no matter how wise, no matter how prudent and cautious, we all have an Achilles' heel. Security is not the lot of man. Readiness, alertness, responsiveness—these are the sole defenses against the blows of fate.

I smile to myself in putting the following to the honorable members of the Court, prompted as I am to take the bull by the horns. Would it please the Court to know that by common opinion I pass for a sane, healthy, normal individual? that I am not regarded as a "sex addict," a pervert, or even a neurotic? Nor as a writer who is ready to sell his soul for money? That, as a husband, a father, a neighbor, I am looked upon as "an asset" to the community? Sounds a trifle ludicrous, does it not? Is he the same *enfant terrible*, it might be asked, who wrote the unmentionable *Tropics, The Rosy Crucifixion, The World of Sex, Quiet Days in Clichy?* Has he reformed? Or is he simply in his dotage now?

To be precise, the question is—are the author of these questionable works and the man who goes by the name of Henry

Miller one and the same person? My answer is yes. And I am also one with the protagonist of these "autobiographical romances." That is perhaps harder to swallow. But why? Because I have been "utterly shameless" in revealing every aspect of my life? I am not the first author to have adopted the confessional approach, to have revealed life nakedly, or to have used language supposedly unfit for the ears of school girls. Were I a saint recounting his life of sin, perhaps these bald statements relating to my sex habits would be found enlightening, particularly by priests and medicos. They might even be found instructive.

But I am not a saint, and probably never will be one. Though it occurs to me, as I make this assertion, that I have been called that more than once, and by individuals whom the Court would never suspect capable of holding such an opinion. No, I am not a saint, thank heavens! nor even a propagandist of a new order. I am simply a man, a man born to write, who has taken as his theme the story of his life. A man who has made it clear, in the telling, that it was a good life, a rich life, a merry life, despite the ups and downs, despite the barriers and obstacles (many of his own making), despite the handicaps imposed by stupid codes and conventions. Indeed, I hope that I have made more than that clear, because whatever I may say about my own life, which is only *a* life, is merely a means of talking about life itself, and what I have tried, desperately sometimes, to make clear is this, that I look upon life itself as good, good no matter on what terms, that I believe it is *we* who make it unlivable, *we*, not the gods, not fate, not circumstance.

Speaking thus, I am reminded of certain passages in the Court's decision which reflect on my sincerity as well as on my ability to think straight. These passages contain the implication that I am often deliberately obscure as well as pretentious in my "metaphysical and surrealistic" flights. I am only too well aware of the diversity of opinion which these "excursi" elicit in the minds of my readers. But how am I to answer such accusations, touching as they do the very marrow of my literary being? Am I to say, "You don't know what you are talking about?" Ought I to muster impressive names—"authorities"—to counterbalance these judgments? Or would it not be simpler to say as I have before, "Guilty! Guilty on all counts, your Honor!"

Believe me, it is not impish, roguish perversity which leads me to pronounce, even quasi-humorously, this word "guilty." As one who thoroughly and sincerely believes in what he says and does, even when wrong, is it not more becoming on my part to admit "guilt" than attempt to defend myself against those who use this word so glibly? Let us be honest. Do those who judge and condemn me—not in Oslo necessarily, but the world over—do these individuals truly believe me to be a culprit, to be "the enemy of society," as they often blandly assert? What is it that disturbs them so? Is it the existence, the prevalence, of immoral, amoral or unsocial behavior, such as is described in my works, or is it the exposure of such behavior in print? Do people of our day and age really behave in this "vile" manner or are these actions merely the product of a "diseased" mind? (Does one refer to such authors as Petronius, Rabelais, Rousseau, Sade, to mention but a few, as "diseased minds"?) Surely some of you must have friends or neighbors, in good standing too, who have indulged in this questionable behavior, or worse. As a man of the world, I know only too well that the appanage of a priest's frock, a judicial robe, a teacher's uniform provides no guarantee of immunity to the temptations of the flesh. We are all in the same pot, we are all guilty, or innocent, depending on whether we take the frog's view or the Olympian view. For the nonce I shall refrain from pretending to measure or apportion guilt, to say, for example, that a criminal is more guilty, or less, than a hypocrite. We do not have crime, we do not have war, revolution, crusades, inquisitions, persecution and intolerance because some among us are wicked, mean-spirited, or murderers at heart; we have this malignant condition of human affairs because all of us, the righteous as well as the ignorant and the malicious, lack true forbearance, true compassion, true knowledge and understanding of human nature.

To put it as succinctly and simply as possible, here is my basic attitude towards life, my prayer, in other words: "Let us stop thwarting one another, stop judging and condemning, stop slaughtering one another." I do not implore you to suspend or withhold judgment of me or my work. Neither I nor my work is that important. (One cometh, another goeth.) What concerns me is the harm you are doing to yourselves. I mean by perpetuating this talk of guilt and punishment, of banning and proscribing, of whitewashing and blackballing, of closing your eyes when convenient, of making scapegoats when there is no other way out. I ask you point blank—does the pursuance of your limited role enable you to get the most out of life? When you write me off the books, so to speak, will you find your food and wine more palatable, will you sleep better, will you be a better man, a better husband, a better father than before? These are the things that matter—what happens to *you*, not what you do to *me*.

I know that the man in the dock is not supposed to ask questions, he is there to answer. But I am unable to regard myself as a culprit. I am simply "out of line." Yet I am in the tradition, so to say. A list of my precursors would make an impressive roster. This trial has been going on since the days of Prometheus. Since before that. Since the days of the Archangel Michael. In the not too distant past there was one who was given the cup of hemlock for being "the corruptor of youth." Today he is regarded as one of the sanest, most lucid minds that ever was. We who are always being arraigned before the bar can do no better than to resort to the celebrated Socratic method. Our only answer is to return the question.

There are so many questions one could put to the Court, to any court. But would one get a response? Can the Court of the Land ever be put in question? I am afraid not. The judicial body is a sacrosanct body. This is unfortunate, as I see it, for when issues of grave import arise the last court of reference, in my opinion, should be the public. When justice is at stake responsibility cannot be shifted to an elect few without injustice resulting. No court could function if it did not follow the steel rails of precedent, taboo and prejudice.

I come back to the lengthy document representing the decision of the Oslo Town Court, to the tabulation of all the infractions of the moral code therein listed. There is something frightening as well as disheartening about such an indictment. It has a medieval aspect. And it has nothing to do with justice. Law itself is made to look ridiculous. Once again let me say that it is not the courts of Oslo or the laws and codes of Norway which I inveigh against; everywhere in the civilized world there is this mummery and flummery manifesting as the Voice of Inertia. The offender who stands before the Court is not being tried by his peers but by his dead ancestors. The moral codes, operative only if they are in conformance with natural or divine laws, are not safeguarded by these flimsy dikes; on the contrary, they are exposed as weak and ineffectual barriers.

Finally, here is the crux of the matter. Will an adverse decision by this court or any other court effectively hinder the further circulation of this book? The history of similar cases does not substantiate such an eventuality. If anything, an unfavorable verdict will only add more fuel to the flames. Proscription only leads to resistance; the fight goes on underground, becomes more insidious therefore, more difficult to cope with. If only one man in Norway reads the book and believes with the author that one has the right to express himself freely, the battle is won. You cannot eliminate an idea by suppressing it, and the idea which is linked with this issue is one of freedom to read what one chooses. Freedom, in other words, to read what is bad for one as well as what is good for one—or, what is simply innocuous. How can one guard against evil, in short, if one does not know what evil is?

But it is not something evil, not something poisonous, which this book *Sexus* offers the Norwegian reader. It is a dose of life which I administered to myself first, and which I not only survived but thrived on. Certainly I would not recommend it to infants, but then neither would I offer a child a bottle of *aqua vite*. I can say one thing for it unblushingly—compared to the atom bomb, it is full of lifegiving qualities.

                                                                Henry Miller